THE VERSATILE VOICE
OF
ELLEN GOODMAN

"Someday, I would like to see a television series about a family that sits around the set watching a series about a family that sits around the set."

"Many, many people who are sexually 'free' to do what they want are confused about what it is they want to do. There is increasing discomfort at the idea that people know each other in the biblical sense before they know each other in the emotional sense."

"The story of Jean Harris and Hy Tarnower...resonates with jealousy, rejection, pain, insensitivity. With her fourteen years and his other women. Her pride and his other women. Her self-esteem and his other women."

(more...)

"It is plain old hostility that assumes that a woman can only get to the top on her back instead of her merit...If women can sleep their way to the top, how come they aren't there?"

"It isn't just the criminal offensive that affects our lives, it is our own growing defensive. When we learn to turn on the alarm, put the jewelry in the refrigerator, push down the buttons in the car, think twice about walking down a street, our lives are diminished."

"Most of us grew up expecting a stable world. I don't think we were betrayed; at worst, most of our parents believed they could build us that world. They thought we needed to be assured instead of prepared. Instead, we were surprised."

"This isn't a subject I'm dying to leap into. Just whispering 'teenage sex' is like yelling fire in a crowded theater. Perfectly sane people panic. Reason rushes out the exit doors and we are left stranded in the murkiest emotional alleyways."

"I suppose we make kids the repository of our highest ideals because children are powerless. In that way we can have ideals and ignore them at the same time."

"Once upon a time, it was only card-carrying members of the Legion of Decency who went around sputtering words like 'disgusting,' 'obscene,' 'indecent'...Now I find myself applauding a friend who got two teenage kids kicked out of the R-rated *Dressed to Kill*."

"The Grateful Wife began to wonder why she should say thank you when a father took care of his children and why she should say please when a husband took care of his house. She began to realize that being grateful meant being responsible."

"The Anita Bryant saga is not just another tale of disillusionment and divorce. She is part of a long tradition of women who enter the public sphere only to 'defend' the private one: conservative women who become part of change."

Fawcett Crest Books
by Ellen Goodman

CLOSE TO HOME

TURNING POINTS

AT LARGE

ELLEN GOODMAN

FAWCETT CREST • NEW YORK

ACKNOWLEDGMENTS

This is my chance to say thank you. On this page, I can "acknowledge" the people who have nourished my work, encouraged me.

My impulse this time is to start by thanking people I don't even know, the people who read my column. They are, in a real sense, responsible for this book.

Last year, when I was awarded the Pulitzer, I had three almost simultaneous reactions: pleasure, amusement, appreciation. Now, I told a friend, I knew the first line of my obituary. Now, I told an interviewer, I had a sense of how much things had changed. Ten years ago, what I write about—values, relationships, women's issues, families, change—would not have been taken "seriously" by the newspaper world.

To a certain extent I have been active in that change, but I have also benefited from it. People want to see their real concerns reflected back in the daily paper. They have been part of my dialogue on social issues, and for their interest, I am grateful.

It is editors, however, who have given me access to readers. The continuing support and interest of the editors who run my column have sustained me.

There are people in my immediate work life who are also a part of this book. Tom Winship, my editor and mentor at the *Boston Globe*, is always "there" for me. Bill Dickinson, the head of the Washington Post Writers Group, which has syndicated my column since 1976, manages to be gracious under the deadlines of our mutual life. He and Anna Karavangelos, and the rest of the Writers Group, make it all run smoothly.

It is Micki Talmadge who keeps my trains running on time. She has been my assistant, associate, and friend in every sense of the word.

This column is one person's point of view. But my view is an amalgam of many lives, private and public. The web of friends and families enriches me. My family takes both pride in my work and heat from it. They are also—especially my sister, Jane Holtz Kay—named and nameless "sources" in this book.

I have another ready resource of both pleasure and rootedness in the younger generation. The lives of my cousins David and Adam Weinstein, of my nieces Julie and Jacqueline Kay, enlarge me. My daughter Katie's insight, her emerging self, is richly intertwined with my own through these pages. I am lucky in my "choice" of children.

I am also lucky to have friends who nurture and goad me. Pat O'Brien, Otile McManus, and Bob Levey eat with me, think with me, argue with me, worry with me. Sometimes we do all four at the same time. We are, by now, part of each other's history. Thank you is too mild a word, but I offer it in partial payment.

To Bob, for being my best friend

CONTENTS

PART 2
WOMEN IN THE AGE OF TRANSITION

PART 3
OF MEN AND WOMEN

PART 4
OUR DAUGHTERS, OUR SONS

PART 5
PERSONALS

PART 6
THE HARD QUESTIONS

PART 7
PUBLIC LIVES

PART 8
THOUGHTS AT LARGE

PART 9
GROWING PAINS

INTRODUCTION

It's been two and a half years since I last sat down to introduce a book of columns, to reflect on my own reflections.

This is a long time as newspapers divide it—nearly 900 editions of daily news. But it's a short time for those of us who try to step back a bit, to keep some perspective on all the new-ness.

During these years, there has been a sea change in the country, in this formless thing we call the "mood" of the nation.

It seems as if the 1970s collapsed into the 1980s. The decade of self-improvement hardened into the decade of survival. The concerns about fulfilling ourselves turned to concerns about filling our tanks, our burners, our pocketbooks. Fewer people are worried about the meaning of success, and more are trying to dress for it. The options of the seventies are now the hard choices of the eighties.

There is a new supply of complex questions and a new group promising easy answers. I am increasingly intrigued by the questions and suspicious of the answers.

The columns in this book chronicle much of that change. They observe the life of a people born with great expectations and dealing with limits. They tell of the overeducated young faced with underemployment, of people who married

forever dealing with separation, of people trying to do-good
and frustrated at bad consequences.

I follow, like a scorekeeper, the conflicts and ambiva-
lences of our lives. These years, as I reread the columns,
seem particularly ripe with them. We have seen women
strike down the fifties Supermom myth only to find themselves stuck with the eighties Superwoman myth. We have
heard a divorced President from a reconstructed family become national spokesman for the traditional. We have
watched people press for equal rights and be granted, instead, equal responsibilities.

During this time, I have also passed from one decade to
another, the thirties to the forties. When Gloria Steinem
was told she didn't look forty, she answered, "But this is
the way forty looks." This book is to a certain extent the
way forty looks. At forty, I am in between generations,
values, stuck with seeing both sides.

At forty, living in a time of great polarization, I am more
interested in mediation. If I carry a placard at all, it says
simply: "Wait a minute, it's not as simple as that." I am
convinced that most of us commute between "positions,"
that we are more complicated than political name tags, more
complex than ten-point programs. I am simply more interested in the grays than the black-and-whites, more involved
in tracking some sane path through a thicket of confusion.

In that sense I live and work At Large, across a wide
range of interests and positions. There are many aspects to
any one life and I have long refused to separate the public
from the private, the humorous from the serious.

In the course of a year, my dog bites the electrician, my
daughter turns twelve, I worry about my weight and the
bomb, attend congressional hearings in Washington and seal
gatherings in Casco Bay. We create a life out of so much
and I have to work "at large" to reflect this.

But I have also called this book *At Large* because of how
my own life has changed in the past years. The pace of it
has stepped up, there are more deadlines from other places,

more conversations and observations from other datelines. I began writing even these words on a plane.

This collection and the last, *Close to Home,* are truly bookends to my life and work. I am rooted at home, in the rhythms of my family life, and also exist in a public world.

The pieces here show that. They talk about the people I have known—an Understanding Woman, a Grateful Wife and a Helpful Husband, my family, friends—as well as the people I have never met—Jean Harris, Mother Teresa, John Lennon. They deal with life-and-death issues in my own home and in the Congress. They discuss matters which are both public and private, argued in the bedroom and the boardroom, the kitchen and the court: love, work, sexuality, children, war, peace.

A column grows continually the way a person does. Old interests, like cells, slough off: new ones take their places. In looking back over these pieces I see both this change and continuity.

The one constant is a desire to find a context and a meaning. If journalism tells us two things—what is happening and what it means—I am one of the people trying to figure out what it all means. It is my job but also my second nature.

Writing a column is both a luxury and hard work—the luxury and the hard work of reporting, reflecting, thinking, writing. I have by editorial fiat 750 words twice weekly, whether I am confessing how I fall asleep at dinner parties or dissecting the legal relationships of parents and children. Sometimes I can take only a nibble of a huge subject at a time, so I come back for seconds and thirds.

In some of these columns I ask questions, to try and define the shape of our concerns. In others I "wonder." In most of them I distrust certainties and yet struggle for solutions. This book is a brief record of these struggles, of our times and my times, of my own journalistic wanderings "at large."

PART 1

The Way We Live

Preservation of the Eighties

Here we go again. No sooner do we end one Me Decade than another one comes peeping around the corner . . . armed to the teeth.

Goodbye to the Era of Self-Improvement, hello to the Era of Self-Preservation. Good-bye Hedonists; hello pessimists. The Me People of the seventies were learning to actualize themselves, but the Me People of the eighties are learning to defend themselves.

Yes, indeed, fellow trend watchers, the true religion of the decade is not going to be est or evangelical, it's going to be Survival. Already 50,000 self-proclaimed Survivalists from coast to coast are hunkering down for the Apocalypse. They aren't preparing their souls to meet doom, they are preparing their bunkers to escape it.

What the hot tub was to the seventies, the bunker will be for the eighties: the emotional escape hatch.

The Survivalists' visions of disaster differ. For some it is nuclear, for others economic, for still others class and race warfare. But the solution is the same: The Survival of the Outfittest.

While the other little piggies are building straw huts and singing in the sun, Survivalists are bricking in for months to be spent munching dried foods, sipping canned water and counting their ammunition.

Survivalists see the handwriting on the wall, or at least the typewriting in the mail-order catalogues. The Urban Survival Arsenal, a review of the weapons "you need," pictures us in fortified bunkers while squads of "dope-crazed savages" lie in wait outside.

"What are you going to do?" it asks. "Are you going to sit there like an idiot . . . or are you going to read the Urban Survival Arsenal and be prepared to exact a mighty toll as you retreat?"

The message is to exchange self-fulfillment for self-protection, roller skates and rolfing tables for rifles. As Survivalist Fred Kurpsie, fondling his weapons, told CBS News, "This will stop a man, kill a man."

Good Neighbor Fred finds his inspiration, no doubt, in the books hot off the Delta Press publishing list like *The Brass Knuckle Bible* and *Kill or Be Killed*.

Well, we should have seen it coming. On the best seller lists the books on how to flatten your stomach are being replaced by books on how to increase your Krugerrands.

The optimistic self-obsession of Wayne Dyer has been topped by the pessimistic self-obsession of Douglas Casey. While Dyer, the man of the seventies, boasts that *The Sky's the Limit,* Casey, the man of the eighties, offers tips on *Crisis Investing* for those who want to make big bucks on everyone else's bad times.

I suppose it was inevitable. This is the decade of the paranoid "haves." The fever is part of the national cult of self-defense. Survivalists are probably acting out the impotence and anxiety felt by many others.

But Survivalism is the frontier spirit gone mean; individualism turned hostile.

In the new Me Decade, sharing your feelings is out; hiding your assets is in. The people who were once into personal growth are being replaced by the people who are into personal hoarding.

If the mentor of the seventies Self was a psychologist, the mentor of the eighties Self is an urban guerrilla warfare instructor. If the seventies Self looked down his belly button, the eighties Self looks down a rifle barrel.

Frankly I'm spooked by the people who are sure The End is At Hand . . . for everyone else. I'm spooked by people waiting for the chance to defend their dried food and turf against the marauding hordes. I'm spooked by people who spend their energy embracing the end instead of avoiding it.

The people who move from worrying about disaster to preparing for it, will end up looking forward to it. Like people who put a date on Doomsday, they have an investment in being right.

While the rest of us try to solve problems, they put their money on the collapse. They bet that it won't be the righteous but the selfish who inherit the earth.

I find nothing new in this message. It's the oldest cult on earth: every man for himself. And to my ear, at least, that isn't a sermon of survival. It's the same old pathetic preaching of humanity's defeat.

NOVEMBER 1980

Such Empty Options

The man is keeping his options open. He has been doing it for some time now and it is, I suppose, what he does best.

Through the decade I have known him, he has let good women and great chances slip through his hands like water. But he has held onto his options like a lifeline.

In fact, you might say that at thirty his most long-lasting, deeply held commitment is to noncommitment. But perhaps that is too pat.

The option tender is, after all, a man of some charm. He wears the appropriate suit and air of interest. He carries the right briefcase and credentials. He has a good sense of taste and humor. And he travels light.

There is nothing wrong with him, nothing at all. Just something different. How can I explain it?

The option tender is a man who works carefully at his job, but always has a résumé out. The option tender is a man who enjoys seeing a woman, but always has an eye out.

He doesn't get involved. He responds to affection with alarm and to praise with wariness. What one person calls connections, he calls bonds. And if one person values commitment—well, he values options.

The man is not unaware of himself. He once described

life to me as a kind of one-plate buffet table. If you fill up
your plate at the beginning, you won't have any more room
at the end of the table. What, he asked earnestly, if the
shrimp cocktail is in the last dish?

He prefers, you see, to leave some space for what might
come next. So he serves himself only the stingiest spoonfuls.
The option tender says that this way he is keeping his life
open-ended.

He is not the only one. I am told that he belongs to a
kind of subculture, a whole generation living in a permanent
state of potential.

I am told, moreover, by people like Gail Sheehy that
they have a label. They are called now the Postponing Generation, as if there were an Andromeda strain of delayed
adolescence running through their age group. But I wonder
if postponing can become incurably habit-forming.

The option tender had a father once. I knew the man.
He had married at twenty-two, fathered at twenty-three,
gone to war at twenty-four. By thirty he had three children,
one mortgage, and a job which he turned into a vice-presidency after fifteen years of hard labor. By fifty-four he was
dead.

"Locked in," the son had told me at his father's funeral.
"He spent his whole life locked in." His father's plate was
overloaded, and he had fallen under its weight.

So, the son mixed guilt with terror. He built his father's
life story into his own life plan. Where his father was locked
in, he would be open. Where his father had burdens, he
would have space.

We all do that. Whatever else, we tell ourselves we won't
make the same mistakes as our parents. We are much more
conscious of what was missing in their lives than what was
present. Much more conscious of what was bad than what
was good.

We don't make their mistakes. We make our own.

The Workaholic Heart Attack Victim has become almost
a cliché, a negative role-model, if you must, for a whole
generation of sons.

He is, to young men, what the displaced homemaker is to young women: The Ghost of Christmas Future.

The man's sister, who watched her mother become a widow at fifty-one, also knows what she doesn't want to be when she grows up. An unemployed widow, an unemployable divorcée. Her protection against the ghosts is work. His protection is . . . keeping his options open.

The thirty-year-old man doesn't describe it this way. He says that where his father had obligations, he has freedom; where his father had responsibilities, he has opportunities; where his father had a wife, three children, a mortgage and a vice-presidency, he has . . . his options.

But what I wonder is simply this; Where is the line between being locked in and frozen out? When do options become emptiness? When do you realize that the only way to keep a full table of choices is to keep an empty plate?

When does the option tender who has everything in potential realize that he holds nothing in the palm of his hand?

NOVEMBER 1979

Hung Up

It's not that I have anything against psychiatry. Some of my best friends have been shrunk as if their heads were 100 percent cotton. When it was over, they fit better.

But I worry about those members of the mental "help"

professions who take every public problem and wash it into a private one. I worry, too, about the lay people who spin-dry each social illness until it looks like an emotional dis-ease. I worry about the rest of us who wring every fear into a phobia.

It has become, if you will excuse the expression, a social disease.

At Three Mile Island, for example, we have people busily turning a nuclear accident into a neurotic one. It's a year now since the incident at the Pennsylvania plant and we still have no scientific solution to the technical problems. What we do have is a $375,000 grant from the federal government to study chronic stress.

I have no objection to turning the area into a psychiatric lab. It's better than being a radioactive lab. But I have the creepy feeling that by the second anniversary of Three Mile Island, we'll be experts in "living with nuclear plant stress" and rank amateurs in getting rid of the source.

The same thing has happened with the DC-10. Since last winter, I have entered these planes only against my better judgment and my instructions to the travel agent.

When I talked about this fear with a flight attendant on a 727, she agreed. But then she told me that those attendants who refuse to work on the plane are being offered, you guessed it, psychiatric help. The airline wants to ground the fear, you see, instead of the engine. Never mind that there may be more to fear than fear itself.

The same thing happened to a woman who was being sexually harassed by the men at her plant. When she com-plained to her boss, he referred her to a psychiatrist.

I understand that in the world there are people who are nuts. But I am also sure that the world can make people nuts. The "helping professions" are sometimes less con-cerned with the causes than the treatment. But we all have a tendency lately to focus more on the individual than the environment.

Take inflation (please!) as an example. We are now hav-ing a national anxiety attack about money. We have people sinking into debt or terrified about the future of their fixed incomes. I am sure that they will all be taking tranquilizers, and reading articles on anxiety. Someone will surely come up with a perfectly reasonable program for dealing with inflationphobia: jogging and brown rice.

Inflation—like DC-10s, and Three Mile Islands, and Cold Wars—is bad for your mental health. But there is a difference between dealing with these problems as social diseases or as psychological ones. It's the difference between giving the unemployed jobs or giving them leaflets on how to explain to their children why they aren't getting birthday presents.

The whole psychiatric, psychobabble approach to major social problems makes me cringe. It puts the responsibility on the person who often is least powerful. It smacks of blaming the victim.

It's not that mental problems aren't real. They are. But there are a host of anxieties for which the best treatment is rubbing dollars bills all over your body.

There are other problems which need more action and less analysis. I know a couple who spent six sessions at a marital counseling service discussing their arguments over housework. For the same price, they could have hired a cleaning service. But the cleaning service isn't covered by health insurance.

For the past ten years, we have had a tendency to look at a lot of our problems as personal, private, psychological when they may be environmental, social, public.

We all have a tendency to shrink our problems to manageable size by placing them inside our heads. We learn to cope with the world instead of trying to change it.

I sometimes suspect that mental health in America is like mental health in Russia. In the USSR you get labeled crazy, maladjusted or whatever, if you disagree with the government. In the United States, you can get a psychiatric referral if you freak out over the chemicals in your backyard, or the agent Orange in your past, or the Not-So-Jolly Green Giant in your wallet.

Psychiatry is a growth industry in this country. Like any expanding business it starts creeping into new areas. We seem to launder more and more anxieties into syndromes. The only thing we should be shrinking is the market.

MARCH 1980

Watching the Grasshopper Get the Goodies

I don't usually play the great American game called Categories. There are already too many ways to divide us into opposing teams, according to age, race, sex and favorite flavors. Every time we turn around, someone is telling us that the whole country is made up of those who drive pickup trucks and those who do not, and then analyzing what this means in terms of the Middle East.

Still, it occurs to me that if we want to figure out why people are angry right now, it's not a bad idea to see ourselves as a nation of planners and nonplanners. It's the planners these days who are feeling penalized, right down to their box score at the bank.

The part of us which is most visibly and vocally infuriated by inflation, for example, isn't our liberal or conservative side but, rather, our planning side. Inflation devastates our attempts to control our futures—to budget and predict and expect. It particularly makes fools out of the people who saved then to buy now. To a certain extent, it rewards instant gratification and makes a joke out of our traditional notions of preparation.

It is no news bulletin that the people who dove over their heads into the real-estate market a few years ago are now generally better off than those who dutifully decided to save up for a larger down payment. With that "larger down payment" they can now buy two double-thick rib lambchops and a partridge in a pear tree.

But inflation isn't the only thing that leaves the planners feeling betrayed. There are other issues that find them actively pitched against the nonplanners.

We all know families who saved for a decade to send their kids to college. A college diploma these days costs about the same amount as a Mercedes-Benz. Of course, the Mercedes lasts longer and has a higher trade-in value. But the most devoted parent can be infuriated to discover that a neighboring couple who spent its income instead of saving is now eligible for college financial aid, while they are not. To the profligate go the spoils.

This can happen anywhere on the economic spectrum. There is probably only one mother in the annals of the New York welfare rolls to save up a few thousand dollars in hopes of getting off aid. But she would have been better off spending it. When she was discovered this year, the welfare department took the money back. She, too, was penalized for planning.

In these crimped times, the Planned Parents of the Purse are increasingly annoyed at other parents—whether they are unwed or on welfare or just prolific. For the first time in my own time, you can hear families with few children complaining out loud at the tax bill for the public schooling of families with many children.

One man I heard even suggested charging tuition for the third child. He admitted, "It's not a very generous attitude, I know. But I'm not feeling very generous these days." He is suffering from planner's warts.

At the same time I've talked with friends whose parents prepared, often with financial difficulty, for their "old age" and illness. They feel sad when this money goes down a nursing home drain, but furious when other people who didn't save get this same care for free.

Now we are all aware that if many people don't plan their economic lives, it may be because they can't. It does no one any good to keep the cashless out of college, to stash the old and poor into elderly warehouses, to leave the "extra" children illiterate. We do want to help others, but we also want our own efforts to make a difference.

There is nothing that grates a planner more than seeing a nonplanner profit. It's as if the ant had to watch the grasshopper get the goodies.

Our two notions about what's fair end up on opposite sides. It isn't fair if the poor get treated badly, and it isn't fair if those who work and save, plan and postpone aren't given a better shake. We want the winners to be the deserving. Only there is no divining rod for the deserving.

The hard part is to create policies that are neither unkind nor insane. It is, after all, madness not to reward the kind of behavior we want to encourage. It we want the ranks of the planners to increase in this massive behavior-modification program called society, we have to give them the rewards, instead of the outrage.

MARCH 1979

EST:
Energy Saving Tips

In the spirit of the times, your family newspaper has brought the moral equivalent of war marching into every home to the beat of John Philip Sousa. As journalists, we have just profiled several red-blooded patriotic American families who are Licking the High Cost of Energy.

During the gas crisis of the past summer, for example, we offered the stirring example of Mr. and Mrs. Moonshiner, who brew their own gasohol and carry their entire family of twelve to church on a single moped. Well, today as the days grow shorter, and we all begin to sing our own September song, "Baby It's Cold Outside," we have the hearthwarming tale of Bob and Sue Down.

The Downs are typical Urban Homesteaders who assumed they would get a divorce as soon as they finished renovating their brownstone. But just as they had stripped the last wall down to its brick, they discovered EST: Energy Saving Tips.

They now have a renewed sense of commitment. In the sharing spirit of EST, the Downs told this reporter (exclusively) some of the handy hints which you, too, can use to get through the next winter with lower fuel costs. To begin with, last year Sue (fondly known as Goose) Down signed up for the energy-saving hours program with her local utility. She now does her family wash (in cold water, of course) between the hours of 11 P.M. and 4 A.M. on Sunday, Tuesday or alternate Fridays.

This has been an inconvenience because during the evening hours the Down thermostat is turned to 55 degrees. But it has not proved unpleasant since she took the dryer exhaust out of the wall. All that warm air which was once cast wastefully into the night now heats the laundry room and dries her hair. "You do get some lint in your hair," Goose says, "but it saves a bundle on the blow-dryer."

As long as she is up at that hour anyway, Goose is also able to turn the dishwasher off before it goes onto that old energy-guzzling cycle, dry. By opening the door at the right moment, the dishes dry by themselves and the moist air humidifies the kitchen while defrosting the meat for their next night's supper.

Bob also helps. At the beginning of the year, he took out a license as a draft detector. He now has a duly registered caulking gun. Although he is a bit quick on the trigger—"last week he sealed the toaster-oven"—the energy bill reflects his energy.

He has insulated every window with (1) weather stripping, (2) a storm window, (3) an insulated five-layer shade, (4) a large piece of plastic and, of course, (5) his own polyester window quilt created to match the tapestries which now hang on every formerly chilly wall.

Every sunny morning Bob goes to the east window and removes the insulated shades and polyester quilts to let the sun stream in across his plant-filled greenhouse windowsill. After dark he boards it up again. This he figures, conservatively, saves $14.57 a month on his fuel bill.

The Downs' two teenage girls also keep chipping away at those pennies. Since the family that saves together stays together, they help by putting the plug in the bathtub while they shower. When both girls are through, they leave the warm water in the tub until it cools down to room temperature, thus growing some interesting molds around the ring of the tub.

The girls find they can study in this nice warm room by

putting a plank across the sink and using the twenty-five-watt night-light. "This year Ducky (their seventeen-year-old) will be saving even more energy by having her boyfriend Josh move in. At first we were worried about that, but Ducky pointed out that women only have 330 BTUs while men have 390 BTUs. So we could see where it made energy sense. Not to mention energy cents!" she quips.

Ducky and Josh will need every ounce of heat they can generate since Ducky's old room has been closed off ("just between October and April") and they will be living in the seaweed-insulated attic.

All the Downs have changed their clothing habits. Since one-fourth of the body warmth is radiated through the head they wear ski masks throughout most of the day. During this interview, for example, Bob wore his Eddie Bauer 100 percent goose down facial mask.

During the average winter evening they each retire into their long, quilted body bags. Duck demonstrated for us how quickly you can move in a body bag once you get the hang of it. Goose, who used to cut quite a figure among the Perrier and spinach salad crowd still wears cashmere camisoles and a flannel teddy (not the bear, the underwear).

She and Bob once again share a double bed instead of twins, for obvious reasons, but she confesses it hasn't done much for their sex lives. "I think it's the socks," she says. Asked whether things will get dull again now that they have dodged every draft and cut their fuel bill by two-thirds, Bob says no. Their goal is to see if they can heat the entire house for a whole month with one pot of soup and a hundred-watt light bulb. To see how this family makes it through the winter keep your energy eye on this hot spot. We're hoping for a 100 percent Down victory!!

SEPTEMBER 1979

Read Gourmet, *Eat Scarsdale*

As a citizen of a country where the national spectator sport is Watching What You Eat, I am part of a lingering minority who still regard food as fun.

I know that is radical, but there you are. Surrounded by messages to read *Gourmet* and eat Scarsdale, I do not like to feast solely with my eyes. In fact, my all-time favorite diet was written by F. Scott Fitzgerald: "Gave up spinach for Lent."

I am not a gluttonous eater, you understand, but a constant one who thinks of a fast as three hours without food. This is because I was raised on Winnie the Pooh who was, in turn, raised on demand feeding. His internal clock didn't register lunch time or dinner time but, rather, "Time for a Little Something."

The reason I do not have the same shape as my little mentor is that Winnie hit the honey pot and I tend to chomp on things, like carrot sticks, that make noises inside my head.

Nevertheless, I am absolutely inundated and depressed by messages warning me that food—too much of it or the wrong kinds of it—may be bad for my health.

Which brings me to the point. Every night on my way home, when my mind is filled with lovely thoughts of A Little Something, I pass a six-foot-high male midriff bulge.

This particular bulge is brought to me on a sign paid for by the Blue Cross–Blue Shield people and it is captioned with the following two words: Hazardous Waist.

I have a theory about the double message of this sign. It is that, living in a world which seems dangerously out of our control, we have become obsessed with defending our own bodily turf. When we can't do anything about the big hazardous wastes out there, we worry about the hazardous waist around our middle.

The waistline gag would not go over big at Love Canal. But even there, I will bet you some people are counting calories while their chromosomes are under attack. They are like the man photographed jogging in the shadow of Three Mile Island during its darkest days.

The urge to protect our own lives is part of human nature. If we can't control anything else, at least we think we can control our weight.

And our shape. And our health.

This vague obsession with our selves isn't either the hedonism or the masochism it's cracked up to be. It's self-defense. We draw a Maginot Line around our bodies and regard anything that goes into them as potential intruders.

The news is full of stories this week that deal with food as if it were a foreign agent. They divide our problems into eating and exercising, calories and cholesterol, pounds and preservatives, sweeteners and sodium.

The National Academy of Sciences reports that the cholesterol we were supposed to give up may not be bad for us, but too much salt and too many pounds are. Another researcher tells us that the bypass surgery performed on 20,000 people a year may control their obesity but cause their arthritis.

In the *Journal of American Medicine*, someone writes that we can help our hearts by walking briskly and carrying a six-and-a-half-pound stick. In the *New England Journal of Medicine*, someone else says that the secret to preventing heart disease may be eating Chinese black tree fungus.

Meanwhile, at Arizona State University middle-aged pigs

on polysaturated and polyunsaturated diets are forced to go jogging.

The fact is that if you are what you eat these days, you are confused.

In an odd way the urge to take charge of our lives has led us headlong into the arms of the "experts." But as Irish essayist Robert Lynd once said, "The last man in the world whose opinion I would take on what to eat would be a doctor. It is far safer to consult a waiter, and not a bit more expensive."

The National Academy of Sciences report offers at least one thought close to my heart: "Good food . . . should not be regarded as a poison, a medicine or a talisman. It should be eaten and enjoyed."

Yes, indeed, I think it's Time for a Little Something.

JUNE 1980

Bamama

My friend will get another degree next week. She will become a B.A., M.A., M.A., or as we fondly call her, a Bamama.

This latest degree will raise her academic temperature and the quality of her résumé. In fact, as of June 4, my friend Bamama will become officially qualified to be unemployed in yet a better class of jobs.

Let me explain. When she got a B.A. in philosophy four years ago at the cost of $12,000 (them was the bargain basement days), Bamama had the choice between becoming an overeducated waitress or an overeducated office worker. So she became an overeducated day-camp counselor and went back to school.

The next year, for $4,000, she got a degree in library science. Now, qualified as a librarian, she won a job as an overeducated part-time library assistant. In her off-hours, she became an overqualified clerk at a cheese counter. Rumors that she arranged the cheddar according to the Dewey Decimal system were greatly exaggerated.

In any case, her course was clear. Before she entirely coated her brain as well as her arteries with brie, she went back to school. Now, $5,000 later, she is qualified not only as a librarian, but as a school librarian, teacher, administrator, etc, for a school system in need of an efficient, caring, well-educated Bamama. No such luck or, rather, no such system.

So, Bamama has done the only logical thing: applied for and been accepted for a Ph.D. program. With that degree, Bamamaphd, three years older and deeper in debt, would be qualified as a college professor and might, therefore, be able to find a job as an overqualified school librarian.

She had, you see, followed the life pattern of Woody Allen, who says that success has meant that he is now turned down for dates by a better class of women. Bamama may be particularly adroit at choosing a career track on which 90 percent of the stations have been closed. But the problem is not uniquely hers.

There are more than one million Americans getting bachelor's degrees this year, more than 300,000 getting master's degrees and more than 32,000 getting doctorates.

They and/or their parents are up to their ears in debt. The economy is up to its ears in the overeducated underemployed.

Eighty percent of the recent college graduates, we are told, are doing work which was once done quite capably by people without college degrees. The point is that you don't need the degree to do the job. But nowadays you do need the degree to get the job.

College graduates may be getting the jobs once filled by nongraduates, but they are not automatically filling the spots once guaranteed by a degree. There is more educational competition at every level. In fact, by 1985, 2.5 college graduates will be competing for every "college" job.

This is the name of the 1980s war game called Defensive Education. As economist Lester Thurow put it: "As the supply of more highly educated labor increases, individuals find that they must improve their own education qualifications simply to defend their current income position. If they do not go to college, others will and they will not find their current job open to them."

This is described as the "tiptoe syndrome" in Michael Harrington's book *Decade of Decision*. At any parade, the people in the second row stand on tiptoe to see over the heads of those in the front row. Then everyone else behind them stands on tiptoe, just to stay in the same position.

As more and more people go to college, a degree no longer guarantees who will get ahead. But the lack of a degree still can determine who will fall behind. We keep raising the education threshold to the job market.

This is the sort of new truth that makes us feel trapped and cynical and furious. Trapped into paying a fortune, not for advance but for defense. Cynical about the real motivation for "Higher Education."

Meanwhile, even as we play the game, the gap between our education level and job level grows and is filled with the discontent of the "underemployed."

Remember the movie *Goodbye Columbus?* There was a moment when the father, who owns a trucking business, shakes his head watching his son work. Finally he sighs, "Four years of college, and he can't load a truck."

Just a few years ago, that was funny. But at the current rate of the education escalation war, the kid won't even be able to get a tryout without a Ph.D.

The Breakdown of Private Lives

Not long ago, I talked to a friend who was newly sepa-
rated. The thing that surprised him the most, he said, wasn't
losing his home. He was prepared for that pain. It was rather,
losing his privacy.

His wife, he said, casually traded the secrets of their
marriage to others. She littered cocktail tables with the pretzel
crumbs of their last scenes. His flaws, his absurdities, were
exchanged like the calling cards of the newly single: You
show me yours, and I'll show you mine. It was a bizarre
violation.

I suppose we have all had some similar kind of experience. Perhaps as a child we told something to our parents
and saw it repeated to other adults as a "cute anecdote." As
a grown-up perhaps we told a secret to a friend and found
it transformed overnight into neighborhood gossip.

The pain of betrayal is much greater when the traitor has
been an intimate. It is horrid when we let someone into the
front yard of our lives and he bulldozes the fence.

Yet it happens all the time in private life, and especially
in the private life of public people.

"Gossip," wrote Harvard law professors Samuel Warren
and Louis Brandeis way back in 1890, "is no longer the

resource of the idle and vicious, but has become a trade which is pursued with industry as well as effrontery." And they hadn't even read *Jackie Oh!*

Today the invasion of privacy has become big in the book business. The most popular of the gossip books are now the most destructive—the ones written by intimates, the Split and Tell authors.

This spring alone we've been treated to Sheila Weidenfeld's breach of faith with the Gerald Fords. We've been offered the memoirs of a lover, publicly reveling like some necrophiliac in his month with Marilyn Monroe, telling us the state of her stomach muscles and her insecurities.

But the worst of this genre is the latest, a classic work of self-indulgence by Margaret Trudeau, appropriately named *Beyond Reason.*

When Margaret Trudeau left her prime-minister husband to "find herself," she wore the full regalia of delayed adolescence. It was embarrassing and yet understandable. Now, at thirty, this relentless flowerchild titters her ghost-written silliness across North America.

She confesses all: the times her husband sniffed her hair for marijuana; their passion for caviar; his jealousy; her infidelity, rebelliousness and unhappiness. Clinging to immaturity as if it were her permission slip, she writes a book that is—as she describes the scene of her Las Vegas tryst— "quite outstanding in its vulgarity."

Autobiography without literary merit is gossip. And in this graceless work, Trudeau trades on her estranged husband's fame in order to tread on it. Surely the timing, publication in the midst of an election campaign, is determinedly destructive.

If the child-woman had merely exposed her own inanity, the book would be no more than humiliating. Yet she chose to sacrifice her husband and her children to her "honesty." As the law professors put it, this is an "effrontery," a gross invasion of privacy, privacy she doesn't own.

Each of us, says Robert Smith, the author of *Privacy,* "needs an environment in which we don't have to be accountable for what we do." We need privacy in which to explore each other and ourselves. We need privacy and intimacy.

Vulnerable to invasion by big government, big business and bigger computers, we fall back more needfully on our families, our friends, the network of trusting relationships we call our Private Lives.

Yet for the most public of us, from Ottawa to Washington, violations occur more frequently than parking tickets.

"This kind of privacy has disappeared for public figures," says Smith. "I don't think Teddy Kennedy can sneeze without someone, even very intimate associates, marking it for future use. It means that people are much more cautious. There are absolutely no moments of candor. We don't give them any time when they are truly backstairs at the White House."

When he married this child-woman, Trudeau was surely of an age to know better. Yet he doesn't deserve this mistress of indiscretion. This is infidelity of a much deeper and more unforgivable sort.

Margaret Trudeau has broken new ground on the privacy front. She has introduced the estranged wife as tattletale— not merely on the cocktail party circuit but in the best-selling confessional. It is, to put it bluntly, much worse to do this to people you have loved.

At the end of the book, she writes: "I realize I don't come out of this story very well." It is her only understatement.

APRIL 1979

Don't Just Stand There, Do Something

I once worked in an office with a sign that read: "Don't Just Stand There, Do Something." I always wanted to rip that thing off the wall, but it occurs to me now that it was the perfect American slogan, a motto worth being immortalized in needlepoint.

Americans seem to do "something" pretty eagerly and often pretty well. But we "just stand there" very badly.

We get as antsy when our government is doing nothing as when our kids are doing it. We are much more in tune with busy-ness, action, and we prefer living with at least the illusion of purpose.

"Even if it doesn't work," wrote Henry Miller, "there's something healthy and invigorating about direct action." And most of us would agree.

I suppose that's half the reason why we were so distracted by the way Carter handles—or doesn't handle—foreign policy. What he calls restraint looks a lot like passivity.

How do you spell relief in America? A-C-T-I-O-N.

Jerry Brown knows that, too. Since he decided to run for the presidency, he talks a lot less about lowering our expectations and more about raising our eyes to the heavens, or to the exploration of the solar system. He waxes on about expanding, as well as accepting.

29

"Lower Your Expectations" wouldn't, after all, make a very good bumper sticker.

Most of us are the inheritors of a Can-Do philosophy. We instinctively prefer the sort of questions posed by Karl Malden in that silly American Express ad: "What will you do? What *will* you do?"

But now we come smack up against the realities of what we can't do—like dictate events in foreign countries and devise perfect social solutions in our own. We even have to think about when the best thing to do might be nothing.

I don't know many people who truly believe that idle brains are the only devil's workshop. Brains working overtime may be more dangerous. Someone once wrote to me that, "A million professional sunbathers do a whole lot less harm than one very busy criminal or even at times a well-intentioned social planner."

It's true that doctors, social workers, members of Congress are asked, maybe for the first time, to do less. Medical people are criticized when they intervene too eagerly in terminal illness. Congress is criticized if it regulates too much. Social workers are criticized if they "do good" to excess.

It's hard to know these days when inaction is a cop-out and when it's the better choice. It's hardest, though, to do nothing, even when it's "right."

We run into this sort of problem all the time, even with our kids. When should we intervene, "help" with their homework or their social problems or their moral decisions? When do they need our advice and authority? When will our best efforts work? When will they only build a fine resistance? When do kids have to figure things out for themselves?

But even if the best policy is a hands-off policy, it can be agonizing. The agony of not doing.

"Action may not always bring happiness. But there is no happiness without action." How far off the mark was Disraeli? For many of us, inaction always feels like repression of will, a conscious suppression of the innate desire to *do something*.

I suppose that's not the worst of human flaws or of national flaws. It's one that can make us act precipitously, even make mistakes, but it also makes us flexible and searching.

Today, however, we live with a justified fear of mistakes and fear of inaction. So we feel increasingly trapped in the undecided zone between standing there and doing something.

MARCH 1979

Primal Screen

Someday, I would like to see a television series about a family that sits around the set watching a series about a family that sits around the set.

It might not make the Nielsen top ten, but it isn't such a strange idea. Especially when you think about what's going on right now.

Night after night, inside the tube, warm and wiggly families spend their prime time "communicating" like crazy and "solving problems" together like mad. Meanwhile, outside the tube, real families sit and wait for a commercial break just to talk to each other.

About the only subject that never comes up before our

glazed eyes is what the medium does to our family life. But, I suppose we already know that.

According to a recent Gallup Poll, television comes out as a major heavy in our family lives. On the scale of problems, TV didn't rate as bad as inflation, but it ran neck-and-neck with unemployment.

According to a recent Roper Poll, it even causes fights. When people were asked what husbands and wives argued about, money was the champion. But television was a strong contender.

Husbands and wives were far more likely to fight about television than about that old standby, sex. But, considering how much more time we spend in front of the tube, that may not be such a shock.

To a certain extent, we blame the programs. In the Gallup Poll, for example, people worried most about the over-emphasis on sex and violence. But surely half of those fights between husbands and wives must be about the more fundamental issue of turning it off.

Deep down below our poll-taking consciousness, we know that the worst aspect of our addiction isn't what's on TV, but how long the TV is on. We can't help but be aware of what happens when we spend more time facing the screen than facing each other.

In that same Gallup Poll, a large number of us said that the way to improve family life is by sharing—sharing family needs, recreational activities and chores. But when you are watching, you aren't doing. The only experience you are sharing is a vicarious one.

I am absolutely convinced that the average wife feels tuned out by the twelfth consecutive weekend sports event because she *is* being tuned out. The average kid develops that distant, slack-jawed, hypnotic, hooked stare because he or she *is* hooked.

In the same way, the people who spend night after night in front of the tube should worry about it. They've become an audience and not a family. Television simply presents us with one model of family life. Watching it makes us fit another model.

But the striking thing in all of this research about how we feel and behave is the role of choice. On the one hand, we have real anxiety about what TV's doing to us. On the other hand, we allow it to happen.

We choose to turn it on and each other off. We choose peace and quiet when we let the kids watch TV instead of running around the living room. We choose to "relax" in the semi-comatose slump.

The average viewing time of the American child between six and sixteen years of age is twenty to twenty-four hours a week. A large percentage of parents place no restrictions on either the number of hours watched or the type of program viewed.

At the very least, we behave as if we were powerless to wrench each other away.

I grant you that there are a lot of things that touch on our families that are totally out of our individual control. We can't regulate foreign affairs. We can't set the price for oil. We have about as great a chance of controlling inflation as we do of capping Mount St. Helens.

But a television set has a dial and a plug. And we have hands. It is absurd to let our feelings of impotence in the world start creeping into our private lives.

Just once, we ought to create a private show about a real-life family that kicked the habit.

JULY 1980

Hostages in an Urban Fortress

He has three keys dangling from one end of his key chain.
The top one, he explains, goes into the extra safety lock.
The round one turns off the burglar alarm. The bottom one
opens the door. When he was a kid, he tells me, the back
door of the house was always unlocked. His own kids are
taught never, never, to open the door to strangers.

She is seated next to me on the airplane. She looks over
and says I should put my gold chain in my pocketbook when
I get to New York. Haven't I heard about the kids ripping
necklaces off women? I take it off.

She is traveling on business again. At the registration
desk the clerk tells her that they have a new escort service.
Someone is available to accompany her every time she goes
to her room. Once she would have refused, now she accepts.

They are not paranoid, these people. Nor am I. We do
not cower in distant suburbs afraid to come to the city for
dinner. In fact we all live in cities, and have evolved over
time a certain pride in urban survival.

And yet something has changed.

Maybe it was the thirteen-year-old son held up on the
way home from school by seventeen-year-old boys. Maybe
it was the fourth time the car window was broken and the
third time the stereo was stolen. Maybe it was the purposeful

murder of John Lennon or the random murder of Dr. Michael Halberstam.

Or maybe there are simply too many incidents too close to home to brush off anymore.

But our resilience has been worn down, and so we shake our heads when we read Chief Justice Warren Burger's words to the American Bar Association: "What people want is that crime and criminals be brought under control so that we can be safe on the streets and in our homes and for our children to be safe in schools and at play. Today that safety is very, very fragile."

If Burger was out of place delivering an eleven-point program as if he were an attorney general, he nevertheless clarified something that we already know: The urban spirit is turning into a fortress mentality.

We've all heard it in a dozen small, anxious ways. In the dinner-party gossip about crime that now matches, story for story, the gossip about love affairs. Which family on the street has broken up? Which family broken into?

The same people who talked incessantly about making a profit from their real estate now talk incessantly about protecting their real estate. Today they improve their homes with iron bars instead of bushes. They add locks instead of shutters.

There is an edge to life, sane and sad, of self-protection. The man who put on his necklace as a sign of free expression in the seventies takes it off for safety in the eighties. The woman who bought silver in the fifties as a tribute to financial security hides it in the eighties as a tribute to insecurity.

I don't mean to suggest that we are obsessed, that we quake in fear. We don't. But our guard is up more often in more places.

On the street, we may fantasize a plan of self-defense. In the elevator, in the ladies room, in the subway, an image of danger may flit across out consciousness for just a moment. We may begin almost superstitiously to avoid some place that seems dangerous to us, whether it's a red-light district or an underground garage.

I have not even mentioned gun permits and California self-protection courses in the use of tear gas.

"Are we not hostages within the borders of ourselves because of alarms and locks?" asked Burger.

Yes.

It isn't just the criminal offensive that affects our lives, it is our own growing defensive. When we learn to turn on the alarm, put the jewelry in the refrigerator, push down the buttons in the car, think twice about walking down a street, our lives are diminished.

The man looks at the burglar alarm keys in his hand. He hates them. I tuck the chain inside my pocketbook and resent it. The woman is escorted to her room and feels smaller. All of us are somehow less free.

NOVEMBER 1980

For Goodness' Sake

There was something ironic about the story to begin with. Once again, the United States was guilty. But this time we were guilty of the international crime of doing good.

The headline put it this way: U.S. Criticized for Aiding Refugees. The story went on to list the countries and quote the officials who blamed us for our policy of rescuing the boat people.

We were told that our action merely encouraged more people to flee from Vietnam and so, in a sense, it was our fault that the ranks of the homeless were swelling. Under this reasoning, the ones who refused these people admission, pushed them out to sea, sent them back to bailing were actually the good guys.

Well, forgive me if I don't buy that. Perhaps my level of American guilt is falling below par, but this is the sort of Darwinian morality that I find repulsive . . . and common. All around me.

I see "doing good" labeled "butting in." We are told that the only moral stance these days is noninterventionist—the survival of the fittest. Things are upside down. Good is bad and bad is good, and we are left in the wrong.

When I was a kid, this country exported do-goodness. The crates were stamped with the words: Made in America. Maybe our marketing plan was too global or too naive. We wanted not only to rebuild Europe but to "save the free world."

We were, I am sure, too sanguine in our sense that we could do no wrong. But now we are frustrated, even embittered with the sense that we can do no right.

It occurs to me that we are thwarted by our inability to use our power. Not the flexing muscles, CIA sort of power, but the power to help.

Some of our frustration comes, justifiably, from a trial and error sophistication. We have become, as we should have, far more aware of consequences. When we reduce the rate of infancy death, we may increase the rate of malnutrition. When we "save" a country from one dictator, we may deliver it to another. When we rescue a boatload of people adrift in the sea, we may in fact be the hope that encourages others into it.

But we have also become too cynical about our motives, cutting down our kinder impulses. We are overwhelmingly aware now of the times when we "did good" in the national interest. We are self-conscious about the times when our bleeding hearts made good business sense.

Well, I am hardly a flower child, but I think that caring is also a motive, and the desire to help others is also an urge. Edward Wilson, the sociobiologist, wrote in his book that altruism is also innate, as natural an instinct as self-interest. He has a case.

I am not going to read you the line about people being basically good. I don't think people are basically anything except a collection of possibilities pushed into action by the right button.

When a woman in Florida gets arrested for shoplifting food because she is hungry, people deluge her with cans. When they see the Save-the-Children photographs in the magazines, they respond. When they read about people pushed from port to port, their instinct is to help.

It is popular to note that these people may also regularly vote against foreign aid and food stamps. But if their own lives are not mean enough to have killed off the energy and interest in others, they care.

But what happens when time and time again we see more of the negative consequences of doing good than the positive? What happens when time and time again we are criticized for helping, lambasted for reaching out?

At some point, surely, we feel and behave as if we were isolated. We retreat to increasingly narrow concentric circles, to the places and people we can affect, to the guiltless region of inaction, to ourselves. Instead of improving the world, we improve our serve.

It's important not to flip from naiveté to cynicism. It's true that we can't "save the world." Our "causes" are often random and shallow. There are consequences from the most well-meaning action that may require more help, even indefinitely.

But retreating leaves the world a harsher place. In the case of the boat people, there is no benign neglect. Not even the defensive judgment of those who made the headlines can convince me that it is more moral to let people drown. We know better, instinctively.

AUGUST 1979

Indecency Is Legion

This is the sort of column that is supposed to begin with the words, "I'm not a prude but..." However, I'm not so sure anymore. I think I am becoming one of those little old ladies in tennis shoes who go around brandishing umbrellas at X-rated people.

I realized it first in one of those boutiques where people try on clothes to a disco beat. But this time, the stereophonic sound wafting over the racks resembled the sound track of a porno flick in which the lead female says nothing but "Oh, Oh, Oh." It made disco seem subtle.

What I wanted to do was walk up to the manager and tell him that if he didn't switch off the hard-core station, I'd walk out the door. What I did, however, was to walk out the door.

Then, a few days later, I personally girl-cotted Jordache jeans from my daughter's dressing room, because of the ad they have running. This ad features a teenage girl mounting a teenage boy, piggyback style. Jordache has brought the values of *Lollytots* magazine into such good gray publications as the Sunday *New York Times*. I personally refused to support the kidporn of the ad world.

As if this weren't enough, last night I found myself ranting and raving about the Calvin Klein TV ads that pan slowly up to the crotch of fifteen-year-old Brooke Shields and say something like, "I have fifteen pairs of Calvins in my closet. If they could talk I'd be in trouble." Suddenly I wanted to drown Brooke Shields in the nearest blue lagoon.

Once upon a time, it was only card-carrying members of the Legion of Decency who went around sputtering words like "disgusting," "obscene," "indecent." But once upon a time, a prude was someone who knitted clothes for dogs. Once upon a time, "indecent" was the word for a wife who undressed in front of her husband with the lights on.

Now I find myself applauding a friend who got two underage kids kicked out of the R-rated *Dressed to Kill*.

You don't have to be a parent to be appalled at the teeny-bopper stations playing the ten-minute orgasm, or the clothing industry marketing fifteen-year-olds into sex-for-sale objects. But it helps.

Growing up, especially in the second decade of life, is mined with explosive changes, physical and emotional. It's the time when young people are supposed to gain competence, to learn who they are in the world and how they'll survive.

It's an even tougher business today when kids are unemployed and kept in age ghettos of schools. The teenagers I know are often acutely aware that they are regarded as useless, if not downright dangerous.

There is no way for them to test living skills. The rites of passage have been reduced to drinking, driving and sex. The only value they seem to have is as consumers. So they are being, quite literally, sold sex along with their deodorant and shampoo and eyeliner and movie stubs.

The contradictions are really stunning. Television is filled with alarmed programs about teen-age pregnancies—and sponsored by the sex merchants. The movies show Foxes and Little Darlins doing it "naturally" in Blue Lagoons or Caddy Shacks, while the marquees suggest "parental guidance" or an eighteen-year-old chaperone.

The worst part of the sex mania is the message—as one-dimensional as the one I heard on that record. There is little aura of kindness or awakening sensuality. There is virtually no sex on television that isn't sniggering or exploitive, bumps or grinds.

As parents, many of us try to spoon-feed our children messages about the human context in which we live our sexual lives. Meanwhile they stand hip deep in televised "jiggle" jokes and X-rated "acts." Like some complicated sauce, sex is reduced, over the media flame, to "doing it."

For too long the people leading the protest have been the sort who want to ban D. H. Lawrence and repress sex back to a necessary evil. As a First Amendment junkie, I defend the right of consenting adults to read and behave as they will. But I don't have to like the messages or ignore the marketing of sex, especially to kids.

I can rage against it. And if that makes me a prude, pass me the umbrella.

SEPTEMBER 1980

Plastic World

The moment of truth came at 3 P.M. on our second day in The Magic Kingdom of Disney World. There, in the middle of Fantasyland, a small brown bird got up and flew away.

Now I know that small brown birds do this sort of thing all the time. But not, I assure you, in Disney World.

In Disney World, they may sing, they may bob their heads, kick their legs, move their beaks, blink their eyes and flap their wings. But they do not fly away. And so, I stood there for several dumbfounded seconds, looking for his wire.

We'd been in Disney World long enough.

For two days we'd been awed and delighted by a world in which anything was mechanically possible, but a world in which the only Real Thing was the Coke.

The hotel we were in was so committed to the Dutch motif that anything that wasn't nailed down was molded in the shape of a wooden shoe. There, we swam in a pool in the shape of a windmill. From this absolute tulip of a spot we shuttled back and forth to the Magic Kingdom. And there, too, everything was in the shape of something else.

Each bush was a topiary version of a dragon, or an elephant balancing on its trunk. Trees were carved into crocodiles. Wax was molded into Presidents. An entire zoology department was created out of the endangered species known as plastic.

Disney World is nothing if not homage to the Mickey Mouse that lurks in each of us, an advertisement written to the Genuine Imitation. It is a tribute to the lifelike. As opposed to, say, the live.

Am I grousing? No, I loved it. I loved the rides, loved the fantasy and the monorails. It is the cleanest, most trains-run-on-time amusement park in the world. Like the thirteen million other Americans who'll visit this year, I was awed by the creations of Frontier Land and River Country and the sheer cleverness of the people who created all the characters of the cartoon world from Peter Pan to Cinderella.

Still, you don't have to be a Save-the-Snail-Darter fan to see something weird about the idea of taking acres of natural land and carving out artificial streams and waterfalls—each with its own plastic inhabitants.

And you don't have to be a Restoration Bug to notice that million of tourists every year gasp with awe at the reproduction of Main Street—just like the original one being torn down at home.

Over $700 million was invested in this place, and there are enough Mickey Mouse T-shirts sold there every year, I'm sure, to double the bank account of the Sierra Club. The $50 million that went into building the Space Mountain could save a whole lot of other mountains. If only it were profitable.

Well, I refuse to fume about the inconsistencies and contradictions of society. It's too simplistic. You can't take the money from Tomorrow Land and use it to save whales.

But standing there, watching the flight of the brown bird, I thought of that 1960s song, "Pave paradise, put up a parking lot." The writer was way off the mark. If we were to pave paradise, we'd put up a perfect imitation. Plastic apple and all.

We are much more fascinated with the man-made than with the natural. We are more impressed with what we have made than with what is just there. We are constantly making improvements on nature and applauding our cleverness. We prefer our animals to be anthropomorphic and our mice to be Mickeys.

We also seem to get much more excited about making something "new"—even if it is a New Historical Village—than saving something old, like a house or a train station or a drug store on the corner.

It's a form of human narcissism, I suppose. We find teeny transistors more marvelous than seeds, Disney lands more extraordinary than natural ones. But it is the sort of pride that can be shaken by a small brown bird in a big plastic world.

MARCH 1979

Social Nibbling

They were sitting under the fern next to mine. I began fern-dropping.

The woman ordered Perrier on the rocks with lime. The man wanted his straight up. Ah yes, it would be another three-Perrier lunch during which business would be discussed under properly misted hanging plants, over tastefully appointed tables with white plates and green napkins, sprinkled by yard-long pepper mills.

That is the way it goes now at urban lunch spas that

stretch under some giant greenhouse from one coast to the other.

The menu was nothing if not discreet. The fare it offered with such artistic flourish was, of course, restrained. Modest. No roast beef would ever bloody its plates. No french fry would grease its side dishes.

The platters were lean enough to pose for the camera; the luncheon menu so light that it cost more per ounce than caviar.

When the woman's soup came to the table, it was a clear broth with six discreet rings of scallion floating on the top. The man and woman glanced at the French bread the waiter brought, as if it were a gate crasher. Too polite to kick the interloper out, they merely ignored it.

Finally, the lunch arrived. His was spinach with a smattering of mushrooms and a sprinkling of egg whites. Hers was watercress and Boston lettuce with a modest touch of Stilton.

They nibbled through the pasture of choice greens, talking enthusiastically about their health regimens. Placing the watercress neatly into the lean frame under the silk shirt, she shared the wonders of running. Filling his European-cut body with spinach, he talked about his stationary bicycle and his universal exercise machine and the assorted pushups and downs of his mid-life.

I, sitting under my own fern, began wondering if pieces of the plant would be macheted and arranged charmingly under a dressing on a platter in front of me. I wanted to tell the waiter that F. Scott Fitzgerald once recommended giving up spinach for Lent.

Suddenly I had an urge for a hot oven-grinder with a side of onion rings and ketchup, hold the hot peppers. Suddenly I longed for coconut pie; I hate coconut pie.

It occurred to me that to order anything more massive than the five-inch square of blue fish offered to me would be to commit a social gaffe of urban enormity. The bouncer would, no doubt, get rid of me.

It occurred to me, furthermore, that the right sort of

people do not eat food in public anymore. They merely graze and water themselves.

Self-control, we call it, with a straight face. In the middle of international chaos, we manage to worry about staying in shape. When everything is out of control, we try to control our waistline. Self-discipline chic.

If I had called a halt to all the munching, and polled the people under the ferns, I would surely have found ethical relativists and physical absolutists. I would have found uncertain people in an insecure environment who maintain food regimens and exercise—religiously.

Their hair shirts would be warmup suits and their Ten Commandments would begin with "Thou Shalt Not Eat Pasta." They would arrive at the morning weigh-in as if the scale were an altar offering proof of their virtue.

The grandparents of urban life in a safer time competed with overindulgence, orgies of oysters. Now, in stress, we compete with underindulgence, twigs of watercress: from excess of feasting to excess of fasting. We whip ourselves in shape and are still called hedonists, flagellate ourselves for what we eat and are still labeled narcissists. We regard the sins of the flesh as inches that must be worked off. Maybe we are Me-sochists. Who knows.

The man and woman finished their tea and, ducking the fern, arose, lean and hungry, from the luncheon fast. Another challenge won.

My own leaves arrived. I forked them and thought about what A. A. Milne once wrote: "What I say is that if a man really likes potatoes, he must be a pretty decent sort of fellow." I'll nibble to that.

The Reagans Are Not The Waltons

Now it's the Reagans' turn to stand up for their family portrait on the podium and in the press. And now it's our turn to hear again that the sum of the Reagan parts do not add up to a whole.

Digit by digit, here is the rundown.

The "family" consists of one man, with four children—three biological and one adopted—from two marriages.

The second wife, Nancy, was the only child of a mother who was divorced in her infancy. The four children have only two things in common: They are all college dropouts and have all dropped in different directions rather far from the family tree.

Maureen, thirty-nine, has been twice divorced, is an ERA organizer and is an actress.

Michael, thirty-five, has been once divorced and sells gasohol and races boats.

Patricia, twenty-seven, is a rock musician, composer, actress with an antinuclear bumper sticker on her car and a live-in man in her past. Her song of the moment is, appropriately enough, "No Place Left to Hide."

Ron, twenty-two, is a ballet dancer, who lives in New York with his woman friend.

In short, the family that took center stage Wednesday night was not quite vintage perfect.

The Reagans have lived through the normal difficulties and estrangements of divorce and remarriage, and the normal growing pains of adolescence and rebellious adult children.

Now none of this would be surprising or certainly shocking, except for the fact that the Reagan people have set themselves up as defenders of the Ye Olde Time Soda Shoppee family life.

So, there are two schools of thought on why Reagan is preaching something entirely different from what he practiced. The first, The Conspiracy Theory, is that the man is a rank hypocrite playing to the audience holding tickets on the right side of the theater.

The second, The Honest Confusion Theory, is that the Reagans are a walking expression of ambivalence laced with a shot of denial.

Being of benign mind and body, I vote for the second theory.

It seems to me that any number of people have been through earthquakes in their private lives that haven't even made a crack in the walls of their philosophy. They hang onto their ideals as if they were the reality, and regard any personal deviation like a bad accident. They prefer to forget that it happened.

Ronald Reagan is hardly the only man who believes in the permanence and sanctity of marriage, even in his second permanent marriage. Nancy Reagan is hardly the only woman who prefers to forget the woman before her.

Nor are they the only people who believe in the closeness of family life, while experiencing distance with their own children. After all, nostalgia grows out of a sense of loss, not of fulfillment.

The nostalgia constituency is always greater than the number of people who are actually living the lives of the Waltons. It's part of the tension in millions of us to fill and fit both our old ideas of how we would live and how we do live. It's the tension between the ideal of stability and the reality of "accidents."

The only real tradition in family lives is the notion of a tradition, an ideal past in which values were passed down from one generation to the next as easily as pocket watches.

Reagan, for example, looks back to his own parents' lives as a time of stability and caring. But his parents' marriage, between a Catholic and Protestant, must have unsettled his grandparents. In turn, surely, Reagan's divorce startled the older couple in Illinois, and Patricia Reagan's live-in mating startled Ronald and Nancy.

There is a curious pattern by which each generation redefines the traditional, while believing in it. A pattern by which each looks back on the last with nostalgia and forward to the next with anxiety.

"I don't think any of us is doing anything so alarming," said Patricia Reagan. And she is right.

The Reagans up there on the platform were a crazy-quilt pattern of reconstituted family life. They had been through change and had struggled to accept their distances and differences while remaining a "family."

They are like a lot of us. But I wonder if they know it.

JULY 1980

"Old Boys"
Will Be Boys

In every female life there is an inevitable confrontation with something called The Secret All-Male Club.

For most of us, the big moment comes in fourth grade when the boys who can say no more about the opposite sex than "Girls are Yucky!" suddenly hang a notice on some door or other that rules: NO GIRLS ALLOWED.

This is the one crucial bylaw of every male club.

Well, for a time, the fourth-grade boys succeed in making their female classmates mad and little sisters sad. But one day the girls find out what is going on inside the club.

What is going on inside is this: The fourth-grade boys are sitting around, giggling , and telling dirty jokes. Stupid dirty jokes.

This discovery prepares women for the future. From then on, whenever faced with all-male societies, they are equipped with two crucial pieces of information:

(1) The most important word in the expression "Old Boys Club" is *boys*.

(2) What they are probably doing inside is sitting around, giggling, and telling dirty jokes.

The "old boys" who moved into power last week also have their "club." It appears that the president, the vice-president, the attorney general and the secretary of defense all belong to an exclusive male society in San Francisco known as the Bohemian Club.

The Bohemian Club is so all-male that its members do not even hire women to work at their 2,7000-acre redwood retreat. They are so all-male that they are being sued for sex discrimination. This they admit, with nary a blush.

Their defense rests on the sole idea that the club members would be "inhibited by the presence of women." Inhibited from what, you ask?

Well, it appears that one of the Fun Things that the upper-crust bohemians do is produce dramatic events where members dress up as women and, you've got it, tell dirty jokes.

The club's attorney, for example, a distinguished silver-haired fellow, recalled in detail his own artistic triumph as a wood nymph. "We wore wings and body stockings." This, he maintains, he could not have done comfortably in front of women.

Do not be alarmed. As far as I know, none of the august members of the Cabinet have donned the old tutu and taken to the kick line. At least there are no photographs extant.

They are merely following tradition. The truth is that the more upper crust, top drawer, preppy, and elite a man is in America, the more likely he is to belong to a club whose basic ritual is cross-dressing and telling dirty jokes.

In my own town, which drips with ivy, the exclusive Tavern Club holds theatricals during which assorted sober souls who turn the financial wheels of the Northeast can be seen in what they do not call drag.

At Harvard, the exclusive Hasty Pudding Club has existed for years on the single joke of all-male and relatively blue-blooded chorus lines. In such places do the future leaders of America kick up their legs and let down their hair, so to speak.

No less an expert than John Spooner, stockbroker, author and Duchess of Woppery in the Hasty Pudding Production of 1959, describes all this male activity as a throwback to dubious prep-school practices. I am more inclined to pathos; it occurs to me that the elite are so self-controlled that their female side can only burst out into these hysterical rituals of release.

But I don't want to suggest that all men do when they get together in their clubs is play dress-up. They also play sports, and sports fans. For many years the big event of the season at The Harvard Club of Boston was an all-male Boxing Night. On that evening, some of the most highly respected professionals in Boston—men who transplant our kidneys, transform our laws, and translate our finances— would don black tie , and sit down to dinner while two less-fortunate souls beat each other up in the center ring.

Boys, as they say, will be boys.

Out of these places and out of this mind set, the chains of the old-boy network are forged. It is surely no surprise that these chains reach all the way to Washington. But perhaps, never has the cast come in such numbers.

If the Boys from the Bohemian are true to their society, keep your eyes on center stage. This Cabinet may put on quite the show.

JANUARY 1981

Cant and Recant

Sooner or later it was bound to happen. Sooner or later the liberals would run out of New Frontiers of guilt and seize upon the last one: their own liberalism.

For decades, the liberal conscience was like that insatiable bacteria engineered to gobble oil spills. It went about devouring guilt about racism and sexism, class and carcinogens, phosphates, leaded gas and assorted social ills that spread out across the surface of society.

Liberals held the genetic patent on guilt. They were the pseudomonas of politics.

So, they were predestined to turn inward and devour themselves. What is more typical and quintessentially liberal than feeling guilt about liberalism?

Now, if you have been away or depressed, you may have missed the chorus of mea culpas, or the parade of the culpable meas. But let me assure you that it's going around. You cannot pick up the paper or the telephone these days without hearing from someone who has given up the ghost along with the Volvo, and publicly confessed to "going too far."

Being a liberal is out; being a Repentant Liberal is in.

A Repentant Liberal is one who has actually read a corporate ad and agreed with an article telling him "Where the New Deal Went Wrong."

A Repentant Liberal is one who has, at least once, felt uncomfortable for ever having wanted a *great* society.

A Repentant Liberal is one who has said out loud either "I really do have to learn more about economics," or "Right now social programs are a luxury."

A Repentant Liberal has one of the following:

(1) A kid in college who didn't qualify for a loan because the parents earned "too much" money.

(2) An elderly relative left behind in a "changing" neighborhood.

(3) A friend who knows a guy who used food stamps to buy steaks.

(4) A boss who got her job "because she was a woman."

(5) A banker who won't give them a mortgage.

(6) A brother-in-law who works for the GSA.

(7) A kid in a big-city public high school.

I am not downgrading the latest set of qualms vibrating across the shaky left wing of the country. At some time or another, I have said, or had, almost all of the above.

It is absolutely clear that every major change has what the policy makers call "unintentional consequences"—what you and I would call "rotten side effects." The liberals didn't add the warnings to their original labels.

But now it's all obvious. The pie isn't getting any bigger and so it's harder to share with more people. It's become clear that the program helping those who cannot work may also help those who will not work; the regulation set up to help a consumer can hamstring a producer.

It's hard to defend one set of rights without attacking another; hard to act affirmatively for some without affecting others negatively. We all know that now.

The liberal agenda, like some massive public building, came in way over cost. Like the John Hancock building in Boston, the building is up but the windows keep falling out.

Still, there is something appalling about the rash of liberals asking forgiveness for their good intentions. They seem to have bought the idea, with alarming ego as well as speed, that they are responsible for the bleak state of the nation.

Never mind the cost of the Vietnam war or Arab oil. Never mind the fact that big corporations have been as malignant and incompetent as big government. Never mind that authority can be as threatening as anarchy. Never mind the fact that at the moment the only alternatives to tired old liberal ideas are equally tired and old conservative ideas.

We seem to be choosing this year between the sound of cant and the sound of recanting. Frankly, I'd rather hear the slightest murmur of a new idea, a new way to do something more than muddle through.

The Repentant Liberals are people who say, "It would be nice to be humane, but we have to be realistic." But surely it's possible, even in this peak season of pessimism, to devise new ways to be both.

SEPTEMBER 1980

Checks and Non-Balances

Let me begin this story by confessing that I haven't had a balanced checkbook since November 4, 1973. And even then it was a coincidence.

My checkbook is, in short, a scandal.

Other people I know have clauses in their wills specifying who may and may not read their diaries or go through their closets. I, however, have left a request that my checkbooks be cremated. I want the ashes strewn over the desks of assorted bank officers who will not be mourning my departure.

After years of checks and nonbalances, I have discovered that the only way out of a mathematical disaster is to occasionally close one account and open another. I have left a trail of broken bank accounts across the length and breadth of my city. I am the Donna Juan of the checkbook set.

I don't confess all this because I'm proud of it—although I think it does take some misguided strength of character to get through sixteen years of school and still be unable to work the percentage button on a calculator.

But this is simply my way of explaining why I should have been grateful when the payroll department at the office offered us something called Direct Deposit Payroll plan. Someone like me needs all the help she can get.

According to the form on my desk, all I have to do now is sign on the dotted line. Every week until retirement, my paycheck will be directly (do not pass Go, do not lose $200) deposited into my bank checking account. This plan will eliminate the middleman, or in this case, the middleperson, with all of her various accounting flaws, which are legion. And mathphobic.

But something about this plan gives me the creeps. I have a feeling it's another step on the big long road back to indentured servitude. Pretty soon we'll have no more control over our paychecks than the man who sold his soul to the company store.

I can only distantly remember the days when most people used genuine green money. Today, only the Amish pay their bills with cash on the barrel head. The dollar has not only shrunk; it's become as quaint as a barrel head.

It's been replaced by paper money called checks and plastic money called credit cards. We now pay for goods with plastic money and then pay for our plastic money with paper money. We only use the real stuff for highway tolls, school lunches and parking meters.

I suppose I sound like William Jennings Bryan bemoaning the passage of silver, but I'm uneasy as we now pass out of the era of the check and into the era of the digital. We're exchanging our name for a number, and our paycheck for a printout.

Our paycheck is already decimated by conveniences. The government long ago instituted what might charitably be called its own "direct deposit system" under which we pay income taxes and Social Security. Payroll deductions, they tell us, are for our convenience. The office credit union will also deduct loan payments from our paychecks. Just to make things easy.

Meanwhile, the same bank that issues credit cards as a customer service will also deduct the payments for those credit cards from our checking account. As a customer service.

It is possible to have some banks pay your bills without a check or a signature. You tell them who to pay. One computer then gives a batch of numbers to another computer. And, Look Ma, no hands!

It's only days now until the banks offer to decide which bills should get paid, thereby saving us the inconvenience of playing end-of-the-month roulette. And if we finally end up in the red, like Cleveland, they will surely help us to declare ourselves Bank Rupt. Another customer service.

I don't want to get paranoid about all this. But it seems the only role we have left in the economy is in the pick up and delivery of our own paychecks. The only difference between us and the people who work for room and board is Pay Day.

For a few fleeting moments once a week we are able to believe that we have earned money. We even believe we have some control over the redistribution of income—at least our own. For those moments we are able to harbor fantasies of cashing in the check to buy something wildly extravagant—like a pack of gum.

And for those few fleeting moments, I say hang the convenience, never mind the state of my checkbook and excuse me while I rip up my application for direct deposit. A sense of balance is more than a column of numbers.

FEBRUARY 1979

Nagging Negatives

I am standing in the Atlanta airport. It is 11 o'clock in the morning and I am sober. But I am hearing voices.

At first this fact doesn't alarm me. After all, many people routed through this airport for no apparent geographical reason have been known to hear voices. Most of the voices are saying things like, "Why, Lord, do I have to go through Atlanta to get from Memphis, Tennessee, to Lexington, Kentucky?"

But these are not my own personal voices. These are public ones. From the ceiling high above my head, a well-bred, well-modulated alto, speaking in tones decidedly un-southern, is giving me advice.

I am to stand to the right on the moving sidewalk. I am to walk on the left. I may take the train to Terminal A.

She/it repeats these directions calmly, over and over, never losing patience. I do what she/it says.

Aboard the train, another voice, this time a baritone, tells me that I must prepare to disembark. I do what he/it says. I almost, but not quite, tell him/it to have a nice day.

It is only later, after the disembodied voices are silenced and I am seat-belted into the next flight, that I start to giggle. Why was the airport talking to me?

I realize that this was not some isolated event, some certifiable crazy Wizard of Oz sending orders out of a programmed loudspeaker. It isn't unusual at all. We live in a world in which more and more THINGS are telling us what to do.

This is the age of the spoken word, the era of ear pollution. From cradle to grave we are at the mercy of talking elevators, streetcars, telephones, toys and computers.

A small friend of mine has a Baby Beans doll that demands "play patty-cake." She obeys. This same delightful child has a barnyard sound-effects machine that will quiz her on what the piggie, doggy, kitty says.

A slightly taller friend of mine has a teaching computer that gives her spelling tests in a thick Texas accent. It asks her to spell a word. If she types it correctly, the machine drawls, "That's right, now spell *witch*."

These two children find nothing unusual about this. But then, children have come a long way from the time, fifteen years ago, when my nephew looked up at the voice coming from the intercom in his bedroom and said suspiciously, "What do you want, wall?"

Today the kids think this is normal.

As for the games grown-ups play, there is a new car—the Datsun 810 Maxima—that comes equipped with a female voice. This voice reminds the owner politely, and in English, "Please turn out the lights."

There is also an epidemic of elevator voices in department stores that tell, without ever being asked, precisely what you will find on any given floor. And if that isn't bossy enough, the banks are now devising money machines that will literally tell when to place your card in the hole and take your money out.

Even if we manage to avoid the din of daily life, we aren't immune. They now have voices that can follow us to the graveyard. There is a company in California making talking gravestones. Press the button, and sappo! The last words, last instructions, last guilt-trips come soaring out over the heads of the dearly beloved gathered together.

I am sure that the proliferation of these talkies has something to do with automation or illiteracy or both. Voices don't have pension plans and disability payments. Nor do people have to read them.

But I don't like it. I want to arrest the elevator for invasion of privacy. I want to tell the built-in nag in the dashboard that it's none of her business if I leave my lights on. I want to tell the know-it-all in the toy that piggies don't really say oink-oink anyway.

What I want is a real live person. Tell me, ceiling, is that too much to ask for?

MARCH 1981

Hard Times

I was thinking of a real new year, the sort of year that comes awash in toasts, swaddled in hope. But 1981 has arrived middle-aged, rather wary and worried.

There is a tightness around the edge of Americans this January, a tenseness in the national jawline. People aren't eager to embrace 1981. They are braced for it.

In this transition from one year to the next, perhaps one era to the next, there is a feeling of mid-life closure in the cold air. I see people putting up the storm windows of their lives, laying down the insulation for the tough weather ahead, battening down for bad times.

Maybe this is a first for Americans. I don't know. We used to be pretty good at futures, good at looking ahead, optimistic, expansive, even with a touch of idealism.

But this is not a year when excitement seems very appealing. We have had enough surprises lately and most of them have been bad. They've come in supermarket checkout lines and evening news reports.

The world seems out of control. Out of our control. Other people have kept Americans hostage. Other people have helped push up inflation rates.

Now there is a rather hard-edged urge for order, for books to go by and guidelines to hang onto, and for somebody—somebodies—to be in charge.

I don't know quite how to describe the symptoms. But they are legion and all around us.

In November we voted against weakness. We opted for the man who promised to take charge. By December his inner circle talked openly about the character they wanted in those hired for this new government. They were looking, they said, for the S.O.B. factor.

For 1981, yes, tough guys are in again; softness is out. Certainty is in; doubt is out. True or False Questions are in; essays are out. For better and for worse, the atmosphere is changing, the reins are being tightened.

In the past year, I saw three books sticking up for the power of parents. Some of the same people who supported children's rights in the 1970s are supporting parents' rights in the 1980s. Americans want to be in charge again, at least of their children.

The same urge for "order" and authority has struck at women's rights. The S.O.B. factor, if you will, can be seen in the blatant new macho spirit. At home, too, we are told by the pro-family movement, "somebody" has to be in charge. That somebody is the husband, father, man.

The season is not ripe for negotiation, compromise and sharing. This is the year for authority, control and power.

In the trend world, it's the time of cowboys. In television, we cheer for J.R. In foreign policy, it is a moral majority for missiles. In the schools, it is cut-rate regulation. In crime, it is civilian patrols and juvenile sentences.

Even theologians who deal with the mysteries of eternity, the complexity of the world, and the ethical dilemmas of human life are now told to go by The Book.

The man of this new year is the one in the surreal Betamax ad. He sits in a cool armchair holding his remote-control tuner aloft under the motto: "Experience the freedom of total control."

It's no surprise that hard times breed hard lines. Under pressure we all retreat. We replace growing with coping. We react to the troubles outside by defending our own turf with dozens of rules and tens of commandments.

If we cannot create order in the world, we try to create its image at home. If we are afraid of the future, we assume some safety in tradition. Afraid of uncertainty, we give and take orders.

But there is a desperate age to this transitional winter. This 1981 comes in, middle-aged and worried, with its spine already stiffened and its posture defensive.

Its mind is fixed on survival. Its method is control. This is not the bubbly stuff of a happy new year.

JANUARY 1981

PART 2

Women In The Age of Transition

Superwoman, Supertired

In one moment, she wrapped it all up, the whole decade of change, the remaining problems, the new anxieties. Betty Friedan, the founding mother, the astute and caring observer of the women's movement, stood in front of a New York audience last month and said: "We told our daughters you can have it all. Well, can they have it all? Only by being Superwoman. Well, I say *no* to Superwoman!"

By any media calculation, the audience was a collection of superwomen. They wore their raised consciousness layered with two-piece suits. Yet they broke into spontaneous applause. They, too, were saying no to the Superwoman myth.

That moment is as good a place as any to stop and assess, to review and preview.

For all the social change in the past decade, all the rhetoric and action, we have moved from one national ideal of True Womanhood to another—from Supermom to Superwoman. The girl who was told that when she grew up she should get married and have children and keep house is now a grown-up woman being told that she should be married, have children, keep house and a job, or better yet, a career.

While mothers at home have felt increasingly pressured for "not working," mothers in the work force feel increasingly pressured by the double burden. They have been "liberated" to the Russian model—have a new role on top of an old one.

Every study shows the same things. The overwhelming number of working mothers do the overwhelming amount of housework and child care. They may not have it all, but they seem to do it all.

Why has the change been so lopsided? I have asked that question a hundred times and heard a dozen different answers, ranging from the psychological to the economic. One feminist psychiatrist says that women spent the decade proving themselves. A sociologist believes that the person who initiates the change—the person who goes to work even out of necessity—accepts the personal responsibility for it.

A woman from a working-class neighborhood in Baltimore tells me that women are stretching their own energy to cover both their traditional and nontraditional values: the desire or demand to make Christmas pudding and a salary. An economist offers a different theory: "The average woman earns fifty-nine cents to her husband's dollar. She sees her time as worth less and overworks herself. She gets it twice."

And last week a union leader said: "Remember three things. One: A lot of women with lousy jobs hope they'll be able to quit. By doing everything, they think they're keeping their options open. Two: The home is the only place some women have any power. They sure don't want to let go of that. Three: Never underestimate the power of the men in their lives to resist."

Perhaps single mothers were the first to wipe off the upbeat Superwoman makeup that covered the lines of fatigue. But now it seems to many women that the Superwoman model who looked so chic at the beginning of the decade looks worn at the end.

In 1970, women had just begun to agitate collectively for new choices. But in 1980, the "daughters" who were to "have it all" face new choices that are still limited, frightening as well as attractive.

Many women, especially those "up against the clock" of their thirties, approach motherhood with fear and trembling.

Those for whom homemaking, even temporary, is not a psychological or economic possibility see only two choices: superdrudge or childlessness.

In Washington, a forty-five-year-old woman says ironically, "I saw my mother frustrated at home. My daughter sees me overworked. I'm not such a great role model myself."

Superwoman was in part a creation of the self-help, self-reliant, self-improvement seventies. This was the flip side of the so-called Me Decade. It was not new narcissism, but new isolation masked as independence.

"I used to take pride in being a Superwoman," said a Manhattan woman listening to Friedan that afternoon. "Now I see it, not as a personal victory but as a failure. A failure of my relationship with my husband, a failure of the work world, maybe even a failure of the society that just isn't adjusting to the way we live."

The Superwoman myth is exploding like an overstuffed sofa. Women are no longer willing to look inside themselves for all the answers and all the energy. At the turn of the decade, they don't want a Superwoman pep talk any more. They long for something more precious and more realistic: a support system—of families, the workplace and the community—to fend off this cultural kryptonite.

DECEMBER 1979

The "Selfishness" of Emma Dunmire

Emma Dunmire is one of those people the President has described as selfish.

She fits his description—selfish member of special-interest group—because she has the egocentric nerve to oppose the budget cuts he has outlined.

The forty-eight-year-old mother has the gall to come to the defense of that group of human beings known as displaced homemakers. These are women who made one terrible economic "mistake." They stayed home to take care of their children.

In Ft. Myers, Florida, Dunmire has run "Rediscovery," one of the thirty-one nascent programs across the nation for caretakers who have been left in the lurch by death, divorce, desertion, disease. Once a displaced homemaker with 4 children of her own, Dunmire has seen 300 women come into the program with little work experience and less self-esteem. She has seen them leave with a decent résumé, a prop of self-worth and a job prospect.

"We're talking here about really getting people back on their feet," she says.

It took four years for people like her to make the term "displaced homemaker" a respectable one, years to set up legislation, years to get programs operating.

Now they see it all going down the drain. At best, pro-

grams like Rediscovery will find their budgets amputated
so that they can barely limp along.

So Emma Dunmire, selfish special-interest groupie that
she is, now knows what the rest of us had better understand:
This administration, which lauds the traditional role for
women, is making this choice riskier and riskier every day.
There is no single job in America more economically per-
ilous today than that of full-time motherhood.

The proposed budget cuts are aimed dead-eye at women
who are now, or have been for most of their lives, mothers
at home.

Who will be hurt by cuts in food stamps? Women with
children.

Who will be hurt by cuts in Aid to Families with Dependent Children? Women with children.

Who will be hurt by cuts in Medicaid, cuts in day care,
cuts in child nutrition? Women with children.

This mother is threatened now with the specter of work-
fare—forced labor at dead-end subsistence-level jobs—if
she wants to stay at home. She is threatened with slashes
in child-care deductions and training programs if she wants
to go to work.

The cuts in programs to the poor affect mothers most,
because they and their children are the poor. Two-thirds of
the households headed by women with children receive welfare benefits. One-third of today's generation of children is
likely to live in homes headed by women receiving welfare
benefits before they are eighteen.

An enormous number of the mothers in this country are
one man away from welfare.

But the Reagan proposals may have an even more devastating effect on the older women who have spent most of
their adult lives taking care of others. "Our safety net of
programs," insists Reagan, "is intact." But the safety net
never caught these women.

There are four to six million displaced homemakers in
the country; many are caught between AFDC and Social
Security. For many of them, displaced homemaker pro-

grams were a road to economic independence. This road is now virtually shut.

At the same time, the subsistence rut of economic dependence is pitted with new, treacherous holes. The proposed cuts in Medicaid, the proposed cuts in benefits to veterans' dependents, the possibility of raising the age of eligibility for Social Security are all directed at older women hanging on by their fingernails. There is no net over this abyss.

The older a woman is, the worse the story gets. One out of every two women can expect to be widowed by sixty-five. One-third of all widows lives below the poverty line. The average income for a woman over sixty-five in 1979 was $59 a week.

The plan to cut minimum Social Security will hurt these older unemployed women alone the most. Only 15 percent of those who receive benefits are "double dippers," living off two pension plans. The bulk of them are women who spent a bare minimum time in the work force and now live off those payments.

These are the true stories, these are the true prospects for the traditional woman's role the Reagan Administration so praises. These are the risks for a young woman who wants to be a full-time mother in the brave new world of fiscal responsibility.

Once again protection turns out to be a sham and the caretakers of our society end up at the bottom of the heap. There, if they sift among the proposed budget cuts, they can find a pretty clear message: Any woman selfish enough to want to take care of her own children had better find a husband who will never leave her, and never get sick . . . and never, ever, die.

MARCH 1981

Being a Secretary Can Be Hazardous to Your Health

They used to say it with flowers or celebrate it with a somewhat liquid lunch. National Secretaries Week was always good for at least a token of appreciation. But the way the figures add up now, the best thing a boss can do for a secretary this week is cough up for her cardiogram.

"Stress and the Secretary" has become the hottest new syndrome on the heart circuit.

It seems that it isn't those Daring Young Women in their Dress-for-Success Suits who are following men down the cardiovascular trail to ruin. Nor is it the female professionals who are winning their equal place in intensive care units.

It is powerlessness and not power that corrupts women's hearts. And clerical workers are the number one victims.

In the prestigious Framingham study, Dr. Suzanne Haynes, an epidemiologist with the National Heart, Lung and Blood Institute, found that working women as a whole have no higher rate of heart disease than housewives. But women employed in clerical and sales occupations do. Their coronary disease rates are twice that of other women.

"This is not something to ignore," says Dr. Haynes,

"since such a high percent of women work at clerical jobs." In fact, 35 percent of all working women, or 18 million of us, hold these jobs.

When Dr. Haynes looked into their private lives, she found the women at greatest risk—with a one in five chance of heart disease—were clerical workers with blue-collar husbands, and three or more children. When she then looked at their work lives, she discovered that the ones who actually developed heart disease were those with nonsupportive bosses who hadn't changed jobs very often and who had trouble letting their anger out.

In short, being frustrated, dead-ended, without a feeling of control over your life is bad for your health.

The irony in all the various and sundry heart statistics is that we now have a weird portrait of the Cardiovascular Fun Couple of the Office: The Type A Boss and his secretary. The male heart disease stereotype is, after all, the Type A aggressive man who always needs to be in control, who lives with a great sense of time urgency . . . and is likely to be a white-collar boss.

"The Type A man is trying to be in control. But given the way most businesses are organized there are, in fact, few ways for them to be in control of their jobs," says Dr. Haynes. The only thing the Type A boss can be in control of is his secretary who in turn feels . . . well you get the picture. He's not only getting heart disease, he's giving it.

As if all this weren't enough to send you out for the annual three martini lunch, clerical workers are increasingly working for a new Type A boss: the computer.

These days fewer women are sitting in front of bosses with notepads and more are sitting in front of Visual Display Terminals. Word processors, data processors, microprocessors . . . these are the demanding, time-conscious, new automatons of automations.

There is nothing intrinsically evil about computers. I am writing this on a VDT and if you try to take it away from me, I will break your arm. But as Working Women, the national association of office workers, puts it in their release this week, automation is increasingly producing clerical jobs that are de-skilled, down-graded, dead-ended and dissatisfying.

As Karen Nussbaum of the Cleveland office described it, the office of the future may well be the factory of the past. Work on computers is often reduced to simple, repetitive, monotonous tasks. Workers are often expected to produce more for no more pay, and there are also reports of a disturbing trend to processing speed-ups and piece-rate pay, and a feeling among clerical workers that their jobs are computer controlled.

"It's not the machine, but the way it's used by employers," says Working Women's research director, Judith Gregory. Too often, automation's most important product is stress.

Groups, like Working Women, are trying to get clerical workers to organize in what they call "a race against time" so that computers will become their tools instead of their supervisors.

But in the meantime, if you are 1) a female clerical worker, 2) with a blue-collar husband, 3) with three or more children, 4) in a dead-end job, 5) without any way to express anger, 6) with a Type A boss, 7) or a Type A computer controlling your work day. . . . *You better start jogging*.

APRIL 1980

A G.I. Bill
for Mothers

*O*n Monday Helen Feeney took one last shot at Veterans' Preference and missed.

To no one's surprise, the Supreme Court upheld its own June ruling. It is, they said, perfectly legal for the government to give veterans a lifetime edge on the public jobs list. That for the moment is that.

Now, after years of bucking veterans' preference, it may be time for women to adopt it.

Veterans' preference laws were based on the notion that a soldier reentering the job market shouldn't suffer because of the time he spent serving his country. Eventually, many of these programs became a kind of lifetime affirmative action for a generation of soldiers. But the basic concept was and is a worthy one. The government should have a right to help those who helped the rest of us.

Well, there is another group of Americans who have also taken time out of the work force in order to provide what is generally considered a social good. They are also at a disadvantage when they try to get back in. And they are called mothers.

This, according to Barbara Mikulski's favorite fantasy, should—in the best of all possible worlds—qualify them for their own sort of veterans' preference, their own G.I. Bill for Mothers.

"One of the fundamental tenets that underlies my think-ing," says the feisty U.S. Representative from Baltimore, "is that what we explicitly state as our values, we implicitly deny in our social programs. If motherhood is an occupation which is critically important to society the way we say it is, then there should be a mother's bill of rights."

The basics of the G.I. Bill of Rights gave veterans the chance to pursue higher education, to get a mortgage, to get credit for their army years in their pensions, to have the right to return to a job, to have V.A. medical care, and to have a point preference in the job market.

"We gave them that to compensate for the lost time they gave to their country. Now if we transpose that to women, then we ought to provide them with the same sort of rewards for their time out and caring for their children."

Clearly, not all women need that aid, but many do. "We keep inventing new programs to help these women—dis-placed homemaker programs and all the rest. They're con-sidered gifts when they ought to be a matter of rights," says Mikulski.

Not even this gutsy lady plans to present such a bill. If she did, she would hear a shriek from the Halls of Mon-tezuma to the Shores of Tripoli. "It is not," as she says, "a perfect plan." In fact, it isn't a plan at all, but a point of view.

Still, it isn't a bad place from which to oversee the plight of the woman at home. It has become commonplace lately to cluck about the status of the homemaker. Feminists and antifeminists alike are busily portraying themselves as the Friends of the Homemakers, as if the women were baby seals about to be clubbed to extinction by the opinion mak-ers.

For years people condemned working mothers for ne-glecting their children and then swung around and con-demned full-time mothers for neglecting their minds, their pocketbooks or their futures. We have now settled for the notion that whatever a woman decides is fine, as long as she truly chooses it. We give lip service to choice, as if the choices were free ones instead of tough ones.

The hardest aspect of homemaking isn't the job description, but the insecurity. If one generation looked for security in a marriage certificate, this one looks for it in a résumé.

The homemakers I know who are most at ease are those who know they can reenter when they want to, or when they have to. The young women who have the greatest sense of choice about mothering are those few who have been told the door to the office will still be open. Only they can look at mothering as "time off" or a second career rather than a permanent job disability.

It is odd that the choice to be comfortably at home, in that most private of relationships, depends on access to the public world. But that is the message from the home front. We have veterans here, too, who need more than thank-yous.

FEBRUARY 1980

Masters of Guilt Trivia

*T*he visit had been too short. She left for the plane with a sense of unfinished personal business stuffed between the work papers in one carry-on bag.

But for once the weather was in their favor. Fog had

closed the airport and they returned quickly to unpack their incompleted sentences and half-finished stories.

The two women, friends of mine, felt reprieved, like children with a no-school day. They quickly changed into flannel nightgowns and bathrobes and within a half-hour were sitting by the fire, drinking wine and talking.

The subject for the evening was guilt. Can-you-top-this guilt. If one was guilty about her mother, the other was guilty about her son. If one was guilty about the things she had done, the other was guilty about the things she had not done. If one was guilty about the people she had neglected, the other was guilty about the work she had neglected.

By 8 P.M., each of my friends had declared herself guilty and thrown her sins upon the mercy of the other. By 9 P.M., each had declared the other innocent, while staunchly maintaining her own original plea. And by 10 P.M., they finally asked each other the question I always asked them: Why is it when women get together they always talk about guilt?

It was the teacher, a stickler for the facts, who chuckled, "Oh, that's not all we talk about. We also talk about men."

"Yes," said the other, a writer, "men and work and life and whatever but . . ."

It was guilt which was their baseball talk, their national pastime. They knew verbatim the RBIs and the batting averages of their wrongs. They kept scoreboards on guilts outstanding and guilts appeased.

They were Masters of Guilt Trivia, remembering old wrongs, the sins of omission and of commission, when no one else except another fanatic could even recall the day the error happened.

One remembered the time she had sent her eldest to school with Monday morning-itis and he had come home with the flu. The other knew about the time she'd hung up on her mother when it was really important. They ran the instant replays of their strike-outs and crucial popups, late at night, in the privacy of their minds.

But it isn't a sex-segregated sport, insisted the teacher. Women aren't the only ones who play guilt.

True, said the writer. And yet...

She and her husband shared childcare with ease. For four years they had taken turns with the diapers and hours, the sillinesses and sadnesses of their son. They shared everything...except the guilt.

She was the one who felt guilty if she worked late. She was the one who felt guilty if their son balked at the baby sitter. She was the one who felt guilty if the fog rolled in and closed down the airport. The luxury of drinking wine in a borrowed bathrobe at an old friend's house would eventually be framed in a molding of guilt.

The teacher, for her part, worked at a university with male colleagues who "produced." She had an unfinished book and two children on her conscience. She should spend more time writing. She should spend more time with her family. She should spend more time consulting and advising with her students. The "shoulds" of her life marked the guilt-trip she ran around the bases every day.

These two friends of mine live different lives than their mothers. So do many, perhaps most, of us. Sometimes they think that by both working and mothering, dealing with people and ideas, having ambitions and responsibilities, they have upped the ante on themselves—built whole new astrodomes for superstar guilts.

But other times, private times, in front of a fire with a friend, they also wonder whether guilt isn't the amulet they wear to appease the wrath of the traditional gods.

The teacher confessed that sometimes when she felt her guilt start to slip, she wrapped it around her tighter, like this comfortable bathrobe. She shook her head. Guilt, it seemed, was part of the bargain she had struck with herself.

Yes, said the writer. Maybe that's so. Maybe that's it. We can lead lives different from our mothers or our colleagues as long as we feel guilty about it. Guilt is the scrap we throw to the past. It's the way we acknowledge the "shoulds" of our childhood.

In a convoluted way, their sense of angst had become their proof of innocence, their proof of conscience, their proof of goodness. After all, anyone who feels guilty isn't a truly bad person.

The two women sat and thought a while. Was it possible, asked the writer, that they would feel most guilty about not feeling guilty?

Yes, it was possible, entirely possible, admitted the teacher. Together, the women went upstairs to put a clean sheet on the guest bed.

What would happen if we gave it up?, asked the writer—gave up guilt as if it were smoking or meat? The teacher was quiet and then smiled ironically, as she tucked in the edge of the blanket. "Well, we might have to take up running instead."

MARCH 1979

When Mothers Know Best

I do not usually read the New England Journal of Medicine for kicks. The graphics aren't sexy. The headlines aren't reader-grabbers. Frankly, I have trouble getting into pieces called "Plasma-Cell Dyscrasia and Peripheral Neuropathy with a Monoclonal Antibody to Peripheral Nerve Myelin."

Furthermore the closest you get to humor is an ad, like one for Colace that features a locomotive steaming out of a tunnel under the heading, "The Great Laxative Escape."

Nevertheless the lead story in this biweekly issue could

be straight out of *Punch*. It is, in some ways, the perfect satire of scientific expertise, a case study of how to belabor the obvious.

It seems that no less than five medical doctors, all specialists, working with grants from two foundations and the public health service have startled the medical world with the following information: It's better for women not to go through labor alone.

Stop the presses.

To arrive at this blockbuster of a notion, the men traveled far, to a hospital in Guatemala. There they assigned an untrained lay woman, to stay with each new mother in the experimental group through labor, to hold her hand, rub her back and chat.

The women with a constant companion got through labor and delivery more easily than the women alone, who were only attended by medical people at delivery. They also had a better attitude toward their babies.

So, in a truly risky conclusion the obstetrical-shop quintet said, "The findings of this study SUGGEST the importance of human companionship during labor and delivery."

Well, I don't doubt the sincerity of these doctors, but this is not exactly fresh information. The study reminds me of the old Sean O'Casey story about the Irish woman who listened while two priests described labor as the crowning glory of womanhood. When they were through the woman replied, "I wish I knew as little about it as you do."

It seems to me these men could have gone out into the streets of Cleveland, whence they cometh, walked up to the first two dozen women they met and asked them: Would you feel better going through labor alone or with someone holding your hand? They could have published those answers and used the rest of the grant money to fund a study on How to Use Common Sense in Medical Practice.

Instead they have produced a piece that really should be reprinted as classic in the Annals of American Expert-itis.

We seem to belong to a culture that trusts its experts more than its instincts. Somewhere along the scientific way, we gave up childbirth to the doctors out of fear and trust. Doctors began "delivering" babies as if mothers were merely assembly-line workers strapped to tables in hospital factories until they produced.

Under "modern" hospital policies, very few women had a relative or friend around. Now we have more experts telling us what our grandmothers knew in the first place: this "civilized" childbirth was an abomination.

The new research is like the recent studies "conclusively proving" that chicken soup is good for a cold.

In the medical establishment nothing is true unless it's "proven." It isn't enough that every woman "knows" it's less frightening, and more comforting to be surrounded by people—especially people who care—during labor. They need statistics and charts, and double-blind crossover studies, and chi-square analyses.

In the past ten years, pregnant women have formed one of the most effective "consumer movements" in the health field. They've helped create birthing centers, and resurrect midwifery; they've insisted on getting fathers into the delivery room and indiscriminate anesthesia out of it.

But in many ways, the scientists and not the mothers are still in charge of childbirth. We give them authority, like Elaine May because, "THAT man is a DOCTOR."

There is certainly a need for science and expertise in childbirth, to sort out the use from the abuse of fetal monitors, to curb the epidemic of cesareans, and all the rest.

But even in an overly "experted" society like ours, doctors don't need a report by their peers to believe that a lonely labor is a scary and unhealthy thing. All they have to do is listen.

SEPTEMBER 1980

An Understanding Woman

I know an Understanding Woman. No, not the sort of woman who'll jog along with you a while until she gets tired. I mean a marathon understander.

The Understanding Woman is a good listener and a good human historian. Over the years people have come to her when they were really out of shape and she's paced them over some pretty rough terrain.

She can put pieces together; she can figure out why one person behaves this way and another person behaves that way. She has empathy endurance. And she'll tell you that once you really comprehend someone else's life, it's tough to criticize them.

I've watched the Understanding Woman over the long distance. I've watched with the awe I reserve for feats I can't imagine performing. I am better for an intense short sprint. I fade early. So I've admired the woman's legs, her wind, her stamina.

But lately I've been wondering whether this capacity for understanding is awesome or really kind of awful. If understanding is a good thing, I wonder if she has too much of a good thing. I wonder whether she does the hard work and everyone around her stays flaccid. I wonder if understanding why things happen one way can't become a substitute for making them happen another way.

The last time I saw her I thought about the men in her life. I remember the husband who said he needed space. And she understood.

I remember the guy who was, from time to time, unfaithful. And she understood.

There was also a man who didn't want to get married and have children because, after all, he had already been there. And now there is a man who has difficulty relating to her son because, after all, he has a boy the same age in another state. It is all very understandable.

She isn't the only marathon woman. Understanding can be a great equalizer. It is as if one person's capacity for hurtful or insensitive behavior could be matched, maybe even topped, by another's capacity for sympathetic comprehension.

But I also suspect that a person can spend so much energy analyzing someone else's needs and track record that they analyze away their own. Psychiatrists always say that understanding is the first step of change, but I guess it can also be a substitute for change. A lot of women end up running in place.

This is not exclusively a "woman's problem." There are a lot of men who go the distance every day. But we're trained for it from the time we get our first sneakers.

If you compare them, the men's magazines all deal with things and the women's magazines all deal with feelings. These magazines are our cheerleaders. They shout encouragement when we leave Hopkinton, and they pass water to us over Heartbreak Hill in Newton.

Women are expected to deal with feelings, even the feeling of being dealt with as a thing. We are, for heaven's sake, coached in the art of understanding why men aren't as understanding.

I have another friend who swears that the Understanding Woman is getting exactly what she wants: a chance to be superior in sympathy, to be virtuously martyred. But I think that's too pat and too tough. I think she is struggling to do the right thing, even when it gives her a cramp in the side and shin splints.

You don't have to tell me that understanding is a virtue and that what the world needs now is love. Pass me a Coke and turn the other cheek. But sometimes it's paralyzing.

There's a moment, and it's hard to locate it, when you can understand too much and ask for too little. Anyway, it occurs to me that the Understanding Woman has logged too many miles in other people's shoes.

AUGUST 1979

A Day for the Caretakers

The man was wearing his sincere face. Pretty as a blown-dry greeting card, he looked into the television camera like someone who cared enough to send the very best across the airwaves: his own tele-prompted self.

He reminded the audience that it was almost Mother's Day, and then, in one of those cute asides to his co-host, talked about how worthwhile mothers were. Why, he said, some of them, for heaven's sakes, had skills which "even" he didn't have.

It was unbelievable. The man was oozing pap from every pore. And he didn't believe it for a minute.

The woman lunged for the dial and turned the television set off, which was not at all what she wanted to do. She wanted to throw a lamp at his patronizing puss, but she had too much sympathy for vending machines and parking meters and assorted punching bags of modern frustration.

Besides, she had a better idea. Mother's Day should be reserved—not for calls, cards and flowers, but for a massive reeducation project, the kind that was so popular during the Chinese cultural revolution. In those years, all the bosses and policy makers of the country were recycled through the ranks.

She would like to reassign this fellow to spend Mother's Day in full charge of four pre-school children of her choosing—who preferably had given up their naps and not yet taken to toilet training.

No, she wasn't really all that vicious. Nor was it just Charlie Charming who needed some "reeducation." Sitting in front of the cooling gray screen, she decided that it would be perfect to "reeducate" everyone who had ever devised a policy that offered a piece of patronizing for the caretakers.

She would invite every corporate president with inflexible hours to Cope for A Day, to deal with three emergencies and two dentist appointments and a school play. Then she would insist that every school board member in every town with double sessions take charge of scheduling family life from a first session breakfast to a last session dinner.

And while she was at it, wouldn't it be lovely to have every official who ever signed a piece of public policy that affected people's lives to spend a week living with it!

Never mind the kids playing mother for a day this Sunday. She wanted the caretakers and the policy makers to play Prince and the Pauper.

She paused for a minute and wondered why it was necessary to play games. It seemed to her that the country was organized like some misguided school, committed to a two-track system. Only this time it was divided into Caretaking and Producing—those who dealt with people and those who dealt with things.

The system was fairly simple. It awarded the producers and penalized the caretakers. Two tracks.

The more people were involved in private caretaking, the less likely they were to have any say in the public decisions. The more they were involved in "world" affairs, the less likely they were to have intimate day-to-day experience in nurturing. It was a bizarre double trip.

At the worst extreme, one group of citizens raised their children on Creative Playthings and great expectations, while another group decided whether those children would eventually be killed in a war. One group of people protected their children from junk food, while an entirely different group decided whether solid wastes would be buried in their playground.

She had recently read one of the surveys on nuclear energy that asked the question, "Would you approve of building a nuclear power plant in your community?" After Three Mile Island, the change in attitude wasn't as remarkable as the split in attitudes. Only 46 percent of the men disapproved; 66 percent of the women disapproved.

She claimed no moral superiority for women, never had, but didn't that split have much to do with the values of caring versus the values of producing in a society in which women have been the primary caretakers?

When Ann Trunk, a forty-three-year-old mother of six from Middletown, Pennsylvania, was appointed to Carter's blue-ribbon commission on what went wrong at Three Mile Island, it was a novelty worthy of page one. But the caretakers should be the conductors.

Two tracks. Maybe Mother's Day was the time to connect them so they made one round trip. After all, what we need is a single sane itinerary, with a standard gauge: how we can best take care.

MAY 1979

Young, Pretty
and Uppity

If you could harness the energy devoted to office gossip in any workplace you could probably solve the oil crisis. The Bendix Corporation is no exception.

But the story of Mary Cunningham and William Agee has made the ordinary office viciousness look positively benign. In a matter of days in corporate headquarters, twenty-nine-year-old Mary Cunningham was promoted up to vice-president and then humiliated out of the business. All because of rumors that she and Agee were having an affair.

Needless to say, this story would have bubbled around any water cooler for quite a while. But it also landed on page one of almost every newspaper in America, and for the past week it has been a catalyst for debates between men and women, bosses and employees.

The Cunningham-Agee story is an updated version of the favorite male fantasy about women who sleep their way to the top. It is absolutely ripe with hostility toward uppity women, especially young uppity women, especially pretty young uppity women.

On the surface, the argument is whether Mary Cunningham won her promotion because of "favoritism." But once you get two sentences into the debate you can hear the old subconscious fear and anger rumbling around: The feeling that women really have an "unfair advantage" over men in the business world. The belief that they take that unfair advantage.

I would like to dismiss this notion as the bitter raving of a rejected male executive overdosing on martinis and testosterone. But it's too widespread and too destructive to simply write off.

Just think about all the "unfair advantages." As far as I can see, every promotion to the executive suite is based in part on a personal relationship. Bosses promote the people they like and know.

It's no news bulletin that the ambitious will jockey for casual friendship in the steam room, the golf course, the private club. These are precisely the places often closed to women. Men don't consider that an "unfair advantage."

The other informal path to success is to stop for an after-work drink, or sign on for the out-of-town trip. This is the way a man convinces his leader that he is charming, intelligent, and a good business hustler. This is also the easiest way for a woman to convince her boss that she is another sort of hustler.

The after-work drink and the road trip work for men, but not for women. Men do not consider this an "unfair advantage."

When you come down to it, a woman who wants to diffuse the sex issues had better be plain, happily married and talk about her husband incessantly. At that point, of course, she will probably be passed over for promotion because she doesn't *need* the pay raise.

Women do not have a set of separate-but-equal unfair advantages. It is plain old hostility that assumes that a woman can only get to the top on her back instead of her merit. It is plain old fantasy to envision nubile young business-school graduates cutting through the competition with a little pillow talk.

If women can sleep their way to the top, how come they aren't there? Only 6 percent of all the working women in the country have squeaked into management. Only 600 of the 15,000 people on boards of directorships are female. There must be an epidemic of insomnia out there.

I'm not naive. The workplace is not a convent; people meet and fall in love over stranger things than blueprints. But nobody calls the reporters in when yet another boss sleeps with his secretary. If you look at the sexual harassment statistics, it's women at the bottom who are considered fair game.

The sex issue in work is loaded—against women—precisely because there are so few in any kind of power. Each one is the exception, scrutinized, assumed to have some mysterious power to cloud men's minds.

Did they or didn't they? Are they or aren't they? Does it matter? All I know is that Mary Cunningham is out and William Agee is still president.

There's an old proverb: Whether the rock hits the pitcher or the pitcher hits the rock, it's going to be bad for the pitcher.

Well, no matter what happens, or why, in this sort of collision it's the less powerful person who gets shattered. In corporate America, Mary Cunningham was just another pitcher.

OCTOBER 1980

The Balancing Act

The woman turned to the out-of-town "expert" and asked earnestly, "How do you lead a balanced life?"

It wasn't a trick question or a surprise one. She'd heard it often enough before, especially from women whose lives were changing. But this time the "expert" demurred and hid behind her amateur standing.

Later though, flying home, it occurred to her that she was less sure about the definition of a "balanced" life. What was it now? A balancing *act?* A performance or a pleasure?

Over the past decade she, too, had read all the advice columns filled with handy hints about how The New Woman should lead her New Life. They were recipes concocted out of carefully weighed ingredients: equal portions of men, children, work, and all the rest. Put them all together and you were guaranteed a perfect life every time.

But now they all sounded somehow mechanical, like living-by-numbers games . . . too neat and too dry. She didn't want to play.

She wanted to tell the woman that there was no recipe for a "balanced life." Wanted to say that there is a difference between a life and an act. Wanted to introduce her to men and women who now led lives that fit her fantasies and who still wake up asking, "Is this all?"

Funny.

The out-of-town "expert" remembered the women who had begun questioning their lives ten or fifteen years ago. They were often homemakers then. The notion evolved that if women could shift, put some weight on the outside world, and if men could shift, put some weight on the home world, we'd all find an equilibrium.

But "equilibrium" had proved a difficult territory. Elusive. Hard to stake out.

Waiting in Chicago, she picked up Avery Corman's new book, *The Old Neighborhood*. This time the author of *Kramer vs. Kramer* portrayed a couple right out of *People* magazine. They were two attractive adults with two high-powered jobs and two high-achieving children. But at midlife, they were like compatible roommates who passed each other in the kitchen and made plans through secretaries.

Corman's message was clear. There is a difference between a working relationship and a deep one. There is a difference between a full schedule and a rich life.

Back home, the same amateur expert went to see Jill Clayburgh's new movie, *It's My Turn*. There it was again.

The woman in this Claudia Weill film was a brilliant mathematician living with a humorous and decent man who gave her "lots of space." She was the woman who worked it all out, did everything, had everything. And felt an anxious emptiness.

In the novel, Avery Corman's man returned to his neighborhood roots to see what was missing. In the film, Jill Clayburgh's discoveries came when she fell in love with the "wrong man."

Both of them deliberately upset the "balance" of their lives . . . because it wasn't enough.

These two new works are not diatribes against changing roles. Not at all. Avery Corman's character does not wish to be The Sole Breadwinner. Jill Clayburgh does not long to retreat from her math class to the kitchen.

In a sense, they are both post-liberation stories. Successful women are not a problem but an assumption. Yet, under the new circumstances of their lives, the old question persists: Is this all?

There is less nostalgia than wonder in this question when it's asked by real-life couples. Wonder that the careful sharing of schedules and roles isn't *the* solution, wonder that a "balanced" life can still go out of whack. Wonder that you can have it "all" and want something else.

The amateur expert had never put all that much faith in final solutions. She didn't believe you could create a life pattern to be mass-produced, where one-size-fits-all. She didn't believe that life was in balance for more than a day at a time.

But she remembered what an eighty-two-year-old suffragist and doctor had said at the end of a long interview. "And my dear, when we solve all the problems that come from being a man or a woman, then... *then*, we face the rest of the problem of human existence."

NOVEMBER 1980

PART 3

Of Men And Women

LIVE-IN
MYTHS

"He is not really like that," she said apologetically as her husband left the room.

"Like what?" I asked, wondering which of the many things that had happened that evening she was excusing.

"Well, you know," she said, "cranky."

I thought about that. Cranky. It was typical of the woman that she would choose a gentle, even childish, word for the sort of erratic outbursts of anger which had been her husband's hallmark for the past fifteen years.

He was not really like that. This had been her sentence when they were first dating, when they were living together, and now, since they were married.

When he questioned, minutely, the price tags of her purchases, she would say: "He is really, deep down, very generous." When he disagreed with her politics, veering to the right while she listed to the left, she would cheerily insist that underneath all that he was "basically" liberal.

When he blamed her for the condition of the house, as if he were a lodger, and blamed her for the children's illnesses, as if her negligence had caused their viruses, she would explain, "He is really very understanding."

Even when he was actually his most vital self, amusing and expansive, full of martinis or enthusiasm or himself—

and she disapproved—she would forgive him because he wasn't really like that.

This time, dining with them out of town one brief night, I saw that this was the pattern of their lives together—a struggle between realities. His real and her "really."

I had known the wife since college and the husband from their first date. When they met she was a social worker and he was, it seems, her raw material. Was he the case and she the miracle worker? At times she looked at him that way.

Her husband was erratic and difficult, but he had a streak of humor and zaniness as attractive as Alan Arkin's. Over the years, he had grown "crankier" and she more determined in her myth-making.

This trip, for the first time, I wondered what it must be like to be a text living with an interpreter. To be not really like that. And what it must be like for her, living with her myth as well as her man.

I know many other people who live with their ideas of each other. Not with a real person but with a "really." They doggedly refuse to let the evidence interfere with their opinions. They develop an idea about the other person and spend a lifetime trying to make him or her live up to that idea. A lifetime, too, of disappointments.

As James Taylor sings it: "First you make believe / I believe the things that you make believe / And I'm bound to let you down. / Then it's I who have been deceiving / Purposely misleading / And all along you believed in me."

But when we describe what the other person is really like, I suppose we often picture what we want. We look through the prism of our need.

I know a man who believes that his love is really a very warm woman. The belief keeps him questing for that warmth. I know a woman who is sure that her mate has hidden strength, because she needs him to have it.

Against all evidence, one man believes that his woman is nurturing because he so wants her to be. After twenty years, another woman is still tapping hidden wells of sensuality in her mate, which he has, she believes, "repressed."

And maybe they are right and maybe they are wrong, and maybe they are each other's social workers. But maybe they are also afraid that if they let go of their illusions, they will not like each other.

We often refuse to see what we might not be able to live with. We choose distortion.

Leaving this couple, I thought about how much human effort can go into maintaining the "really." How much daily energy that might have gone into understanding the reality — accepting it or rejecting it.

How many of us spend our lives trying to sustain our myths, and how we are "bound to be let down." Because most people are, after all, the way they seem to be.

Really.

JULY 1979

Vowing To Get Married

She is going to get married.

This is not an announcement, you understand. It is, rather, her statement of intent. The poet has honorable intentions.

In fact, she has been going to get married for years now, almost since her divorce. Often across the telephone line that connects one coast and one life to another, the poet has talked out loud to the journalist about singleness as if she were a transient, somehow awkwardly living "between" marriages.

Tonight she says: "If things work out, we'll get married."

The journalist asks her, "Shall I call the caterer?" and they both laugh through the transcontinental echo. You see, they have been here before.

The poet has said three times in six years, "If things work out, we'll get married." The man in her plural has changed. But not her goal . . . and not her single status.

So, with a sigh of self-recognition, she tells the journalist, "Don't buy a dress yet." There is a pause, while the two friends think in tandem.

The poet is the same skeptic who once wrote a rhyme about the headlines that range like graffiti over wedding announcements: "Woman Has Nuptials." They sound, she said, like parts of the anatomy.

Moreover, this woman has not lived like those emotional migrants who set up tents, desperately trying to end their refugee life. She has rested with her children and her life quite comfortably.

The poet knows the difference between the times you have to compromise and the times when you are compromised. She won't discount her needs to bargain in the marriage market.

Nevertheless she is a single woman committed to the ideal marriage. She is going to get married. Someday. The two talk on and on, defying the telephone company, which promised them economy at night rates.

The journalist is not at all sure that her friend wants to mate again and tells her so. There are times she thinks the poet is merely appeasing the gods of her upbringing by assuring them that she, too, wants what she was taught to want. She wonders if the poet is making a bargain—a promise to remarry in the future in return for living as she choses in the present.

The poet wonders, too. She sees marriage as the question that demands to be answered, even though she knows from experience and observation that it may answer very little.

She knows that marriage carries a weight of its own in our world. If divorce is the context in which we live out our fragile marriages, marriage is the state against which people judge our nonmarriages.

It may be all quite mad, says the poet, but marriage is simply *there*. It is hard, she says, to be unaffected by its powerful presence.

The poet reminds her friend of the times they have told each other, "Everyone we know either gets married or splits." Perhaps it is true; perhaps it is a truism. But it carries with it a self-fulfilling anxiety.

There is just no way to ignore it, says the poet.

The parents of her students get nervous when the children who are living together "premaritally" show no signs of marrying. Her sister asks about her newest love, "How serious is it?" Only marriage is "serious." Every other relationship is, by our social definitions, one which "hasn't worked out yet."

The poet and the journalist have known men who matter more to them than those they were related to by titles. But society takes titles more "seriously" than feelings. An older friend of theirs loved a woman. But when she died, he had no place to mourn. He was not, you see, a widower.

It is odd, living in the State of Flux, with marriages ending in divorces ending in remarriages. No one knows whether the constant is togetherness or aloneness.

The poet on the West Coast believes in the possibility of polishing and perfecting. The journalist on the East Coast believes this: If it is working, don't fix it.

They both see the way the Marriage Issue turns a couple into a ménage à trois: she and he and The Question. The journalist tries to ignore it, which may be absurd. The poet tries to accept it, which may be equally absurd.

Later, after they have spent their budgets and their insights over this long distance, the journalist thinks about her friend's last words: "There is something in me that believes marriage is a more complete commitment. When I look at married people, I don't see it often, yet I keep believing it. What do you do with that?"

Maybe what you do is plan to get married. When, of course, "everything" works out.

APRIL 1980

Taking Turns

Masters and Johnson, the couple who run a kind of Ma and Pa shop in sex research, crossed another threshold last week in their attempt to make what was once outrageous seem perfectly ordinary. No sooner had the public recovered from their scientific dissection of heterosexuality than they moved on to the next frontier, a study of homosexuality.

The rather dour husband and his resolutely charming wife released a study detailing how similarly "gay" and "straight" people function—and dysfunction—sexually.

They found really only one rather intriguing difference, and that was in the way gay and straight couples seemed to choreograph their sexual experiences.

Homosexuals played out sex on a "my turn, your turn" basis. In contrast, the St. Louis researchers said that male-female couples often ran into sexual problems or ended up unsatisfied because they were hung up on the notion of "our turn."

It seems that the goal of filling two needs in one way at one moment is harder to achieve than the goal of filling two needs in two ways at two moments. The search for simultaneous pleasure seemed to be elusive compared to the goal of reciprocal pleasure.

I am hardly an expert on human sexual responses. I am still reeling from Masters' and Johnson's description of ambisexuals. These permanently unattached people who have no apparent sexual preference, who will have sex with anyone of either sex, remind me of Woody Allen's old joke about bisexuals: They double their chance of a date on Saturday night.

But it seems to me that when Masters and Johnson talked about taking turns, the fun couple has come up with a concept that is important not only in our sex relations but in the way we live together. They may have done something even more revolutionary than making the study of sex seem pedestrian. They may have put togetherness in its place.

Many of us were taught that the inseparable couple was the ideal couple. We were assured that the people who play together stay together, and that those who live as a twosome are more likely to remain one. There was the sense that the ideas, friends or pastimes people didn't hold in common were held against each other.

In our culture now, the "I" is seen as self-indulgent or lonely, but the "we" is associated with compromise or self-sacrifice.

There are millions of people who are sure that the only way to keep the "we" healthy is to forsake the "I." There are others I know who are equally convinced that they can only do what they want to do if they do it alone.

I suspect that there was a time in the bad old days when people didn't worry about togetherness because they were constant partners in the business of survival. Now—aside from the partnerships like that of Masters and Johnson—marriage is basically a leisure-time activity. People are afraid of being each other's passing fad, like human Hula-Hoops.

Still, there is something very rigid about the ties that

bind people as tightly as if life were a potato-sack race. The minute one person wants to go one way, the other has to go along, be dragged along or cut the cord.

The notion that the same thing will make two people happy at the same moment is a pleasant enough fantasy—certainly better than some of the ones coming out of St. Louis. But the reality is often mutual sacrifice rather than mutual satisfaction.

The Masters and Johnson method may put our pronouns in new places. There are some things that the most "constant companions" among us should do on our own. If she wants to see *Hair* and he wants to see *The Deer Hunter*, there is no reason to sit miserably through *Halloween* together. If one person wants to have dinner with a friend, it is intrusive to insist on making it a threesome or foursome.

There are other times when mutuality works, and vintage seasons when compromises are perfect for the palate. But there are years, maybe even decades, when taking turns is the most fluid—and perhaps most successful—sort of alternative: when one person is needful and the other plays caretaker, when one person requires privacy and the other grants it, when one person is in a state of siege and the other is voluntary defender. There are moments when we can switch from being needful to needfilled, with the security that our time will come.

Simultaneous pleasure is spelled Pressure. In or out of bed, the togetherness that allows room for the me and the us is called taking turns.

APRIL 1979

Misunderstood Michelle

It is not, to put it mildly, a high moment in the annals of legal history.

Michelle's lawyer has been busy releasing to the press Lee's love letters, carrying such literary gems as, "Oh Baby, I want so much for you, please."

Lee's lawyer in return is threatening to prove that Michelle's "services were defective." Such testimony, he says, "could get down to each and every time she had a headache."

Well, the rancor between actor Lee Marvin and what *People* magazine would call his "ex-live-in-mate" is enough to send anyone for the aspirin bottle.

The lawyers, we are told, are putting "marriage on trial" to prove whether there is a difference between a marital and nonmarital relationship. But if we are to judge from the level of acrimony, they have already proved that there is no difference between a divorce and a nondivorce. One can be every bit as seamy as the other.

The only thing that raises this case out of the mud and into the amusement park is this thing called an "implied contract." Two years ago, the California Supreme Court ruled that unmarried couples could expressly agree to share their property. Moreover, the court said, they could even "imply" such an agreement by their behavior.

So, now, we have a judge spending days trying to read

the clauses and subclauses of a stormy union written in invisible ink.

I haven't seen a lot of "contracts" in court, but I've sure seen a lot of them in real life. Most of the people I know inhabit one or another of the leaky boats known as Relationships. They are usually sure that their behavior, the decisions they've made together, make the nature of their attachment absolutely obvious. Many of them are equally sure that if they bring it all out into the air, the oxygen would dissolve the romance.

But it seems to me that an implicit agreement is most often a series of one-sided illusions. At the very least, half of these unions contain two sets of "agreements": his and hers.

In the Marvin case, for example, Michelle seems to have believed that living together was as good as being married. Lee, on the other hand, seems to have believed that living together was as good as being single.

I have two friends who moved in together many years ago. He looked upon this step as a trial marriage. She looked upon it as, well, moving in together. He was sure that in a matter of time, after they had built up trust and confidence, she would agree that marriage was the next logical step. She, on the other hand, was thrilled that here at last was a man who would never push her back to the altar.

What was "understood" between them was totally "misunderstood." In time, they discovered this gap and each was outraged, convinced that the other was guilty of breach of contract.

This happens just as easily in marriage. One wife may assume that marriage is a contract for their monogamy, while her husband assumes that it is a contract for her monogamy. Another wife may "agree" that the money is theirs, while her husband "agrees" that the money is his.

A homemaker may think of herself as a full partner who saves money rather than earns it and takes care of the details of her husband's life. Her husband, meanwhile, may think of himself as a self-made man.

Michelle Marvin's experience may be typical of the epidemic of what Tom Wolfe described so delicately as "wife-shucking." And Lee Marvin's experience may be typical of the men who are shocked to find their wives fighting for every nickel.

I hate to sound cynical about all this. I think Michelle has a case. There isn't much difference in lifestyle along the continuum from living together to common-law marriage to marriage. Trying to unravel the deals made between two people, married or not, is mind-boggling.

Most relationships begin with the highest, noblest idea about freely given affection, mutual sacrifice, undying love. When they are going fullspeed ahead, it is considered unromantic to read the emergency handbook. Only later do some people realize how far off course they were from the beginning.

It seems to me that any romance that can't handle a bottom-line chat about terms—what's going on here, what have we agreed upon—is in trouble anyway. There's nothing unfeeling about a renewable "contract" or a quadrennial state-of-the-union talk. For all the icky wrangling in the Marvin case the real message is: Be explicit.

JANUARY 1979

When Grateful Begins to Grate

I know a woman who is a grateful wife. She has been one for years. In fact, her gratitude has been as deep and constant as her affection. And together they have traveled a long, complicated road.

In the beginning, this young wife was grateful to find herself married to a man who let her work. That was in 1964, when even her college professor said without a hint of irony that the young wife was "lucky to be married to a man who let her work." People talked like that then.

Later, the wife looked around her at the men her classmates and friends had married and was grateful that her husband wasn't threatened, hurt, neglected, insulted—the multiple choice of the mid-sixties—by her job.

He was proud. And her cup overran with gratitude. That was the way it was.

In the late sixties when other, younger women were having consciousness-raising groups, she was having babies and more gratitude.

You see, she discovered that she had a Helpful Husband. Nothing in her experience had led her to expect this. Her mother was not married to one; her sister was not married to one; her brother was not one.

But at four o'clock in the morning, when the baby cried and she was exhausted, sometimes she would nudge her husband awake (wondering only vaguely how he could sleep) and ask him to feed the boy. He would say sure. And she would say thank-you.

The Grateful Wife and the Helpful Husband danced this same pas de deux for a decade. When the children were small and she was sick, he would take charge. When it was their turn to carpool and she had to be at work early, he would drive. If she was coming home late, he would make dinner.

All you have to do is ask, he would say with a smile.

And so she asked. The woman who had minded her Ps and Qs as a child minded her pleases and thank yous as a wife. Would you please put the baby on the potty? Would you please stop at the store tonight for milk? Would you please pick up Joel at soccer practice? Thank you. Thank you. Thank you.

It is hard to know when gratitude first began to grate on my friend. Or when she began saying please and thank you dutifully rather than genuinely.

But it probably began when she was tired one day or night. In any case, during the car-time between one job and the other, when she would run lists through her head, she began feeling less thankful for her moonlighting job as household manager.

She began to realize that all the items of their shared life were stored in her exclusive computer. She began to realize that her queue was so full of minutia that she had no room for anything else.

The Grateful Wife began to wonder why she should say thank you when a father took care of his children and why she should say please when a husband took care of his house.

She began to realize that being grateful meant being responsible. Being grateful meant assuming that you were in charge of children and laundry and running out of toilet paper. Being grateful meant having to ask. And ask. And ask.

Her husband was not an oppressive or even thoughtless man. He was helpful. But helpful doesn't have to remember vacuum cleaner bags. And helpful doesn't keep track of early dismissal days.

Helpful doesn't keep a Christmas-present list in his mind. Helpful doesn't have to know who wears what size and colors. Helpful is reminded; helpful is asked. Anything you ask. Please and thank you.

The wife feels, she says, vaguely frightened to find herself angry at saying please and thank you. She wonders if she is, indeed, an ingrate. But her wondering doesn't change how she feels or what she wants.

The wife would like to take just half the details that clog her mind like grit in a pore, and hand them over to another manager. The wife would like someone who would be grateful when she volunteered to take *his* turn at the market, or *his* week at the laundry.

The truth is that after all those years when she danced her part perfectly, she wants something else. She doesn't want a helpful husband. She wants one who will share. For that, she would be truly grateful.

DECEMBER 1979

The Mistress of Scarsdale

"*If* you want to know what I think, I think the guy deserved to die!"

The woman says this with blistering vengeance. She is standing at the sink, briskly chopping the six walnut halves of her Scarsdale diet lunch.

"Listen to this," she says, turning back the pages of the paperback to the acknowledgments. She reads down the list: "Suzanne . . . Phyllis . . . Terry . . . Elizabeth . . . Janet . . . Barbara . . . Elaine . . . Frances . . . June . . . Sharon . . . Ruth . . . There are 35 women's names! The creep should have worn a scarlet B for bastard."

The woman puts the last scoop of cottage cheese on the platter and brings it to the table saying, "I don't know if she did it on purpose or not, but I hope she gets acquitted."

I smile at her for a moment, because this irate friend is so rarely belligerent. She is an academic who normally adds historical footnotes and "allegedlys" to her measured opinions. But today she sounds like some advocate of capital punishment for lotharios.

This is what the story of Jean Harris and Hy Tarnower has done. Turned us into voyeurs and partisans of this most compelling case of the "wronged woman."

The papers had been full of more details. There was the engagement ring that led to no wedding. There was the trip to Paris clouded by the letter from another woman. There was the night *she* stayed in, writing diet recipes while he went out partying.

The murder trial resonates with jealousy, rejection, pain, insensitivity. With her fourteen years and his other women. Her pride and his other women. Her self-esteem and his other women. It strikes too many familiar chords to simply play in the background.

So Jean Harris has become a kind of upper-crust blues heroine. Everywoman whose man done her wrong. Everywoman who ever found the inscription on the cuff links, the letters in the drawer, the clothes in the closet. Everywoman who responded by saying only, "I wish—the same old wish—there were more ways I could do things for you."

She was forty-three when she met the New York cardiologist. Whatever the scars of her childhood and marriage, she was and is also a vital, witty magna cum laude from Smith, dubbed Big Woman by her sons, and Integrity Jean by her students.

It was this woman who was attracted to and wooed by the urbane man with his roses, his wine cellar, his dinners, his trips . . . and his little black book.

I don't know whether she came to this relationship with her own low crop of self-esteem or whether he eventually cut her down to size. He sounds like a bait-and-switch artist of great experience—a man able to hook women on charm and promises of stardom and then transfer them back into his chorus line. We've all seen men like that.

But I still don't see this as some classic heroic tragedy. I see it as the sorry common soap opera of the woman who hung on too long for too little.

We've all seen them, the women who gradually settle for what a man gives rather than what she wants. The woman whose self-image slowly splits into warring halves: head-mistress of Madeira and scorned mistress of Scarsdale, Integrity Jean in her work life and Jealous Jean in her love life. We've seen what's left for the losers in this internal war of the ego, a final revealing request: "I wish immediately to be thrown away."

By fifty-seven, after fourteen years, Jean Harris had learned too well how to swallow mouthfuls of humiliation in return for tidbits of attention. By fifty-seven, she had learned to misuse her pride to pretend she didn't mind. It's not all that unique.

Inevitably when anyone tamps down jealousy, anger, and pain, the pressure builds up. Cover fourteen years of it with pills or pride, and sooner or later it will explode into some form of destruction.

So forgive me if I don't think Jean Harris is Everywoman Wronged. To me, she's Everywoman who didn't know when or how to go. She's Everywoman who ever stayed with a bastard "because I love him"—and called this romantic.

She is, finally, Everywoman who ever hung onto a relationship by her fingernails while her self-esteem eroded like a crumbly windowsill on the eighteenth floor.

Eventually, like all of them, she fell into an abyss.

FEBRUARY 1981

"What Are You Thinking?" "Oh, Nothing"

The couple were seated at the window table eating their dinners. She was looking at him. He was looking at his plate.

"What are you thinking about?" she asked finally, engaging him with a half-smile, cocking her head flirtatiously, her fork poised in the air.

He returned her smile for a minute and said, "Oh, nothing," and went back to his dinner. His wife, with a glimmer of disappointment, a hint of hurt, pierced a heart of lettuce and joined him in a somewhat silent meal.

I watched the scene next to me like the audience at an ancient play. I had heard it, overheard it, before. I recognized the body language from other tabletops and sofas. Women leaning forward, men sitting at a slight remove. Wives grinding the conversation in gear, husbands disengaging.

Where are you going? Out. What are you thinking? Nothing.

But what made it all so much more poignant this time was that this husband and wife were in their eighties. It was white hair that she tipped flirtatiously, a lined hand that was raised in this gesture. It was possible, I calculated, that for fifty years, for sixty years, she had wanted to know what he was thinking, wanted to reach into his mind, and he had given her "nothing."

Of all the set pieces of dialogue that go on between men and women, theirs was dismally common.

I have watched so many women leaning toward their men, as if their need pressed them into a dangerous incline. So many women asking for intimacy. So many women wondering, Is he thinking of her, of them?

I have seen the men, too, more removed or perhaps contained. So many men resisting this womanly intrusion into their privacy. So many men uneasy with this incessant need for what her magazines called "communication." So many men thinking of "nothing."

I didn't know this couple, never saw them before and may never see them again. I didn't know what silences and words have passed between them over the years. But they fit into some test-pattern. The wives who want to talk and the husbands who want to read. The wives who want to talk and the husbands who want to watch football. The wives who want to talk and the husbands who want to eat silently.

I wondered if this hasn't been a deeper rift between men and women than pay scales or legal rights. A double standard of intimacy, of need for connections and sharing.

I know, it's a generalization. I know it's changing. The male stars now are not John Waynes of strong silences but men who have words spilling out of the cracks of their old images. The extraordinary aspect of the characters in the movie *Ordinary People* was that the father—not the mother—kept reaching out, wanting more, feeling more. Like Dustin Hoffman in *Kramer vs. Kramer* or Richard Dreyfuss in *The Goodbye Girl*, the fantasies of "women's movies" are about men who ask the questions, demand the connections, need.

Yet in real life it is the old dialogues and acts that hold the center stage. In *Unfinished Business*, author Maggie Scarf says that women build their lives on attachments. The investment of a woman's self in others is as striking as ever... and as fragile.

Women's depressions were largely triggered by personal loss, personal failure, she said. Men's depressions were largely triggered by work failures. The differences were still so strong that she wondered if they were innate.

I don't believe that these human gaps are riveted by our genes. But the difference is there, painfully obvious, and painfully lingering. I wonder about all the decades trapped now between this woman's need and her husband's "nothing." Between so many needs and so many "nothings." I wonder about the differences between all the "us and thems"—women and men.

There is one moment, one exchange of doubt, between women in Margaret Drabble's *The Middle Ground* that passed my mind as I watched the white-haired couple sipping the last of their coffee:

"'Do you think,' asked Evelyn, 'really, seriously think that life is very different for men?'

"Kate stood still and thought apparently earnestly, shaking her head without any flippancy at all and no facial expression whatsoever: 'I don't know. The truth is, I do not know.'

"'No,' said Evelyn. 'After all these years of thinking about it, neither do I.'"

OCTOBER 1980

Just a Guy Who Can't Say No

The most amusing footnote to the whole silly, slightly smarmy Gay Talese business is the author's surprise that everybody doesn't love him.

"I was staggered by the personal attacks on me, on what they thought was my infidelity," he is heard gasping coast-to-coast and channel-to-channel.

Here, after all, is a man who went massage-parlor hopping, sex shopping and sampling across the country, wrote about it and talked about it constantly... and his wife still loves him. Why don't the critics?

He has, he whines touchingly, "run up against small minds, a liberalism that is liberal about everything but sex."

Well, frankly, I suspect their marriage has survived because it is more symbiotic than "open." We have one husband who needs constant proof that he is loved No Matter What He Does, and one wife deeply into proving it.

As a friend of theirs told me, "Nan once wanted to be a nun, but she's settled for being a saint." If Gay Talese feels he is living out the male fantasy life, Nan is his male fantasy wife.

But if *Thy Neighbor's Wife* has not been embraced by the critics, it's for a different reason. The book is just not about "the redefinition of American morality," as it is billed by the author.

Rather, it is largely a series of sexual biographies of middle-aged men who grew up in a repressed atmosphere and who seem to identify the sexual "revolution" with the Right to Do It All.

Reading the book is like being trapped in a time warp. His characters, from Hugh Hefner of *Playboy* to Al Goldstein of *Screw* magazine to John Williamson of the Sandstone community, are Gay Talese clones who regard the world of swinging, swapping, consumer sex "like a kid given free run in a candy store."

They are still fighting against the old should-nots and repressions of the 1950s, while the rest of us are wrestling with the new shoulds and confusions of the 1980s.

In a scene toward the end of the book, Talese describes this: "The initiators were almost always men, the inhibitors almost always women."

Well, this was the basic social pattern of male-female relationships before the so-called sexual revolution. Men were supposed to try; women were supposed to resist. This dynamic set up a pattern of sexual hostility which has painfully permeated our relationships, even marriages, for generations.

But Talese and his cronies define sexual liberalism as simply getting rid of the nay-saying. In this he isn't alone. Nancy Friday's new book, *Men in Love,* another best seller, relays a recurring fantasy of many of the men who wrote to her: the woman who wouldn't say no.

When I asked Friday her own definition of "sexual liberation," her first response was that a sexually liberated woman wouldn't say no when she felt yes. But among the young generation you hear more wondering about whether they have said yes when they felt no. Many, many people who are sexually "free" to do what they want are confused about what it is they want to do. There is increasing discomfort at the idea that people know each other in the biblical sense before they know each other in the emotional sense.

In the first wave of any "revolution," people batter down

the old standards, and often confuse anarchy with freedom. Talese, for example, defines freedom as the victory of the old male posture of "initiating" over the old female posture of "inhibiting." His is an impersonal and grim world of sex as a consumer item.

His men seem pathetically stuck: stuck in the traditional male mode; stuck in sad old fantasies; stuck as eternal adolescents proving they can do what Mommy told them was naughty.

There is, however, another and kinder vision of liberalism that also has come out of this "revolution": the interweaving of our sexuality with the rest of our emotions. And this is sorely missing from *Thy Neighbor's Wife*.

In a truly breathtaking quote, one of Talese's characters describes his wife mockingly as a typically traditional woman who couldn't have sex "without becoming emotionally involved." But sex is about involvement. Sex is about the binding and delicate feelings that build trust in ourselves and others. It's about vulnerability and pleasure.

A book about sex that never touches its meaningful core— the involvement called love—is an odd chronicle of the emotionally impotent. That is why it is so unlovable.

MAY 1980

An Ideal Mate—for Someone Else

The fact of the matter is that he had once been a bully. She says this squeezing the lemon viciously until the last juice drops into her iced tea.

It isn't that he wanted to be a bully. It just grew out of his need to be in charge, to have things work smoothly—which is to say, his way—and out of her growing resistance.

I listen, nodding, remembering. In my mental picture of her husband from the scrapbook of their marriage, he is always wearing a tie. But then, he was the sort of man who looked like he was wearing a tie even in a sports shirt. He could be rigid in a hammock.

The woman talks on intensely, as if it were one day and not five years since they'd split.

He thought of himself as fair minded, she says, scrupulously fair minded. But to him life was a book he had to keep. In the last years of their marriage when she tried to change the original deal—his dollars for her services—he reacted as if he'd caught her hand in the till.

Each time she raised a foot to take a new step for herself—school, work—he accused her of aiming at his shin.

Yes, I say impatiently, rattling the ice cubes in my glass. This is all ancient history. Each of you has new lives now.

But that's the point, she says, leaning suddenly across

118

the table. He has changed, really changed. You wouldn't believe it. The children came home from vacation with him and his new wife. They dropped hints about his transformation that rattled across the floor of her old images.

The new wife teases him and he laughs—at last—at himself. The new wife cooks and he cleans, without a comment. The same man who once played through women golfers as if he were General Patton, now plays *with* them. The man who sabotaged her first interview, now races to the post office at deadline with his new wife's grant proposal.

My friend leans back in her chair, resting her case. There is something in her voice both wondering and resentful, amused and angry. Her ex-husband had become what she had wanted him to be...with someone else.

Be fair, I say. She too has changed with the new husband in her life. Stopped apologizing...stopped defending... stopped preaching. She has blossomed and relaxed in his acceptance.

For a moment I look at her and wonder. Would the former bully be shocked at his former wife? Would her second husband's first wife be equally amazed at his new life? Isn't it possible that there is a chain of ex-lovers, husbands, wives, friends, carrying around thousands of old images of people who have changed?

I suppose so, particularly now, says the woman, an edge of sadness to her voice. She knows a man who never got an apple out of the refrigerator of his first life and became a gourmet cook in his second. Her brother, who wouldn't "let" his first wife work, wins the award as Most Supportive Man with his new woman. People are as likely to change as they are to repeat patterns—which is both frustrating and reassuring.

My friend and I sit and talk about the investments, the time, the children. Between the three families there have been five children disrupted and relocated; six adults disillusioned and reconstructed...the chain stretched out.

Why is it easier at times to break up a relationship than

to break out of its patterns? she asks, directing her question at the tea or the air. Maybe it is just that people store up warehouses of bad feelings they can't empty, she answers herself. Maybe patterns firm into ice cubes of expectations that freeze us all.

It's possible, I say. We can start out in a new place without having to machete our way through old assumptions. But sometimes I wonder, too, whether we simply mesh in different ways with different people.

My friend had a theory when she was divorced, that people are simply threatened by change. They read every shift in their partner as a criticism or a betrayal or a threat. Now, in her second marriage, she hopes it isn't true.

Maybe, she offers, her first husband's second wife never saw him as a bully and so he doesn't behave like one. Maybe they had learned something. Maybe they were simply better suited.

We run through lists of "maybes." And then she looks up again. What if we all begin to change again? she asks uneasily and sighs. This time I hope we can become different people in the same place.

Yes, I say, raising the dregs of my tea, we'll both drink to that.

JULY 1980

Men in Search of Balance

There is a cartoon by Ed Koren in the December 10 New Yorker which carries a slightly delicious, slightly malicious tag line to the decade. Two furry, liberal, mid-life-crisis-aged husbands walk into the kitchen where their wives are standing over the eternal hot stove. Side by side, martini glasses in hand, benign smiles in place, they announce: "John and I are sick of hearing about women and their problems."

The irony, the honesty, the self-revelation are all there in that one risky picture. We have come to the end of ten years during which "women and their problems" have been discussed as a subject worthy of panels and government-funded studies and civil rights legislation. Now, underlying the mixed feelings of resentment and unfairness in that cartoon is a desire, even a need, to talk about men and their problems.

There has been something of an expression gap between men and women in the seventies. While books and articles about women's lives created whole new headings in the card catalogue, the few men overtly writing Men's Liberation books sounded as if they were saying what their wives wanted them to feel.

But now we see more and new images percolating up through the surface of men's lives and into the literature and movies. In *The Duke of Deception*, Geoffrey Woolf writes movingly about the sinew of love that runs through even the most difficult father-son relationship. Jules Feiffer creates a pointed and riotous cartoon novel, *Tantrum*, about a forty-two-year-old man who escapes the stifling responsibilities of adult malehood by turning two years old. John Updike goes on tenderly writing about the world of men as husbands, fathers, sons.

In the movies this is the winter of the male "issue" cinema. We have seen Alan Alda laying out the effects of public life on personal life, and Dustin Hoffman turning from an absent (or at least absentminded) father to a tenacious one. Even Burt Reynolds has changed his portrayal of the American male hero from *Semi-Tough* to sensitive in *Starting Over*.

In the real world, the same transitions are taking place. Many men in these ten years have, like many women, changed their ideal of woman. When the ad people at BBD&O surveyed what Today's Man wanted from Today's Woman, they found that "he approves of her going out to work, but wants her to be sure to take care of the household chores and the shopping and the kids."

But as women now say no to this superwife, we also see men, especially those at the cutting edge, beginning to look at their own choices and futures differently. The sons of men who submerged the values of home to achievement are struggling with the question of how to lead a more balanced life.

Corporations report that fewer men are willing to move for the sake of the company and at the cost of the family. Pollsters chronicle the fact that fewer young men seem willing to commit themselves to a success trip.

In a recent issue of *Esquire*, Gail Sheehy analyzed a survey of elite young men—those who would have once been automatically tracked to the top. She found them obsessed with "trade-offs" or the rewards of a top career versus those of a rich personal life. "New Life Choices," the hot topic of women's conferences in the seventies, is now a subject for men: New Tough Choices.

At the same time, from the Harvard Business School to a living room in California, the two-worker couples are trying to figure out how to hold down two jobs and hold together one marriage. Their decision making has become geometrically more complicated.

As an academic couple in Colorado said: "It was the restaurant business together, or English Lit in Ohio and Economics in Florida." They now run a restaurant.

Some men have experienced relief, others anger, and still others confusion in the fact that today, as Sheehy said, "Men simply cannot call the shots anymore." Some feel that they, too, are being asked these days to carry a double burden.

In fact, the question facing many men carries a familiar ring. Can we have it all? Can we only have it all by doing it all?

At the start of a new decade, it seems that the hopes and conflicts of men and women, especially young men and women, are beginning to dovetail again. Together they may reach out to find support, not only from each other but by changing the environments in which they work and live.

It is clear, at least, that men have found a new and different voice and have begun asking for equal time. In the eighties we will hear a lot more about the problems *of* men than the problems *with* men.

DECEMBER 1979

The Communication Gap

I went back to college this week or, to be more accurate,
back to colleges. For five days I had an intensive course
on the generation born circa 1960. I gathered enough material for a thesis on The Communication Gap Between The
Sexes, Phase II.

On campuses covered with ivy and lined with palm trees,
I met young women who've been encouraged to consider
life plans that will include careers as well as families, as-
piring as well as caretaking. I met young women who talk
regularly with each other in and out of class about marriage
of mutuality, about futures of equality.

But when I asked how often, how easily, these same
women talked about their ideas and ideals with the men in
their lives, I sensed an uneasy quiet.

Gradually, I realized that many of these students maintain
a kind of conspiracy of silence with men. They secrete away
some levels of feelings and hopes until it is "too late," until
false expectations are already set.

This silence grows in part from the old female fears—
can I be ambitious and feminine? can I be "liberated" and
loved?—that live right below the surface of this change.

Vulnerability and uncertainty, the anxiety about being
accepted and acceptable, are most acute in the first years
away from home. To many of these students, words like

women's rights, equality and, surely, feminism, are too risky to say in mixed company.

The fear is something they brought with them from home to campus, from childhood to adulthood. After all, most of these twenty-year-old daughters of forty-five-year-old mothers grew up in traditional, or transitional homes.

More than one talked freely about the double messages delivered by parents. One mother still tells her daughter regularly to make a partnership marriage. Yet the mother lives as junior partner with the man who is, after all, the daughter's father.

Another father urges his daughter on to success, a flourishing career. Yet the same man expects and wants service from the woman who is, after all, her mother.

In their families, far more was said about changing roles to daughters than to sons.

Now, in college, too, "women's issues" are still largely a single-sex subject. The classes, the lectures, the guidance sessions are overwhelmingly taught by women to women. Few teachers—like few parents—talk with young men about the real lives they will jointly lead.

The job of communicating with men, changing their ideas, again falls onto women. It falls heavily into the middle of all other issues raised in that emotional world we call a relationship.

The old reluctance of women to share their new aspirations is also founded in the very real continuing gap between the expectations of men and women.

I know that men have changed in tandem with the times. When Helen and Alexander Astin did their study of incoming freshmen in 1971, 52 percent of the men and 31 percent of the women agreed that "the activities of married women are best confined to home." When they asked again last year, only 34.7 percent of the men and 19 percent of the women still agreed with that "confinement."

But a gap between men and women exists even on this

easy question. It grows into a chasm as the issues of sharing and partnership become more complicated.

So, the new silence has grown out of the old silence. The students, male and female, are the latest victims of two-track talking, two-track teaching.

After my week at school, I wonder what will happen if young women don't learn that they have much more to fear from what they don't say. I wonder what will happen if more campuses don't involve their male students in thinking about lives gauged together, rather than on these separate tracks.

We may graduate a whole new generation, sadly unprepared to live together. We may graduate another crop of men who will be stunned and saddened at middle age, to discover that their wives do not, did not, want the life plan they thought was mutual.

Is this pain and disillusionment being nurtured now in the soil of our silence?

MARCH 1981

Being Loved Anyway

From time to time, my Uncle Mike likes to pass on the wisdom of one generation to another. In his own fashion.

On the subject of enduring love, for example, he and my aunt are role models of believability. They like each other.

They have a good time together. And they have managed it for roughly forty-one years.

So, when someone asks him the secret, he is more than willing to share the fact that he modeled his own success on his father's.

"My father would get up in the morning, look in the mirror and say, 'You're no bargain.'"

This, I think, would make a hell of a Valentine.

Maybe I'm just tired of people who pick at each other's imperfections like pimples. Maybe I know too many people trying to figure out if their mate is living up to expectations. Maybe I've met too many "6"s who think they are slumming with anything less than a "10." But I think he is on to something.

If you start your day looking your own flaws in the face, you might work up a pretty good appetite of gratitude before breakfast. If you know you're no bargain in the morning, by evening you could be atwitter with appreciation for someone who actually loves you anyway.

From my own, not particularly vast, experience and my uncle's advice, it seems that this is the glue of any long-term attachment: Being Loved Anyway.

There are at least two ingredients to the sticky stuff: (1) you have to know your own worst, and (2) you have to find someone who also knows it, but doesn't think it's all that awful. Being Loved Anyway, you see, is not being regarded as perfect but being accepted as imperfect.

I don't suppose that sounds very romantic. Other people may want sonnets to their perfection and flowers for their pedestal. They may want doilies of adoration.

But frankly, adoration would make me nervous. I'd keep waiting to be discovered.

I have a friend who got involved with a man who was in awe of her. It was outrageously flattering—for about three months. The problem was, she said, she couldn't yell at her children in front of him. The problem was, she had to keep washing her hair. She simply couldn't live up to it.

To this day, she refuses to trust the durability of any relationship in which she is still regularly shaving her legs.

I have another friend who, as they say in the shrink trade, has difficulty getting close. He is sure that someone will find out that his heart of darkness is made of mud, rather than chocolate.

But because he never lets anyone in, he never trusts anyone in love with him, since, by definition, she doesn't know him, because if she did know him, she would reject him. You get the picture.

If there is a constant in life, it must be the human fear of being unlovable. In a recent interview, Phil Donahue was asked for the fourth time what he wanted from love and sighed, finally, "Sometimes I think I invented insecurity." Baloney.

Insecurity was invented by the first kid who was caught being bad and asked his mother, "Do you love me anyway?"

The kid lives in all of us. The kid who is sure she won't be loved if she is bad. This kid is the one making the decision every day between the safety of hiding and the risk of discovery and the security of Being Loved Anyway.

I suppose it cuts both ways. We can't trust our own feelings for someone else until we've been "dis-illusioned," embarrassed, hurt a time or two—and have come out caring.

Now I don't want to make this negative. We shouldn't send all our Valentines to those who love us at our worst. Or those whose worst we love. I know people who have been loved for their weaknesses and hated for their strengths, and it was perfectly dreadful.

We are told that people stay in love because of chemistry, or because they remain intrigued with each other, because of many kindnesses, because of luck. I also suspect that laughing together is vastly underrated.

But part of it has got to be forgiveness and gratefulness. The understanding that, so, you're no bargain, but you love and you are loved. Anyway.

FEBRUARY 1980

PART 4

*Our Daughters,
Our Sons*

Save the Seals...and the Rest of Us

It was lying on the radiator cover in the kitchen in a pile of school papers, under math and ancient civilizations and spelling tests.

The tattered pages belonged to the weekly newsletter that goes out to school children, a publication so cautious that it could barely take a stand in favor of the Ten Commandments. So, too, these words made a bland milkshake of the men running for the presidency.

Still, as I looked at each candidate's picture and brief profile, I saw the words penciled in by children along the margins: "good," "bad," "good," "bad."

Good or bad? How did they know? What were they judging, these young readers of the Casper Milquetoast educational press? It turned out that the children who marked the paper were two-issue voters. They scanned and underlined the profiles to see how the candidates stood on these matters: (1) the environment and (2) peace.

I smiled to myself. Children! Save the seals, stop the wars. Kids and their ideals. Cute. Naive. Simplistic.

Standing there, I was, of course, an adult—sophisticated, tough-minded, realistic...and patronizing.

But as I finished cleaning out the papers, I realized that fundamentally they were right. In the deepest sense, there are only these two interwoven issues: peace and the environment. Save the seals and the rest of us. That's the ball game.

Again they made me think. In one way or another we purposely make children the repositories of our ideals. We allow them to hold up the standards we let slip. We encourage them to believe in possibilities the way they believe in Santa Claus.

Kids. They save Pennies To Fight Pollution, take Walkathons Against War, bake Bread for Brotherhood, are told to be charitable and generous and trusting. And then to grow out of it, as if caring were a pair of jeans.

We raise our children with ethical time bombs, built-in disillusionment alarms. We allow them their ideals until they are fourteen, or eighteen, or twenty-two. But if they don't let go, we worry about whether they will be able to function in the real world. Whether they are hard headed, practical enough.

It is all quite mad. We regard toughness as an adult. We regard cynicism as grown-up.

Adults _know_ that clean air is all very nice, but it must be balanced against jobs. Adults _know_ that helping others is neat, but it may take away their motivation. Adults _know_ that peace is swell, but you may need annihilation to save your national security. Adults _know_ that war is to be feared, but so is the fear of war.

Adults devour this "realistic" junk food, forgetting that ideals may be far more practical.

In our mid-life world, the environment is soft and business is hard-nosed. Peace is flowers, and war is the crushing artillery. The he-man, in all his redundancy, is our role model of mid-life.

In one way or another, most of our leaders had their left-handedness beaten out of them; most of our powerful whipped themselves into adulthood like G. Gordon Liddy.

So, we watch President Carter hyperventilate through his press conference, sure that he has done the right thing because it was the hard thing. He has, he would say, grown in his job and turned out more aggressive, less trusting. We call this the process of maturing.

Somewhere we learn that only by conquering our childhood instincts will we be admitted into the realm of adulthood, taken seriously. Those who refuse are forever regarded as childlike, Peter Pans . . . soft.

In our most common parenting scenario, we instill ideals into our children, resent it when they challenge us for not living up to them, and then feel reassured when they give ideals up, like sleds or cartoons.

I suppose we make kids the repository of our highest ideals because children are powerless. In that way we can have ideals and ignore them at the same time. We can assuage our conscience and maintain our status quo.

We keep placing our hopes in the next generation, always the next generation. I look at the papers in front of me and smile. Peace and the environment. They call this kid stuff.

MAY 1980

Drafting Daughters

My daughter is eleven, and as we watch the evening news, she turns to me seriously and says, "I don't like the way the world is doing things." Neither do I.

My daughter is eleven years and eight months old, to be

precise, and I do not want her to grow up and be drafted. Neither does she.

My daughter is almost twelve, and thinks about unkindness and evil, about endangered species and war. I don't want her to grow up and be brutalized by war—as soldier or civilian.

As I read those sentences over, they seem too mild. What I want to say is that I am horrified by the very idea that she could be sent to fight for fossil fuel or fossilized ideas. What I want to say is that I can imagine no justification for war other than self-defense, and I am scared stiff about who has the power to decide what is "defense."

But now, in the last days before President Carter decides whether we will register young people and whether half of those young people will be female, I wonder about something else. Would I feel differently if my daughter were my son? Would I be more accepting, less anguished, at the notion of a son drafted, a son at war?

Would I beat the drums and pin the bars and stars on his uniform with pride? Would I look forward to him being toughened up, be proud of his heroism, and accept his risk as a simple fact of life?

I cannot believe it.

So, when I am asked now about registering women for the draft along with men, I have to nod yes reluctantly. I don't want anyone registered, anyone drafted, unless it is a genuine crisis. But if there is a draft, this time it can't just touch our sons, like some civilized plague that leaves daughters alone to produce another generation of warriors.

We may have to register women along with men anyway. Women may not have won equal rights yet, but they have "won" equal responsibilities. A male-only draft may be ruled unconstitutional.

But at a deeper level, we have to register women along with men because our society requires it. For generations, war has been part of the rage so many men have held against women.

War is the hard-hat yelling at an equal rights rally, "Where were you at Iwo Jima?" War is in the man infuriated at the notion of a woman challenging veterans' preference. War is in the mind of the man who challenges his wife for having had a soft life.

War has often split couples and sexes apart, into lives built on separate realities. It has been part of the grudge of self-sacrifice, the painful gap of understanding and experience between men's and women's lives. It is the stuff of which alienation and novels are written.

But more awesomely, as a male activity, a rite of passage, a test of manhood, war has been gruesomely acceptable. Old men who were warriors have sent younger men to war as if it were their birthright. The women's role until recently was to wave banners and sing slogans, and be in need of protection from the enemy.

We all pretended that war was civilized. War had rules and battlegrounds. War did not touch the finer and nobler things, like women.

This was, of course, never true. The losers, the enemies, the victims, the widows of war were as brutalized as the soldiers. Under duress and in defense, women always fought.

But, perhaps, stripped of its maleness and mystery, its audience and cheerleaders, war can be finally disillusioned. Without the last trappings of chivalry, it can be seen for what it is: the last deadly resort.

So, if we must have a draft registration, I would include young women as well as young men. I would include them because they can do the job. I would include them because all women must gain the status to stop as well as to start wars. I would include them because it has been too easy to send men alone.

I would include them because I simply cannot believe that I would feel differently if my daughter were my son.

FEBRUARY 1980

Adolesc...
It's a Mess

When Franklin Zimring, a law professor at the University of Chicago, was thirteen years old he went through the Jewish rite of passage called a bar mitzvah.

"On that day I became a man," he says, and then adds ruefully, "but the next week at Sunday school they still took my attendance."

The point he was making was a simple one. In America today there's no single threshold birthday to adulthood, no benchmark that separates the child from the grown-up. In fact, the laws, the attitudes and court actions governing the transition could come right out of the verse from *Chorus Line:* "Adolesc...it's a mess."

I think of that as I leaf through some of the news stories sitting on my desk. This month in Mississippi, for example, a fourteen-year-old boy was tried as an adult for four robberies. He was sentenced to forty-eight years in jail before public outrage reopened the case. Meanwhile, in Pittsburgh, a college sophomore successfully sued his father for monthly "child" support, despite the fact that he was nineteen years old, a voting adult.

Now, in Washington, the Supreme Court is going to decide whether a minor needs the consent of her parents for an abortion, and in Massachusetts and elsewhere state legislatures are debating whether eighteen-year-olds should still be allowed to drink.

These issues are all different, yet they all struggle with the same problem: the age of adult privileges and responsibilities, the line between the child and the grown-up.

The fact is that adolescence, or what some call youth, is now a wildly indefinite time that can range from thirteen to twenty or older. It's typified by something called Semi-Autonomy.

Historian Barbara Brenzel, a professor of childhood and social policy at Wellesley College, says that, "There's an increasing age of semi-autonomy when we're held away from the work place by law or by economic reality, and held apart from marriage by economic constraints and changing social customs.

"For a long time now we're dependent on our parents for shelter and therefore for decision making, but we're on our own for three-quarters or more of the day. What we're trying to do is to make laws that deal with this semi-autonomy, that deal with the different parts of adolescence, the child part and the adult part."

Both she and Zimring suggest that the piecemeal, even conflicting, approach to public policy on adolescence may be the best. As Zimring puts it: "Any policy which is not eclectic is ridiculous." The notion of a national bar mitzvah could be less rational, less helpful, than dealing with these issues one by one.

Under the piecemeal approach, for example, it seems reasonable that a girl who can get pregnant without parental consent should be allowed to have an abortion without that consent, even if she couldn't have an appendectomy without it. It seems reasonable, too, that in criminal cases we should be able to protect ourselves from the hardened violent criminal of sixteen as well as from the one of eighteen. But we should make enormous leeway for the nonviolent criminal of fourteen.

Drinking laws are an easier area for making semi-policy about semi-autonomy. If you regard adolescence, as Zimring does, as the learner's permit period of life, the question isn't how old is old enough to drive or drink. "The proper question," he says, "is how old is old enough to start to learn."

Phased-in laws make a great deal of sense. The federal gun-control law allows people to own hunting guns at eighteen and hand guns at twenty-one. A law which allows people to drink only wine and beer first—perhaps even the old 3.2 beer—may be a sound idea. A law which makes a distinction between drinking in a bar and buying in a package store is another phase-in alternative.

They make more sense than the artificial "rationality" of setting eighteen as the age to drink, drive and get drafted.

After all, if there is one time of life defined by inconsistency it's this lengthy adolescence, delayed adulthood, and we may need laws as flexible, protective and gradual as the process of maturing.

As Zimring suggests, "It may be that the only thing the law can do is what adolescence does. Which is, at best, to muddle through."

MARCH 1979

Parents Have to Grow Up Too

*H*is *children are growing up. This is not exactly a news* bulletin, he tells the woman on the bench next to him. It's what children do. It's their thing.

Still, he says, facing the baseball diamond, he thought this growing up would all be gradual. Instead, his kids seem to lurch from one age to the next the way the oldest takes the corner in his driving lessons. They shift from one gear to the next with the most unnerving sound effects.

He remembers when his eldest was only three. The nursery school boy holding his hand said hello to someone on the street. How could the boy know someone the father didn't know? Even then, he felt these tiny electric shocks of independence.

Now they were going through rites of passage again. The oldest is getting his license. The youngest is heading for junior high school.

On cue, the thirteen-year-old came up to bat. In a matter of weeks, months, the boy had gotten it together...the wrists, the stance, the eye. It was as if his body had been preparing for today's final exam. He passed it with a solid double.

The father watched him as only parents watch their own. Too proud one minute and too critical the next. To be a parent is to know excess. But today he felt something else, between wonder and wistfulness, between love and loss.

Maybe, he says to the woman, he is going through a kind of adolescence himself. Maybe parents go through a second one with their kids: caught here between the pleasure of seeing them grow and the pain of letting them go.

He chronicles the little things. The projects they bring home from school have changed. A butcher-block table replaces the first raw wooden-block candlestick. A sixteen-page civics paper replaces the crayons. The boy heading off for camp once had anxiety; now he has a list and extra socks.

While they talk and watch, the teams change sides. The thirteen-year-old swoops by to pick up a glove and heads for third base. Someone hits a line drive at him and the boy drops it.

The father is on his feet in a second and then back down again. He tells the woman: Two years ago the boy would have been in tears; now he recovers quickly. The woman tells him: Two years ago you would have been compulsively coaching; now you are a spectator.

Yes, he says, we are both growing up. But, he adds grumpily, the difference between my son and me is that I have been his age and he has never been mine. The two laugh. This is a difference that makes no difference.

Yes, once upon a time, this man thought he knew a great deal about fathering. He had, after all, been a child, had a father. He pictured himself guiding his children around the potholes of his own youth. He would pour everything he had learned about life into their heads so that they would be protected from the worst.

He thought his life would be a foundation that they would build on from where he left off, like skyscrapers.

But his children are more like he *had* been than like he wished he had been.

Now, gradually, he was beginning to accept what Doris Lessing once wrote, that "his son, all of them would have to make the identical journey he and his contemporaries had made, to learn lessons, exactly as if they had never been learned before."

In turn, he was learning the lessons his father had learned before him: about the intensity of feeling and wanting for his children, about the need for letting go.

The game ended. The lanky younger son loped over. He handed the forty-two-year-old man a glove and a ball. He took $3 to buy pizza with the team and took off. Halfway across the field, the boy yelled, "Hey Dad, thanks for coming."

The man waved after him. It was OK. It was what happens. They grow up.

JULY 1980

Sugar-Coated History

The sounds leaked into the kitchen like cold air around the edges of an unsealed window. Despite their insistence on closed doors and lower decibels, the two mothers could hear the well-worn grooves of the record announcing, "Grease is the w-o-o-r-r-r-d."

In the living room, the two girls were giggling and jitterbugging to the music in their best ten-year-old rendition of a 1970s version of the 1950s.

But in the kitchen, their mothers groaned.

The mothers were, however, women who had given up

absolute censorship over their children's lives. They had reduced their rating power from R to PG, and so they didn't interfere.

Instead, they stayed sequestered in the kitchen, while their daughters lyrically professed for the 110,000th time that year: "Look at me/I'm Sandra Dee/Lousy with Virginity!"

It was worth a groan of mythic proportions. The girls were typical *Grease* recidivists. The ads for this never-ending movie asked, "How many times have you seen it?" Each could answer, "Three times!" The mothers, however, had seen it only once—a sentence that was long enough.

The children loved the music. The adults hated the message. The children had seen something refreshingly new. The adults had seen something distressingly familiar.

It had been odd to sit beside the next generation, popcorn in hand, watching an upbeat, high-energy, Technicolor story about the world they had once lived through in its own bleak documentary form.

The adults were not merely annoyed at the mis-writing of history. (Although, why is it that in the fifties revivals, the hoodlum is always the hero and the black leather jacket is always the status symbol?) They were more uncomfortable hearing the smarmy sexual liturgy of the times replayed: "Get much last night?" "Nice girls don't!" "Jugs."

Their children were offered a glossy, sugar-coated, nostalgic package of the worst of their parents' own youth. How many of the 1950s people had found their lives locked into that dynamic: He must insist/she must resist? Some had spent years regrouping from those male-female camps. Some were still polarized, pathetically trying to make connections, using opposite sets of rules.

Now their children gobbled entertainment, song-and-dance routines, about what had caused the parents pain.

Probably each generation resents its own revival. The survivors of the Depression must have blanched while watching Hollywood tapdance across the bread lines. Old union leaders must have been horrified when they saw sunshine stories about life in the old paternalistic mills.

Watching *Grease* in the 1970s was a bit like watching a World War I movie in the 1930s. The mothers wanted a moral, a warning.

Maybe that was it. Maybe all parents have the fear, consciously or not, that their children will be subject to the same injustices, bad judgment, social battering. Afraid to see their children fall into the patterns out of which they had struggled.

Well, perhaps these mothers were making a mountain out of a movie. One record does not a value system make. A revival of an era may even be proof of its distance.

But it was still strangely unsettling to these two survivors of the fifties to hear their children cheerfully, unconsciously, singing about our bad old days.

JANUARY 1979

Rating the Kids

The problem was that she had been visiting New York children.

Not that they looked different from other people's children. They didn't. They were even disguised in blue jeans so that they could pass in Des Moines or Tuscaloosa. Yet the New York children she met always reminded her of exotic plants encouraged to blossom early by an impatient owner.

She had spent one night with two thirteen-year-old girls who went to a school where they learned calculus in French. The next night she met a boy who had begged his parents for a Greek tutor so he could read the *Iliad*. He was nine.

This same boy came downstairs to announce that the Ayatollah Khomeini had just come to power. What, he wondered, would happen to Bakhtiar? Or oil imports?

She wondered for a moment whether this person wasn't simply short for his real age, say, thirty-two. But no, he was a New York child. She'd known many of them at camp and college. They wrote novels at twelve, had piano debuts at fourteen, impressed M.I.T. professors as sixteen. (She was, of course, exaggerating.)

The woman was thinking about all this on the plane. She was flying her flu home to bed. Sitting at 16,000 feet, enjoying ill health, it occurred to her that she was guilty of the sin of child rating.

It wasn't New York children; it was other people's children. It wasn't awe, she knew deep in her squirming soul; it was the spoilsport of parenting—comparing.

Her own daughter was reading *My Friend Flicka* while this boy was reading the *Iliad*. Her daughter regarded math as a creation of the Marquis de Sade, and she was taught in English.

The girl could plot the social relations of every member of Class 5-C with precision, but she couldn't pronounce the Ayatollah to save her gas tank. At ten, she was every inch a ten year old.

The woman hunched down in her seat, wrapping her germs around her like a scarf. When her child was little, the woman had refused to participate in playground competitiveness, refused to note down which child said the first word, rode the first bike. She thought it inane when parents basked in reflected "A's" and arabesques and athletics.

Now she wondered whether it was possible for parents not to compare their children with The Others. Didn't we all do it, at least covertly?

In some corner of our souls, we all want the chid we

consider so extraordinary to be obviously extraordinary. While we can accept much less, at some point we have all wanted ours to be first, the best, the greatest.

So, we rank them here and there. But we are more likely to notice their relative competence than their relative kindness. More likely to worry about whether they are strong and smart enough, talented enough, to succeed in the world. We are more likely to compare their statistics than their pleasures.

And we are always more likely to worry. She had often laughed at the way parents all seek out new worry opportunities. If our kids are athletic, we compare them to the best students. If they are studious, we worry that they won't get chosen for a team. If they are musical, we worry about their science tests.

If they are diligent, we compare them to someone who is easygoing. And if they are happy, we worry about whether they are serious enough. Perhaps the boy's parents wish he could ski.

We compare our kids to the ace, the star. We always notice, even against our will, what is missing, what is the problem. We often think more about their flaws than their strengths. We worry about improving them, instead of just enjoying them.

She thought about how many parents are disappointed in some part of their children, when they should fault their own absurd expectations.

The woman got off the plane in the grip of the grippe. She got home and crawled into bed. The same daughter who cannot understand why anyone would even want to reduce a fraction brought her soup and sympathy. Sitting at the edge of the bed, the girl read her homework to her mother. She had written a long travel brochure extolling the vacation opportunities of a week in that winter wonderland, the Arctic Circle.

The mother laughed, and felt only two degrees above normal. She remembered that Urie Bronfenbrenner, the family expert, had once written that every child needed somebody who was "just crazy" about him or her. He said, "I mean there has to be at least one person who has an irrational involvement with that child, someone who thinks that kid is more important than other people's kids."

Well, she thought, most of us are crazy about our kids. Certifiably.

FEBRUARY 1979

Post-Partum Cheers

S*omebody asked the question. Somebody always asks the* question. It sits so near the surface of our thoughts that the slightest extra heat sends it percolating into the air.

"How do you manage work despite having a child?"

Despite. The word was casually slipped in among the other nouns and verbs, subtly added, as if it were just another conjunction, no more loaded than an "and."

Yet, suddenly, I had a vision of a million small "despites," lying in cribs that blocked some highway to achievement, like those metal barrels on the highways. I pictured a million school-age "despites," innocently tripping their mothers on their way to work. And it made me recoil.

"Despite" the woman's benign tone of voice, I realized that I'd finally had it with The Question. In the past few years we have managed to oversell the burdens and undersell the pleasures of child raising. Now we are also overselling the "despites" and underselling the "because ofs."

People may no longer automatically assume that working mothers are bad for their children. But they do automatically assume that children are bad for their mother's work.

I am aware, of course, of the extra pressure children bring to our lives in terms of time and energy. There is an inherent conflict between workaholicism and a rich family life. Moreover, we have rotten support-systems for working mothers—impossible service industries, impoverished day care. You can read all about it in the diaries of a million angry working mothers.

Yet maybe it's time people began talking about how children have also been good for their work.

I remember going back to my job when my own small "despite" was an infant. Suddenly I was no longer, in some recess of my mind, working "until" I had a child. Whatever had been tentative about my commitment became solid. If I wasn't doing this "until," it was time to do it better.

I'm not alone on this largely unmentioned route. I know many others who gave birth to a burst of ambition or creativity—women for whom childbearing also carried a bio-work-ethic.

For many, parenthood is a passage into maturity, the final internal assumption of adulthood. More than one woman has come through this feeling grown-up and bucking for a promotion.

We've noted that surge in fathers; it's often equally true of mothers. It's a common postpartum expression.

In years of watching working mothers, I've also seen women who move onto a whole new plane of efficiency. Pressure cuts through the nonessentials like a sharp pendulum. If work expands to fill the amount of time available, it also contracts to fill the lack of it. Working mothers take shorter coffee breaks.

I don't want to overdo all this and claim superiority for working mothers. But when people think of children as work traps, it's often because of faulty definitions. We have wrongly defined the "best worker" as the least encumbered: the one who is free to travel and work overtime, the one who has ties to no one but the corporation. We have regarded single-mindedness above all else.

But our work may, in fact, depend much more on skills that are reinforced by living with children: The ability to listen. The ability to judge and to fill unexpressed needs. The experience of having benign authority. The juggling act of doing many things at the same time.

Child raising is a crash course in self-knowledge. It offers connections with a wider world and a deeper set of feelings. These are qualities that are rarely taught in business school and yet are essential in the business world.

But, beyond that, there is simply no way of separating out the working us from the parenting us. How do we manage our work "despite" our children? We are who we have become "because of" our children.

The part of our identity forged by them isn't housebound. It commutes with us to work. The part of us which knows new responsibilities, which has been shaken by new terrors, is also gainfully employed. Not just the part that punches in and out.

Our work and our children aren't worlds that oppose each other across a great "Despite." We need to choose the conjunctions that join, rather than divide, our lives. It's the only answer to The Question.

APRIL 1979

A Gift to Remember

*T*he man stood in the checkout line, holding onto the new bicycle as if it were a prize horse. From time to time, he caressed the blue machine gently, stroking the handlebars, patting the seat, running his fingers across the red reflectors on the pedals.

His pleasure, his delight, finally infected me. "It's a beautiful bike," I said to him, shifting my own bundles.

The man looked up sheepishly and explained. "It's for my son." Then he paused and, because I was a stranger, added, "I always wanted a bike like this when I was a kid."

"Yes," I smiled. "I'm sure he'll love it."

The man continued absentmindedly handling his bicycle, and I looked around me in the Christmas line.

There were carts and carts full of presents. I wondered what was really in them. How many others were buying gifts they always wished for. How many of us always give what we want, or wanted, to receive?

I've done it myself, I know that. Consciously or not. I've made up for the small longings, the silly disappointments of my own childhood, with my daughter's. The doll with long, long hair, the dog, the wooden dollhouse—these were all absent from the holidays past.

I never told my parents when they missed the mark. How

many of us did? I remember, sheepishly, the tin dollhouse, the parakeet, the doll with the "wrong" kind of hair.

Like most children, I was guilty about selfishness, about disappointment. I didn't know what gap might exist between what my parents wanted to give and what they could give . . . but I thought about it.

I knew they cared and, so, even when it wasn't exactly right, I wanted to return something for my gift. I wanted to please my parents with my pleasure.

But standing in that line, I thought about what else is passed between people. Gifts that come from a warehouse of feelings rather than goods.

Maybe we assume other people want what we want, and try to deliver it. Maybe in every season, we project from our needs, we giftwrap what was lacking in our own lives.

My parents, descendants of two volatile households, wanted to give us peace. They did. But I am conscious now of also giving my child the right to be angry. In the same way, I know parents who came from rigid households and busily provide now what they needed then: freedom. They don't always feel their children's ache for "structure."

I know others who grew up in poor households and now make money as a life-offering for their families. They don't understand when it isn't valued.

There are women so full of angry memories of childhood responsibilities that they can't comprehend their children's wish to help. There are men so busy making up for their fathers' disinterest that they can't recognize their sons' plea: lay off.

Every generation finds it hard sometimes to hear what our children need, to feel what they are missing, because our own childhood is still ringing in our ears.

It isn't just parents and children who miss this connection between giving and receiving. Husbands and wives, men and women, may also give what they want to get—care-taking, security, attention—and remain unsatisfied. Our most highly prized sacrifices may lie unused under family trees.

Of course there are people who truly "exchange." The lucky ones are in fine tune. The careful ones listen to each other. They trade lists. They learn to separate the "me" from the "you." They stop rubbing balm on other people to relieve their own sore spots.

Perhaps the man in line with me is lucky or careful. I saw him wheel his gift through the front door humming, smiling. For a moment, I wondered if his son hinted for a basketball or a book. This time, I hope he wanted what his father wanted for him.

DECEMBER 1980

At a
Nuclear Age

The girl is worrying about The Bomb.

It is, a friend assures me, a passing thing. It is, he says, just a symbol of childhood feelings of impotence in a wider and scary world.

But I think it is a symbol of her fear of the bomb.

I saw her staring into space when the idea goose-bumped across her body. She shivered and said simply, "I was worrying about the bomb."

I wanted to say the right thing to her. It is a parental flaw, wanting to say the right thing. We always want to say the right thing and end up telling them to brush their hair. So, about the bomb, I said: "It is worth worrying about." That was dumb . . . unsatisfactory.

She asked for a second opinion. It's what resourceful children do when the first answer is dumb or the source is as historically unreliable as a parent. She looked across the table and questioned a friend of ours: "Do you think I will die from old age, disease, or the bomb?"

My friend was taken aback, but he is congenitally reassuring. At least, he has been reassuring me since I was eighteen and worried about making a fool of myself in *Damn Yankees*. He said then that I would be great. My friend is often more reassuring than accurate.

So, of course, he told the girl that there wouldn't be a nuclear war because it would be disastrous for everyone. People were too sane to drop the bomb.

The girl, however, has had a good deal of experience with the use of ultimate weapons on school playgrounds. She is not convinced that the reasonable human mind is a deterrent to violence.

So it was my turn again. This time the best I could do was wryly point out one of the values of living in Boston, one which goes unadvertised by realtors. In the event of a nuclear war, anyone this close to M.I.T. will never know what hit her.

Double dumb.

What I wanted to be, of course, was both honest and reassuring, both accurate and comforting. But it is sometimes impossible to be both. Ground Zero is not a great comfort, especially if you are eleven years old.

This isn't the first time I have flunked my own self-administered, self-corrected, take-home parenting test. Maybe I'm a tough grader, maybe we all are, or maybe the world has raised the standards over our heads.

It's not just about the bomb. It's hard to be simultaneously realistic and comforting about almost anything that makes life stable, or the future certain.

When we were young, most of us were fed three square meals of certainties. I don't know if our parents believed them all or if they just thought that security, like milk, was good for the children. But it was a pretty constant and even nourishing diet.

We didn't hear much about bad times, bad marriages, bad wars. The survivors of the Depression didn't talk much about it; the survivors of World War II were proud; divorce was a secret scandal.

Most of us grew up expecting a stable world. I don't think we were betrayed; at worst, most of our parents believed they could build us that world. They thought we needed to be assured instead of prepared. Instead, we were surprised.

The way we live is *unexpectedly, surprisingly*, insecure. We live in a state of flux.

And lurking in the background is the epitome of human foolishness and insecurity: The Bomb.

All these things cannot help but affect the way we live with our own children. I suspect that they, too, want a stable, secure world. They want consistency; they want answers to questions and solutions for problems.

But we can't give them what we don't have. Instead we offer ambiguity, contingency plans, history, alternatives. And we call this "preparation for the real world."

I don't know whether they are learning insecurity and fear, or learning how to cope. Or perhaps learning how to cope with insecurity and fear. But I suppose we do what parents always do: our best. We try to share what we know of the world and what we assume they will need to know.

With any luck we will have been too pessimistic.

OCTOBER 1979

PART 5

Personals

The Commuter's Worlds

*F*inally the dirt road in Maine was leading home. The tire touched the first profanity of pavement, and subtly my vacation began slipping away.

By the first tollbooth my state of mind had shifted from neutral to first gear. By the time I had passed all my favorite landmarks—the sign to Biddeford, the bridge labeled Cat Mousam Road—I had slowly and reluctantly begun to relocate my sense of place, my sense of values.

I was going back, to lists and alarm clocks and stockings and school lunches and all the external pressures of the life known as civilization. I was going back to things I had to do.

This time even the skies divided these two halves of my life. Along Route 95, a curtain of almost impenetrable rain separated one world from the other. The day before, this rain on the roof of the house would have been a comforting boundary to the day, a prediction of reading and fires. Now, the rain on the windshield of the car was a hassle, a challenge to overcome.

I turned up the radio, so I could hear the final installment of *Jane Eyre* over the pelting rain, and thought about these different rhythms that mark my own life, many of our lives. Left behind was a world in which I simply lived . . . according to its patterns. Ahead of me was the world of agendas and problems that I was expected to encounter and resolve.

Was it country versus city? Leisure versus work? Nature versus human environment? Both and neither. Vacation is a state of mind as much as a state of the union.

For two and a half weeks in Maine I watched the sky, the cove, the cormorants and a seagull with the gall to steal chicken off our barbecue. I am told that I became an accomplished mud watcher, sitting on the porch, watching the bottom of the cove at low tide for hours. I prided myself on developing a hobby rarely listed in *Who's Who:* I became a fine stick-in-the-mud.

To me, an urban woman who lives much of her life according to other people's deadlines and demands, this was a chance to literally vacate the world of schedules and struggles.

I did not, do not, use my vacation to climb mountains, shoot rapids or fulfill itineraries of some travel agent. I preferred to drift along my inclination down through the circle of goals to the mud of acceptance.

I was content with the harmony we call doing nothing. There was a sense of letting go, being at ease with time rather than at odds with it. I wallowed in the understanding that there was nothing that had to be done beyond watching the clothes dry and casting for mackerel.

But I was also returning. Returning to the energy, the structure, the demands, the pressure. I also chose engagement.

There are, I suppose, these two sides to all of us. The side that wallows like any other organism in the world, and the other side that seeks some purpose "above" that. The side that feels most content in nature, and the other side that feels more energized "on top of the world."

I am aware of this duality, the urge to watch the mud, the urge to build something out of it. Our peculiar human creativity doesn't come from harmony but from wrestling with chaos as well. Every poem and every building was wrested out of raw material by people who refused to accept things as they were.

Too often we work by clocks instead of sunsets and become more attuned to air conditioning than the condition of the air. But there is also in all this the challenge and energy and pleasure of accomplishment.

At one time, I thought these worlds were at odds, that we had to choose engagement or disengagement, acceptance or accomplishment, watching the mud or building with it.

But traveling this kind of road again and again, I realized that they are just two destinations, points along a path of dirt and pavement. Now it is the tension that intrigues me. The search for a balance between comfort and purposefulness, between accepting things and struggling with them.

Driving home, I was reluctant to leave one world for the other, reluctant to put on my city clothes of purpose and structure and struggle. But I knew that I was lucky to be a commuter.

SEPTEMBER 1980

It Keeps
Cropping up

There is an unwritten clause in my contract for this column that prohibits me from writing about my vegetable garden more than once a year.

It is a good clause, a sane clause, an absolutely essential clause. And one which makes me utterly miserable.

I am, you see, a charter member of Veggie Growers Anonymous, a subgroup of perfectly decent Americans with a sense of propriety as well as property who are transformed every summer into garden bores.

You have, I am sure, heard of golf bores. These are the people who putt through parties, recounting every slice of life. You have also met tennis bores who will explain in exquisite, excruciating detail how they turned their grip fifteen degrees to the left and now serve like Bjorn Borg. This fascinating fact is usually accompanied by a demonstration designed to bring down the house. Instead, it brings down the chandelier.

But those of us who spend our summer measuring tomato plants and attacking white flies also can be full-fledged bores. We will, with the slightest encouragement, deliver a State of the Garden Address to any captive audience.

Merely mention the game of squash and one of us will eagerly interrupt, "Speaking of squash, let me tell you about my zucchini."

Tell us that you are trying to get "into your own head," and we will free-associate. "Have you tried my iceberg?"

Ask us, in the midst of bright and witty repartee about world affairs, what is new on the American scene, and we will instantly answer: Sugar Snap Peas.

All of this antisocial behavior is bad enough. But there is more. I, personally, am famous for corralling anyone around my grounds into a footnoted, annotated tour of God's Little Sixteenth Acre. I rival the tape-recorded tours at the art museum . . . in length.

A perfectly innocent gas meter reader of my acquaintance, for example, now knows the relative merits of caged and staked Big Boys. (I am talking tomatoes, not men.) Another man, special-delivering corrections for a magazine article, can tell you precisely why my strawberries died last winter.

The only one who has escaped me this summer is the United Parcel man. As I was treating him to an elegant discourse on the French Intensive method, he retreated wide-eyed down the stairs. How could I know he was thinking Masters and Johnson when I was talking bush beans?

As for my friends and family, from May to November, they are expected to worry and wonder about my garden, and to gasp at science fiction tales of my runaway herbs, including The Mint That Ate New York. (Actually, it hasn't started on New York yet, but watch out, it's headed for Connecticut.)

No one is allowed to just *eat* my little veggies like some sort of barbarian. A tomato is not to be merely sliced; it must be properly sacrificed with a ritual prayer. People must ponder the beauty of the green pepper, the history of eggplant.

I am not at all sure how I became a garden bore. I am definitely not the sort of parent who regales friends with the latest antics of a drooling three-month-old, complete with slides. Furthermore, I find it utterly appalling when people put their pets through show-and-tell in my presence, rolling Rover over and over and over.

Maybe it has something to do with the unexpected. The

only thing we grew in my childhood apartment was refrigerator mold and green carrot tops.

Maybe all the garden bores of America are people who remain surprised that we plant a seed and three months later eat a salad. We are proud as punch; we think we did it; we think this is news; we want to spread the word. We want to spread many words.

But under the terms of my contract, I am only allowed to harvest a measly 750 words each season.

JULY 1980

Buy Now, Gloat Later

Let me begin by saying that I am a woman who grew up believing that it was a mortal sin to pay full price for anything. Of course, over the years I have been extravagant from time to time . . . but only when it was a bargain.

I also belong to a circle of friends who are congenitally unable to tell each other what something costs without also saying what it used to cost, as in, "This blouse is $19.95-reduced-from-$49.95."

Nevertheless, despite this upright background, I found myself standing in a shoestore last week trying on a pair of leather boots so expensive that I felt compelled to ask the salesman whether they came with the rest of the cow (preferably six steaks, two flanks and a tongue). He was not amused.

Even more shocking is the fact that today I am the owner of these boots which, I rapidly calculated, cost me exactly what I took home during the entire first month I was employed.

How did this happen, you may ask, that a person as frugal, not to say crummy, as I ended up with gilded feet? Because, as I stood in front of the mirror, the salesman gently assured me that (1) these might well be the last pair of boots an ordinary human being like me could ever afford and (2) "next year, you're gonna wish you'd bought them" and (3) you should not consider them an expense but "an investment."

Thus, in one brief and hysterical moment, I joined the congregation of people who have redefined the word "bargain" according to the dictionary of inflation. A bargain is not something which costs less today than yesterday. It is, rather, something which will cost more tomorrow.

I am now a bona fide, up-to-date bargain hunter, and member of a new economic cult. We bargain hunters are not merely devout followers of the Windfall Prophet but also people who live under the national mantra: Buy Now, Gloat Later.

Like most new members, I was subtly recruited at testimonial meetings known as cocktail parties where founding members seduced me with the stories of their successes. There were, for example, the inspirational tales of The Homeowners.

These are people who read the real estate pages as devoutly as their ancestors read the stock pages. They clip suburbs instead of coupons. They search the listings with the same obsession that others search the obituaries—to reassure themselves that they are OK.

They win admiration and proper awe by regaling us with how they bought a house and ten acres right after the war with $300 down and a GI mortgage.

Then there are also the Single Killing people. There is,

for example, the famous lady who bought a hand-woven, scrimshaw decorated Nantucket basket in 1959 for $25. She lived to bask in it. Although the basket is no less grotesque than before, it is, she says, pausing for the right effect, now selling for $600.

Most of us are also likely to hear from the Prophets vineyard tender who bought a '61 Chateau Latour for $25 ten years ago. It is now, he confesses to the hushed assembly, worth $200. At that price, he does not drink it, of course, but from time to time he turns it and tallies it.

With these role models, who among us would not immediately rush forward to stand up for the Windfall Prophet? What more does the average inflation-worried American long for then the equal right to buy now, gloat later?

As fully converted New Bargain Hunters, we put our money into sofas instead of stocks, and into boots instead of bonds. We no longer "buy" a bracelet, pocketbook, fur coat, washing machine. We "invest" in one.

Instead of believing in savings banks, we believe in stocking our shelves. We don't worry about what we can have, but how we can hedge. If someone asks in the best West Coast lingo, "What are you into?," we answer: "Things."

Gloating is our delayed gratification.

Of course, there are some limits to the most ardent of the Thing collectors. The only way you can boast about a buy in kindling wood is if you don't light a fire. The only way to make a killing in steak futures is by eating a whole lot of spaghetti.

But as for me, I assure you these boots were not made for walking but for waxing. This year I will feed them mink oil and house them under a glass dome. Next year, when I tell you what they cost, you're gonna eat your heart out.

NOVEMBER 1979

Spring Fever, or a
Case of Restlessness

"*It's just spring fever*," he said, *quite casually*. She bristled with annoyance. She didn't like his instant diagnosis of her feelings. She didn't like the fact that he had labeled it a disease and then implied that she would soon be cured of it.

"Maybe it's healthy," she snapped back. "Maybe I don't want to get over it."

Later, thinking about it alone, she decided that he was probably right. It had been the kind of glorious day that favors spring fever the way a swamp favors malaria. It was a May day, and the guard that northerners wear to protect them from the physical awareness of winter had suddenly dropped like layers of clothing onto the floor.

Around her were littered all sorts of numbing emotional accessories, as if they were the blankets, hats and mittens of winter life. She had the sort of fever that heightens sensibilities rather than thermometers.

The warm May breeze had sent goose bumps across her complacency, and dissatisfaction sprouted up like her new snap peas.

She felt free-floating discontent, an affect without an object. It wasn't the sort of discontent that comes justifiably when something is wrong. It wasn't discontent tied to some-

167

thing that is missing. It came rather from an engorged sense of what might be. She was suffering a shy ache for the possible, the what next.

It occurred to her that people mourn for what might have been at three o'clock in the morning. They long for the might-yet-be when this fever strikes.

It was ironic. It wasn't fair. People who survive the hostility of winter deserve some sort of peace in the spring, the languid pleasure that comes after resistance. They deserve to feel the ease of belonging in the universe, instead of battling it.

Instead they get spring fever. That great yawning want.

Was it just some cosmic joke, some comic reminder that life never quite lets you off the hook? Was it a mystical memo saying that surviving isn't enough, "just living" isn't a good enough reason for living?

Was spring fever a metabolic insistence on *more?*

The woman remembered a few years back when a friend of hers had emerged unscathed from a serious automobile crash. Days after the first giggly gratitude had worn off, this friend had become suddenly restless and searching. Within months she had produced her own life accidents, turning her job over, choosing marriage. Her survival had demanded some justification. She had felt forced to change the norm, pursue some new meaning.

In a smaller way, perhaps, people who merely survive another winter are struck with the same need.

She thought about how many of us live—surrounding ourselves carefully with security systems, battening down all the hatches against the January and Februarys.

Then, suddenly, for no apparent reason, when the snow alert is over and May arrives, security seems so limiting and stability feels like a defeat rather than an achievement. In the place of safety comes the urge to risk, to break patterns, to discover.

In one of his rambling lectures, Alan Watts once said that the most revolutionary question a person could ask is:

"What do I want?" There is a feverishness in that question. It's a self-interrogation worthy of spring.

The people who merely assume that the question has a multiple-choice answer check off jogging or love affairs. They decide that their free-floating discontent is anchored to one of the secure decks of their lives and cut loose— from jobs, families, towns.

But the question always comes back, resisting any final examination. Spring fever, after all, germinates questions, not answers. It is a great, amorphous, rebellious *why*.

No, she supposed it wouldn't last long. Intensity never lasts long. Whether this is a disease or a moment of radiating health, it has a long incubation and short season.

Sooner or later, the elixirs of routines, the pleasant tonics of her life, would "cure" her. She knew that now, though she hadn't when she was younger. This gorgeous discontent was just spring fever and it, too, would pass. She said that with a sense of regret and also, yes, a sense of relief.

MAY 1979

Fathers: Snapshots from a Distance

This Father's Day column began six months ago over a bowl of mussels, a glass of wine and a long talk.

It began because my friend and I were running through the latest episodes of our lives, flipping the pages of our family albums, catching up on the soap opera installments about our parents and children.

There had been another scene between my friend and her mother. That in itself wasn't unusual. Their connection had built-in tension and resiliency. Like the coiled telephone cord through which they communicated, the lines between these two women could stretch to the breaking point or curl up into intimacy in a matter of minutes.

But the picture of her and her mother in this family album was—how can I describe it?—rather like a macrame. It was created out of knots of caring, knots of anger, knots of intimacy. Over the years small, intricate little strings between them had been tied and retied until they formed a whole as difficult to unravel as a six-foot wall hanging.

But somewhere in the middle of this evening, it occurred to me that I had no idea what my friend's father did for a living. Despite a decade of daily contact, despite all I knew about her mother, I couldn't have repeated the slimmest résumé of her father's life.

In that moment I realized that fewer pages had been filled with pictures of him. He had been observed from far fewer angles.

I knew that my friend loved her father and even criticized him at times. But it happened in a rather uncomplicated way. When she profiled him, her voice was less loaded with judgments. She offered a fairly objective frontal view, a snapshot, not a macrame.

I thought about how often this is true. How many of the people I know—sons and daughters—have intricate abstract expressionist paintings of their mothers, created out of their own emotions, attitudes, hands. And how many have only Polaroid pictures of their fathers.

I suddenly had a vision of all our parents, framed. Inside a wooden strip, side by side, would be the mothers—complicated portraits. Next to them would be the fathers—in cool sixty-second focus.

I know that I risk overgeneralizing and offer up any number of qualifications. But, on the whole, the fathers I know are seen through a zoom lens, while the mothers are painted in close-ups.

It is not that fathers are better or worse, not that they are more loved or criticized, but rather that they are viewed with far less intensity. There is no Philip Roth or Woody Allen or Nancy Friday who writes about fathers with a runaway excess of humor, horror . . . feeling. Most of us let our fathers off the hook.

In a dense and often obscure underground book, *The Mermaid and the Minotaur*, Dorothy Dinnerstein says that our psyches are rooted in the fact that most of us were cared for in infancy by women alone. "The early mother," she writes, "is a source, like nature, of ultimate distress as well as ultimate joy. Like nature, she is both nourishing and disappointing, both alluring and threatening, both comforting and unreliable."

She suggests that the extreme dependency of infants produces a range of feelings about mothers, full of the urgency and intimacy that comes from need. If our feelings about fathers have been less intense, perhaps it's because the stakes were lower.

We criticize mothers for closeness. We criticize fathers for distance. How many of us have expected less from our fathers and appreciated what they gave us more? How many of us always let them off the hook?

I bring this up for Father's Day because things are changing. Margaret Mead used to say that motherhood was natural, but fatherhood was a social invention. We have reinvented our definition of a Good Father. He is no longer just a provider. He is now a caretaker as well.

Yet I wonder how much of the reluctance among men for sharing infant care fully has to do with a subconscious understanding of the costs. Caring for infants means being vulnerable and powerful. It means intensity. It means the hook.

It also means sitting for a portrait, rich, complex, not

altogether flattering, full of the subjective eye of the child. And that is much more difficult than posing for a Father's Day photo.

JUNE 1979

Asleep at the Table

Let me begin in self-defense by saying that I have never put a lamp shade on my head, or ended an evening pleading for another chorus of "Melancholy Baby."

That, as they say, is the good news.

But the fact of the matter is that I have a social flaw forgiven only among octogenarians and people suffering jet lag. I fall asleep at dinner parties.

I always have. When I was eight and at a restaurant, my parents would order dinner and two chairs: one for my head and one for my feet. When I was seventeen, I was the only one at the senior prom who went into deep REM instead of high gear during the all-night feast.

If the size of my slippers hadn't eliminated any possibility of being cast as Cinderella, the state of my eyelids would have. I never could have stayed at the ball until midnight.

I come by this trait honorably. After years of politics, my father developed catnapping into a fine art. He could fall asleep in the living room—anyone's living room—and wake up ten minutes later insisting that he had just been "resting his eyes." He always managed to look at this, like everything else, positively. He assured me that falling asleep was a symptom of being profoundly relaxed and self-assured.

But virtually everyone else I know considers it a problem. It seems that those of us who follow our internal bedtimes alienate more hosts and hostesses than if we had whistled "Dixie" while chewing saltines over their shag rugs.

They do not think: Isn't it wonderful that she is so comfy in our home! They think: What a creep! They are insulted. In fact, they generally regard a mummy on the sofa with a hostility otherwise reserved for the Early Exiter. Both are taken as proof of a dull evening.

Because of this, we are all required by the rules of modern etiquette to (1) stay late and (2) stay up. I can do one or the other.

Obviously, I am unfit for the wonderful world of grown-ups. A world in which hosts invite guests to dinner at 7:30, expect them at 8:30, feed them at 9:30 and begin ardent discussions with them at 11:30.

Hopelessly gauche, I arrive at 7:30. am famished by 8:30, desperate by 9:30 and asleep by 11:30.

It is a symbol of adulthood to be able to debate SALT at midnight. The only thing that interests me about Brezhnev at that hour is the "z," or the "zzzzz."

But people do not invite you over to sleep with them, at least not in the literal sense. The only one I know who completely sympathizes with my plight is the husband of one of my best friends who suffers from the same antisocial disease. We have, in fact, often and publicly slept together. Neither of us took it personally.

I wish I could say that this habit was related to late-night feedings, because the parents of infants are excused for dozing wherever they can. They have a note from the pediatrician. But the only midnight snacks my daughter has these days are taken with friends, cousins and other army ants at what is called a sleepover. (A sleepover is an eat-over with as little sleep as possible.)

Still, I think that those of us who fade early and often are not bored, rude or miserable. It's just that we live on our own daylight savings time. We go through life as if everyone else were in California and we just arrived from the East Coast.

We are a much maligned and guilt-ridden minority which sleeps to the beat of a different pendulum.

After all, people are not considered antisocial if they refuse to speak before 10 A.M. We do not shun friends because they doze at dawn and are incoherent at breakfast. Being cranky before coffee is considered sophisticated, adult.

Yet, most of us who sleep after dinner are utterly scintillating over orange juice. We are astute with our eggs. We peak at about 9 A.M. And are made to feel guilty, rather overbearing, for that, too.

I think it is high time that we stopped feeling responsible for the droop of our eyelids. Am I my eyelids' keeper? I intend to hold an elegant breakfast party, promptly at six in the morning. Anyone who is unable to discuss nuclear energy over cantaloupe will be cast asunder.

JUNE 1979

Medicine That Purrs

Not long ago, I read a small story about a cardiac study in Baltimore and filed it away in my mind under the heading "Pets Heal Broken Hearts."

The story was about a biologist, Erika Friedman, who

had studied ninety-two heart patients for a year after they left the hospital. She wanted to see whether there were any special social reasons why some of them did better than others.

It turned out that there was something called a Pet Factor Only three of the fifty-seven patients with pets died during that year, compared to eleven of the thirty-nine without pets.

I am, by habit, wildly skeptical about the sort of studies that end up in pop form. Their authors are usually found a few months later jogging through *People* magazine in expensive terrycloth shorts, followed by their children and their paperback rights. So I have no idea whether the American Heart Association should start filling out prescription pads for budgies and beagles.

Nevertheless, the study piqued the curiosity I've had about people and pets since I bought my first turtle at my first circus. It has often occurred to me that pet owning is not a two-way relationship, but is, rather, two one-way relationships.

I currently live under the same roof with two large, black dogs that eat mail in lieu of the mailman. In my life as a dog owner, I have grown to realize that people and pets do not really have very much in common except each other. I have to give credit for this thought to William James, who once said: "Take our dogs and ourselves, connected as we are by a tie more intimate than most and yet...how insensible each of us is to all that makes life significant for the other—we to the rapture of bones under hedges, or smell of trees and lamp posts, they to the delights of literature and art."

The truth is that we have hung out together for lo these million years out of convenient mutual needs. The need of a pet for a person is as clear-cut as a bowl of food. The only true love song uttered by a dog in the entire history of Anthropomorphism is the one Snoopy howls called "Suppertime." The chorus goes like this: "Suppertime, suppertime, suppertime...."

The average dog or cat will do almost anything to reinforce human supper-giving behavior. Ogden Nash once glowingly wrote:

> "I marvel that such
> Small Ribs as These
> Harbor such a
> Desire to Please."

But to the less romantic among us, this behavior is a matter of thousands of years of natural selection. The dogs that did not "desire to please" ended up in dog pounds that stretched from the Fertile Crescent to the Golden Gate.

But the need of a person for a pet is something entirely different. Except for Doberman pinschers, the average urban-suburban pet owner is looking for a living thing that (1) needs him and (2) can't talk back.

In short, we seek an uncritical constant companion that can never spill the beans. Millions of dog owners commit themselves to a lifetime of walking in the rain simply because the animal on the other end of the leash will never sue it for malparenting. Thousands prowl the streets of Manhattan with scoopers and paper bags in order to have something wagging its tail when they get home. Millions more become devoted to kitty litter so that they can lecture something which will only come back with a purr, and never say, "You're neurotic."

I'm not talking about the crazies, the 141-cat-ladies, and people who build monuments to their Welsh terriers and leave trust funds to their Siamese. They always knew that one dog was worth ten doctors.

We are in this case talking about your better-basic-hamster owner, the full professor who talks baby-talk to his schnauzer and the bureaucrat who worries if he has to leave his bunny at a strange kennel.

This study suggests, just suggests mind you, what we may need for our health. "Taking care" may be as important as taking digitalis. A loyal and friendly companion may be a perfect pacemaker. We all seem to need to be needed, and we thrive on a dose of uncritical companionship. If we can't get it on two legs, we'll take it on four. We'll even take in on the wing.

APRIL 1979

Watching Seals Watching Us

Casco Bay, Maine—At first it is impossible to find them. The seals pile onto the ledges at low tide as if they were part of the rocks. You have to know that they are there, always there, before you can separate them into categories: animal and mineral.

Today, they are lying in a heap of 20 to 30, belly up to the sun, portraits of contentment. From time to time, in the heat that has warmed even this Maine bay, one flips over like a baby, and slips casually into the ocean. Another bellies up the rocks again and settles into a new place.

It is enormously peaceful at our seal-watching post. The cormorants that took off from the water, flapping madly as we came near their home, return. The seals, accustomed to the lobstermen who work their territory, are equally tolerant to us. We, in turn, respect their own sense of distance.

From time to time, their curiosity competes with their wariness and they surround the boat, watching us watching them.

It has been months now since I last seal-watched here.

Yet, they are doing precisely what they did last year, and what they will do next year.

Today I find that reassuring. I have come here directly from Detroit [the Republican Convention], from one world and sense of reality to another. From one culture to another. From the urgency and frenzy of important people doing important things to the timelessness of the bay.

In the week that passed, people made "news." Things changed. A new group came to power. A man was nominated to be president. Another nominated to be vice-president.

At the same time, every day on these ledges, the seals turned their bellies to the sun at low tide, and slid into the water.

Which was real, realer, realest?

Sitting in the boat, drifting too near the ledges, I wonder again whether this place is an escape from reality or an escape into it. Which is the constant? The things that change or those that do not? The world people "make" or the world they live in?

I know the placidity of life at this ledge can be an illusion. It is always easier to have a long perspective on other peoples, other species, other times. In the past year I am sure that much has happened to my small colony of seals: births, deaths, migrations, seasons.

Yet I am much more impressed by their sameness—the same heaps, the same curiosity, the same life cycle. It reminds me of our own, human sameness. That seems to me, realer, surely realer than the drama of the "powerful" and the power of change.

In Detroit, in our public life and public places, we see and hear people who are more impressed by altering the world than by finding a way to live within it. The powerful are, almost by definition, change agents. They assume that we can—should—take hold of events and move them. They are the directors, the shapers.

Even the politicians who last week talked of "the eternal verities" and "fundamentals" and "everlasting" do not think of themselves as passengers in a larger life but as conductors. It comes with the territory of politics.

The others, people who believe that change is a kind of human vanity, are rarely seen on platforms. Those who believe that the current is more powerful and important than our efforts to fight it, or turn it, do not run for office.

I suppose they stop striving, and choose to do no harm. They watch the seals and go with the flow. They turn to simplicity or irony or poetry, not politics. They drop out, or drop back, and leave the world to the makers, the shapers.

Most of us get caught in our own dailiness, importance and change. We do what people have always done: maintain the sense—the illusion?—that we control our lives.

But in this Maine bay, as we find ourselves beached unceremoniously on the ledges, a colony of seals is my reminder of the other reality. I watch the seals watching us as we struggle to push off the rocks. We are too impatient to wait for the tide.

JULY 1980

Passive Smoking

I am, according to the New England Journal of Medicine, a passive smoker. I did not mean to be one. My parents did not raise me to be one. But there you are. *The New England Journal of Medicine* says I am one, and it ought to know.

What I meant to be was a plain old nonsmoker. It fits my self-image better. It fits my habits better.

I am, you see, one of the lucky people who choked on the first green-tipped, personally labeled, sweet-sixteen cigarette that ever touched my lips in 1957. I count this as a piece of biological luck, not unlike my inability to get drunk.

Years ago, I discovered that I fell asleep before I ever found the right lamp shade for my head. So, I end up dozing instead of drunk, the way I end up coughing instead of cancerous.

It is not my virtue but my body chemistry which keeps me from falling down the path of assorted evils. If my jaw would only lock at the sight of assorted chocolates, I would be perfect.

But this morning I am in no position to gloat.

Two men from the University of California, San Diego, studied men and women at work. Some of the 2,000 worked in smoky places and some in smoke-free places. Now, the researchers have published the first study that proves what we knew all along, deep down in our lungs: Nonsmokers are getting zonked by the smokers at work.

Professor James White and Dr. Herman Froeb put it more carefully in their paper. The way they figured it, nonsmokers have about the same amount of small airways impairment as people who smoke up to about eleven cigarettes a day. Sounding like the Surgeon General's warning, they wrote that "chronic exposure to tobacco smoke in the work environment is deleterious to the nonsmoker."

Informally, Professor White said simply, "We know that if a person works around another smoker for a period of time, he will experience lung damage. Now whether it will impair him or cause emphysema, we don't know. But who wants it?"

Not I, said the little red hen. But, at this very moment, I am sitting here at my desk passively smoking.

The man behind me, who is otherwise a charming neighbor, smokes cigars. They are not really offensive, he has explained to me patiently and in some detail, because they are *good* cigars. It's the cheap cigars that smell, he says, pointing one stinking stogie at another. I fail to make this class distinction.

Three yards away, the environmental reporter sits attached to his pipe. The smoke that surrounds it would make the EPA inspector condemn a plant. "It is," he admits, puffing thoughtfully, "a contradiction."

All around me are cigarettes whose smoke is mysteriously attracted to my magnetic personality. I am convinced that whenever I change desks in this city room, the air currents in my office shift and I am once again drifting in the Smoke Stream.

My situation isn't the worst by far. I have a friend who goes home every night and washes that Marlboro man right out of her hair. I have another who actually goes into the garage for a breath of fresh air.

I sympathize with smokers, although I no longer buy them ashtrays. (I have a friend who uses my daughter's dollhouse bathtub for his butts, but I promised not to tell a soul.) I imagine that stopping smoking is like stopping eating.

So, I don't want to ban smoke just because I don't want to work with banned smokers. But I don't want to inhale the stuff, either.

What I would like is to find the national scene more in line with the Minnesota Clean Air Act. What I would like is to extend the airline policy to the ground, wherever possible, and divide the work place into zones.

As *The New England Journal of Medicine* editorialized: ". . . the feelings and psychological reactions of smokers are as vehement as those of nonsmokers. But now, for the first time, we have a quantitative measurement of a physical change—a fact that may tip the scales in favor of nonsmokers."

Well, it's tipped my scale. This morning, at least, one more passive smoker is feeling aggressive.

Dogs Bite, Therefore They Are

On Friday, a dog bit a man.

This is an event so commonplace that it is the very symbol of a non-news story: Dog Bites Man.

We all know that dogs bite. They bite mail carriers, package deliverers, gas meter readers and even, from time to time, an electrician or two. It's one of the things they do, like digging for bones or licking.

They bite, therefore they are. Dogs.

Why was this event different from all other such events? Why was this so startling? Because it was our dog who bit a man.

Did I take it in stride? Of course. I reacted as calmly as if the police had called to tell me they'd picked up my daughter coming out of a bank with a machine gun.

Like a person who discovers that the downstairs neighbor is a mass murderer, I gasped: "Him? But he was such a quiet boy."

In short, I behaved with the same level of surprise shared by a million other pet owners every year when, in fact, their dog bites man.

Despite the absolute banality of it, there is barely a dog owner alive who isn't (1) shocked (2) defensive (3) protective when the faint odor of people is found on his or her dog's breath. Dogs, you see, belong to that peculiar category of modern beasts known as "pets." Their primary function, their reason-for-being, is to give and return affection.

Being fairly docile creatures, dogs learn quickly the same kind of behavior that fills the bill, or rather, the bowl. They do not bite the hand that feeds them.

So, over time, they train us to utter such absolutely inane things as "You know, sometimes I think he's human."

I have personally been heard to say "excuse me" when I pass our dog in the hall. I have also been heard to say at least two of the following statements:

"Don't worry, he's just being friendly."

"If a thief came in, he'd probably want to play ball."

"He'd never bite anyone!"

The false image I lived with until lo this very Friday was imprinted in my brain in the darkness of the Saturday afternoon movies. In the Hollywood of my youth, all dogs were divided into two categories. There were (1) bad dogs who bit good guys and (2) good dogs who bit bad guys.

There were Doberman pinschers genetically programmed to salivate whenever a human appeared. I suspect to this day that they regard the human arm as just another salami.

There were more discriminating German shepherds in war movies. They bared their teeth and strained on their chains to "The Sound of Music." There were Lassie and assorted Disney dogs that only chomped down on certified kidnappers.

The dogs that we choose to live with—unless we own a gas station—clearly belong to the Disney world.

Our dog, for example (the one with a piece of blue jean between his teeth) is "good with children."

Our dog (the one which cost me $82 worth of doctor's bills) has his hair clipped at $20 a shot four times a year.

Our dog (the one currently nicknamed Munch) has a pedigree so long that he can be considered slumming in our middle-class suburb.

Need I tell you that this incident, this sudden revelation that the dog who eats mail might also eat a mailman, dealt a blow to our pride and our favorite myths?

We ask ourselves: Where did we go wrong? Was he making some desperate plea for attention? Was there some social message that he was communicating with his teeth?

But no. Finally, in the dark night of our soul-searching, we realized that we had forgotten only one thing: Dog Bites Man.

Now we have come to terms with reality, come to accept the fact that our Zachary is, after all, an animal.

It is only when I look deeply into his brown eyes that I find myself wondering: What did the electrician do to make my precious poochie so cross?

FEBRUARY 1981

Thanksgiving

S*oon they will be together again, all the people who travel* between their own lives and each other's. The package tour of the season will lure them this week to the family table.

By Thursday, feast day, family day, Thanksgiving day, Americans who value individualism like no other people will collect around a million tables in a ritual of belonging.

They will assemble their families the way they assemble dinner: each one bearing a personality as different as cranberry sauce and pumpkin pie. For one dinner they will cook for each other, fuss for each other, feed each other and argue with each other.

They will nod at their common heritage, the craziness and caring of other generations. They will measure their common legacy . . . the children.

All these complex cells, these men and women, old and young, with different dreams and disappointments will give homage again to the group they are a part of and apart from: their family.

Families and individuals. The "we" and the "I." As good Americans we all travel between these two ideals.

We take value trips from the great American notion of individualism to the great American vision of family. We wear out our tires driving back and forth, using speed to shorten the distance between these two principles.

There has always been some pavement between a person and a family. From the first moment we recognize that we are separate we begin to wrestle with aloneness and to-getherness.

Here and now these conflicts are especially acute. We are, after all, raised in families . . . to be individuals. This double message follows us through life.

We are taught about the freedom of the "I" and the safety of the "we." The loneliness of the "I" and the intrusiveness of the "we." The selfishness of the "I" and the burdens of the "we."

We are taught what André Malraux said: "Without a family, man, alone in the world, trembles with the cold."

And taught what he said another day: "The denial of the supreme importance of the mind's development accounts for many revolts against the family."

In theory, the world rewards "the supreme importance" of the individual, the ego. We think alone, inside our heads. We write music and literature with an enlarged sense of self. We are graded and paid, hired and fired, on our own merit.

The rank individualism is both exciting and cruel. Here is where the fittest survive.

The family, on the other hand, at its best, works very differently. We don't have to achieve to be accepted by our families. We just have to be. Our membership is not based on credentials but on birth.

As Malraux put it, "A friend loves you for your intelligence, a mistress for your charm, but your family's love is unreasoning: You were born into it and of its flesh and blood."

The family is formed not for the survival of the fittest but for the weakest. It is not an economic unit but an emotional one. This is not the place where people ruthlessly compete with each other but where they work for each other.

Its business is taking care, and when it works, it is not callous but kind.

There are fewer heroes, fewer stars in family life. While the world may glorify the self, the family asks us, at one time or another, to submerge it. While the world may abandon us, the family promises, at one time or another, to protect us.

So we commute daily, weekly, yearly between one world and another. Between a life as a family member that can be nurturing or smothering. Between life as an individual that can free us or flatten us. We vacillate between two separate sets of demands and possibilities.

The people who will gather around this table Thursday live in both of these worlds, a part of and apart from each other. With any luck the territory they travel from one to another can be a fertile one, rich with care and space. It can be a place where the "I" and the "we" interact.

On this day at least, they will bring to each other something both special and something to be shared: these separate selves.

NOVEMBER 1980

Age Forty
Inventory

Once, when I studied history for a nonliving, I became fascinated with emigrants. For a time I read everything I could find about the people who left for America, about their profound disruption, their strengths, their heroism.

Perhaps it was my prejudice as an American, but in those days I thought very little about the people who stayed behind.

But lately I've been wondering about the difference between those who emigrated and those who didn't. I wonder whether one person remained in Ireland or Italy or Russia because he was content or because he was resigned. I wonder whether another left because she was desperate or because she was hopeful. Was one person more adventurous or another more committed?

In the most desperate moments—the potato famines, the pogroms—which took the greater strength of character: endurance or uprooting? Who were the heroes and who were the martyrs? The emigrants or those who remained behind?

I am thinking about this, I'm sure, because many of my friends are turning forty. It began happening three years ago and will, at this rate, continue for at least another five.

Forty is, I observe from not too great a distance, an awkward age. It's an age at which people have histories and options. At thirty, they had perhaps less history. At fifty, perhaps fewer options.

But at forty, it hangs in the balance. The status quo is weighed against the possible. The person we thought we might be, still challenges the person we are. At forty, many reassess themselves and their circumstances. They try to come to terms with their limits or to break out of them.

I don't want to force the emigrant analogy. For many of our ancestors, the only option was survival and the only feeling was despair. But for a people who now contemplate leaving lives the way their forebears left homelands, the comparison is fair enough.

I think we have as much difficulty knowing what is right or wrong, what is brave or foolish, destructive or adventurous, resigned or realistic when we look at our modern lives.

I know, for example, a writer who turned forty and decided that he was, after all, only a minor talent. He would never be Will Shakespeare, he said, and settled down to a job writing advertising copy. Was he a quitter or a realist? Did he sell himself short or did he find his place?

I know a woman who turned forty and decided after years of marital indecision and separation that this was her husband, her life—this was "it." It was, she said, okay. Did she settle for less or did she settle down?

On the other hand, there is the forty-year-old man who decided that his history was rot and, to change his future, he left much of his past. How does one judge his action? By just how intolerable his circumstances were? By what his future brings? Did it take more guts to leave than to stay?

My mind curves around all these things like a question mark. It is hard to hold still long enough to make sense of them. I wonder again if we can only judge actions by motivations. Is the person who endures masochistic or virtuous? Is the person who takes off sane or irresponsible?

Introspection is as painful as it is inevitable. At some time in our lives, especially our mid-lives, we take stock like a department store. We face ourselves and our circumstances. We try to be reasonable about our lives, compare what we have (and could lose) with what we might have. We talk about the necessity of compromising and the fear of compromising ourselves. Our satisfactions battle our fantasies.

We try to make rational judgments, I suppose, about protecting the status quo or changing it. But in the end, some of us emigrate to our new worlds and some of us stay with the familiar. And the future historians will have trouble understanding the differences.

AUGUST 1979

PART 6

The Hard Questions

Her Preference Is Merit

On Wednesday, the very last of the weighty legal briefs was hand-delivered to the Supreme Court. Soon the justices will be hearing the saga of yet another citizen determined to fight a powerful affirmative action plan.

But the star of this largely unheralded case isn't an Allen Bakke or a Brian Weber. No, the leading figure is a fifty-four-year-old woman named Helen Feeney. And the "affirmative action" program she is challenging is veterans' preference.

For several years, Helen Feeney, a widow and mother of four from Dracut, Massachusetts, took one state civil service exam after another in search of jobs.

In 1971 she came in second on one exam, and in 1973 she came in third on another. Both scores put her within shooting distance of the job. But both times she was unceremoniously bumped to the back of the line.

In Massachusetts, you see, any veteran who scores even a passing 66 is automatically ranked above any nonveteran, even one with a 99. More than a dozen veterans with lower scores were ranked above her, and she never got the jobs.

Helen Feeney had been a victim of military discrimination once before. As a girl she'd tried to enlist in World War II. But in those days, and female (not any male) under

193

twenty-one needed permission from her parents. Hers said no.

But this time the lady has decided to fight. She maintains that veterans' preference is unconstitutional because it keeps women out of virtually every position except the most traditional "women's jobs." As her lawyer, Rick Ward, puts it: "It guarantees the perpetuation of centuries of discrimination against women."

It's difficult to find anyone, even the opposing attorneys, to deny that this law keeps men at the upper end of the state bureaucracy, here or elsewhere. Since 98 percent of all veterans are male, the preference is theirs.

But the constitutional issues in this case will revolve around two different questions: (1) Was the effect of this law "intentional" or "incidental" on the part of the legislators who wrote it? (2) Does it cross the line between legal "preference" and illegal "discrimination"?

Last year, the Carter administration tried to reform a milder federal law, which adds five points to the scores of able-bodied veterans and ten to disabled. Even this has meant that two-thirds of all middle-level federal jobs are filled by older and non-Vietnam veterans who use their point preference over and over again whenever they go job-shopping.

Carter wanted able-bodied veterans to use the preference only once, within fifteen years of service. But under pressure from veterans, the Congress voted down his reform.

Now Massachusetts is arguing that the legislators who passed a much more extreme law did not intend to discriminate, but were just trying to reward those in military service and help veterans get back into civilian life.

I think, however, the circuit court was right when it said: "It's clear that the commonwealth's motive was to benefit its veterans. Equally clear, however, is that its intent was to achieve that purpose by subordinating employment opportunities of its women."

Any government has a right, maybe even an obligation, to offer remedial help, affirmative action, to those groups at a disadvantage in the job market for special reasons. A veteran who left his job to go to war deserves that help. So, for that matter, may a displaced homemaker who left her job to raise children. So, too, may someone who has suffered from racial prejudice.

But there is a big difference between giving a healthy veteran a helping hand and giving him a chit for life—at the expense of the young, minorities, women and merit.

This particular chit is allotted not only to those who suffered through combat but those who enlisted and enjoyed some of the benefits of military life while serving their country safely behind a desk.

Last year, in the Bakke decision, Justice Powell wrote that a law can give preference to one group, up to a point. At some point, when you have virtually weeded out the other groups, he said, you have exceeded the constitutional grounds.

It seems to me that Massachusetts is guilty of excessive weeding. It's not only unconstitutional, it's unconscionable.

JANUARY 1979

The Emotional
Triangle of Adoption

Not long ago, the adoption of a child was handled like a top-secret real-estate deal. The birth parent signed away the deed to her property, relinquishing her rights forever, and the adoptive parents became the exclusive new owners.

The adoption agency acted as a kind of real-estate broker in this business. In the course of their negotiations, the birth mother was promised anonymity and the adoptive parents were promised a clear title. They were now, and forever more, The Only Parents.

The role of the agency after the deal was closed was simply this: to keep the birth parent free from exposure, and the adoptive parent free from intrusion. And the child was freed from what they felt would be the pain and confusion of having "two mothers" or "two fathers."

The theory was that then everyone could forget the past.

But secrecy never kept anyone from wondering. Over the last few years, as illegitimate birth has become less shameful and roots more meaningful, birth mothers and adoptees have wondered out loud about each other.

Some have gone further. Adoptees like Betty Jane Lipton have written publicly of their search for birth parents. Many birth mothers have formed support groups where they can remember and recover together. And today there are several organizations, like Orphan Voyage or the Adoptees Liberty

Movement of America, which will assist adults in finding birth parents.

So increasingly, adoption agencies find themselves handling requests, pleas and court orders to open up the old sealed records. The changes in attitudes and actions are coming so fast that it may not be possible any longer to respect the old property lines and Do Not Trespass signs.

In Washington, for example, a twenty-two-year-old mother of two, Carolyn Brinker, won the right to see her sealed birth records. Under the terms of the decision, the D.C. Department of Human Resources first will try to find her parents themselves. If the parents are unwilling to meet with Brinker, she will still see the information about her medical background. But if the department can't locate her birth parents within sixty days, she'll be given their names and last known address.

The careful decision is one of the few in which the old "property" has become a principle, and in which the adoptee's "need to know" has been considered paramount.

The cases are delicate ones. In each, we have to balance the right of the adoptee to know his or her own past—especially the medical or genetic history—with the right of the birth parent to privacy, if he or she wishes it. We have to balance the new ideas about the value of "openness" for the adoptee's emotional security, with the old promises of secrecy for the adoptive parents' emotional security. But careful, partial changes like these are under way.

I suspect that it won't be very long now before genetic information is routinely given to adult adoptees. It may not be much longer before birth parents and adult adoptees who want contact with each other can be routinely matched. Nor will it be long before many of the best and worst fantasies of thousands are fulfilled.

We assume that there will be some good effects from all this, if only eliminating the terror of the unknown. But there may also be some difficult implications for the future.

We don't know what the effect will be on adoption itself. This is an era when most unwed pregnant women have abortions or raise their own babies. How many fewer (or perhaps more) pregnant women will consider adoption without the promise of anonymity?

And what will be the effect on adoptive parents? Will the real threat of a "shadow parent" affect their own relationships with their children? How greatly increased will be their fear of loss? As one woman said, "What does this make me, a babysitter?"

The changes demand at least a basic reinterpretation of adoption itself. The dictionary defines the word "adopt" this way: "to take as one's own child." But it isn't that clear any more.

The law reflects a deeper reality, that adoption today is not always the final transfer of a piece of property, but may be the beginning of a lifelong emotional triangle.

FEBRUARY 1979

Who Lives? Who Dies? Who Decides?

Some have called it a Right to Die case. Others have labeled it a Right to Live case. One group of advocates has called for "death with dignity." Others have responded accusingly, "euthanasia."

At the center of the latest controversy about life and death, medicine and law, is a seventy-eight-year-old Massachusetts man whose existence hangs on a court order.

On one point, everyone agrees: Earle Spring is not the man he used to be. Once a strapping outdoorsman, he is now strapped to a wheelchair. Once a man with a keen mind, he is now called senile by many, and mentally incompetent by the courts. He is, at worst, a member of the living dead; at best, a shriveled version of his former self.

For more than two years, since his physical and then mental health began to deteriorate, Earle Spring has been kept alive by spending five hours on a kidney dialysis machine three times a week. Since January of 1979, his family has pleaded to have him removed from the life support system.

They believe deeply that the Earle Spring who was, would not want to live as the Earle Spring who is. They believe they are advocates for his right to die in peace.

In the beginning, the courts agreed. Possibly for the first time, they ruled last month in favor of withdrawing medical care from an elderly patient whose mind had deteriorated. The dialysis was stopped.

But then, in a sudden intervention, an outside nurse and doctor visited Earle Spring and testified that he was alert enough to "make a weak expression of his desire to live." And so the treatments resumed.

Now, while the courts are waiting for new and more thorough evidence about Spring's mental state, the controversy rages about legal procedures: No judge ever visited Spring, no psychiatrist ever testified. And even more importantly, we are again forced to determine one person's right to die or to live.

This case makes the Karen Ann Quinlan story seem simple in comparison. Quinlan today hangs onto her "life" long after her "plug was pulled." But when the New Jersey court heard that case, Quinlan had no will. She had suffered brain death by any definition.

The Spring story is different. He is neither competent nor comatose. He lives in a gray area of consciousness. So the questions also range over the gray area of our consciences.

What should the relationship be between mental health and physical treatment? Should we treat the incompetent as aggressively as the competent? Should we order heart surgery for one senile citizen; should we take another off a kidney machine? What is the mental line between a life worth saving and the living dead? Who is to decide?

Until recently, we didn't have the technology to keep an Earle Spring alive. Until recently the life-and-death decisions about the senile elderly or the retarded or the institutionalized were made privately between families and medical people. Now, increasingly, in states like Massachusetts, they are made publicly and legally.

Clearly there are no absolutes in this case. No right to die. No right to live. We have to take into account many social as well as medical factors. How much of the resources of a society or a family should be allotted to a member who no longer recognizes it? How many sacrifices should the healthy and vital make for the terminally or permanently ill and disabled?

In England, where the kidney dialysis machines are scarce, Earle Spring would never have remained on one. In America, one Earle Spring can decimate the energy and income of an entire family.

But the Spring case is a crucial, scary one that could affect all those living under that dubious sentence "incompetent," or that shaky diagnosis, "senile." So, it seems to me that if there is one moment a week when the fog lifts, and when this man wants to live, if there is any mental activity at all, then disconnecting him from life would be a dangerous precedent, far more dangerous than letting him continue.

The court ruled originally in favor of taking Spring off the machine. It ruled that this is what Earle Spring would have wanted. I have no doubt that his family believes it. I have no doubt of their affection or their pain.

But I remember, too, what my grandfather used to say: No one wants to live to be 100 until you ask the man who is 99. Well, no one, including Earle Spring, wants to live

to be senile. But, once senile, he may well want to live.
We simply have to give him the benefit of the doubt. Any
doubt.

FEBRUARY 1980

Sex Education: In Search of a Partnership

Suppose the question showed up on some national true or false quiz. "Is sex education primarily the responsibility of parents?"

The answer would, I'm sure, be a resounding "Yes."

So Richard Schweiker wasn't taking a great risk in his opening salvo against federal funding for sex education. He said simply, "I don't think it's the feds' role to do it." It is rather, he said, the business of parents.

But there was also something false here in this reasoning. Something false in the underlying notion that parents have ernment with its hosts of professionals took away our job.

In this area, as in so many others, our behavior as parents hasn't met our own expectations. It has never been easy to talk about sex with children. Anxieties and taboos have silenced centuries of parents; ours is not unique. The experts didn't usurp our role. We gave it up.

Parents and teenagers have long been involved in a mutual "strategy of concealment" about our sexual lives. As recently as 1969, only 13 percent of the teenagers who came to birth control clinics had mothers who acknowledged their sexual activity.

Even now we are unlikely to actually *be* the sex educators of our children. In one study 85 to 95 percent of parents of children under eleven have never mentioned *any* aspect of erotic behavior. In another, only a third of mothers and teenager daughters discuss sex or birth control with any regularity.

The people most irate about the "other people" giving sexual values to their children are often the ones least able to talk themselves.

Educators and family planners come in to fill a gap that we left open because of our awkwardness or ignorance. They usually did it with our blessing. In every survey parents have overwhelmingly supported sex education in the schools.

Now all our qualms are coming to the surface. They are often and understandably aimed at the professionals who dealt privately with our children and even identified us, their parents, as the enemy.

As Faye Wattleton, the head of Planned Parenthood, now admits, "In the early sixties and seventies, parents became symbolic of the establishment and all that was repressive. We saw our role as being advocates of young people."

The family-planning clinics often dealt with our children as their patients, dispensing contraceptives. The sex educators often dealt with our children as their students, teaching the "value-free" facts. We often felt excluded.

But parents are changing and so are the professionals. We have all become much more aware of the problems of premature sex—emotional and medical—from the anxieties about intimacy to the trauma of pregnancy. We have all become more sensitive to their real needs for guidance and values.

The professionals who worked to make abortion available to teenagers have become more concerned with making it unnecessary. The educators who worked to answer student questions about sex, now try to answer the most common question: "How do we say no?"

It is becoming more obvious to all of us that young teenagers are still very much a part of family life and parents still have an enormous influence. The latest research suggests that when mothers do talk to their teenage daughters about sex (there is almost no one talking to our sons) the daughters may not only postpone sex but are more likely to use birth control when they have it.

There is also solid evidence that parents are dealing more overtly with teenage sexual activity. Today, more than half of the teenage girls who come to birth control clinics do so with a parent's knowledge.

For all of these reasons, new programs are being developed to help parents deal with these issues. Clinics are learning to deal with teenagers as part of a family system. Religious groups as diverse as Mormons and Catholics, educators as far apart as Massachusetts and California are beginning to encourage parents to come to terms with their own values and to communicate these to their children.

Professionals have learned, as Ruth McDonald of the Educational Development Corporation says, "There is just no way to deal with teenagers without dealing with their parents."

We are at a turning point then, a moment when federal money can be used to support, not undermine, family life. Silent parents and wary professionals are disengaging from some covert competition over teenage sexual lives. It is just possible that we can all become partners in caring.

FEBRUARY 1981

Children Up for Grabs

*Last week Jacqueline Jarrett lost her children. The Supreme Court decided, 6–3, not to review her case. So she has lost custody of her three daughters because she is living with a man she isn't married to.

It didn't matter to the Illinois court that Jacqueline Jarrett had been the primary parent for all the years of marriage or divorce. It didn't matter that everyone, even her ex-husband, described her as an attentive and loving mother. It didn't matter that the three children were comfortable and happy in this new "family."

No, the Illinois court agreed with the father that she had created an immoral atmosphere for the three daughters by living "in sin." And so they ordered the children to move eight blocks and one life-style from mother to father.

But the story doesn't end here. The Jarrett case is a modern tale of conflicting values and conflicting parents. And there are plenty of both going around these days.

There are a million divorces a year in this country now. Another 1.1 million people are living together unmarried and one-quarter of them living with children. The Jarretts are just another accident case at the intersection of these changes.

It is easy to understand the feelings of both parents. The father's rage when his children were living under a different moral structure. The mother's anguish when she was punished by the court, though in her own mind she had behaved responsibly and lovingly toward her children.

These were two parents who differed wildly, irreconcilably, in their moral views. These differences were, I'm sure, a cause as well as an effect of their divorce. They often are.

But when the court was asked to intervene, it sided with the father—and with a vengeance. Never mind any other standard of caring. For the "crime" of fornication—a crime to this day in about nineteen states—a mother was punished by losing custody.

In my view, the Illinois court made the wrong decision. The court record reeked of moralistic judgments, sprinkled with words like "fornication" and "flaunting."

But, as the Supreme Court decision notes, the state court had the right to make that decision. And that is, in some ways, the real story.

More and more often, the legal system is being called on to judge mother against father, life-style against life-style. The cases are all around us, fair and unfair decisions, innovative and conservative, pro-father and pro-mother.

In other Illinois cases, judges have ruled that living together is irrelevant unless the lawyer can prove that it has harmed the children. In Massachusetts, a lesbian mother is no longer "unfit" by definition.

At the same time, in a Chicago courtroom this week, thirty-six-year-old Mildred Milovich—a Brownie leader, a Sunday school teacher, a self-described "Supermom" who worked as a sales representative—lost custody of her children to their father because of her job.

The beat goes on. In one courtroom, a father who left his wife sues for custody of his children because he has remarried and can offer them a "better life-style" than she can on her clerical pay. In another case, a father wins custody because, the court says, boys are better off being raised by a man. Later, that verdict is reversed.

These are not ordinary decisions. There are fewer "ordinary decisions" these days. The standard for custody is now almost always "the best interest of the child."

This is a most elusive standard, made by judges full of good will and prejudice, caring and preconceptions. With the best of intentions, it can also end in the worst of injustices.

In most courts, mothers are still given the edge. But more and more often, custody is up for grabs. The judgments and the judges can be arbitrary. How do you judge which is better or worse for a child: An authoritarian, punitive father or a mother who chooses living together over marriage? A working mother or a working father?

The courts are left to weigh people and life-styles, economics and psyches, according to the loose legal guidelines and their own values. Parents who can't settle, or share, are left to judge-shop, court-hop, and hope.

And the Jarrett case is just the beginning.

OCTOBER 1980

The Kramers: Good Drama, Bad Law

*N*ormally *I am a person who is willing, even eager, to* suspend all rational judgment at a sad movie. I cry, therefore, I enjoy.

Kramer vs. Kramer was this sort of movie, a three-hankie

flick, if I ever saw one. So, I indulged in it like a chocoholic at the Godiva counter.

However, in the cold light of the morning after the binge, the plot weighs a bit more heavily on my mind, if not on my hips. It occurs to me that the scales of Justice were tipped by the heavy hand of Hollywood.

The movie, for those of you who have been busy Star-Trekking, is about the transformation of a fair-weather father into a full-time father. Mommy takes off for California and daddy takes over. Eventually mommy returns, and the stage is set for the ultimate custody battle.

By the time Kramer and Kramer hit the courtroom, we are all on the side of the father. But, in a tribute to the acting powers of both Dustin Hoffman and Meryl Streep, by the end of the pivotal trial scene, both came across as perfectly decent, nonvillainous, equally loving parents genuinely concerned for their child.

Which is more than you can say for the legal system.

Kramer vs. Kramer makes good drama out of lousy law. The judge awards the boy to the mother, because she is a "Mother"—and he does so without even chatting in chambers with this delightfully articulate seven-year-old boy.

Now, I grant you that there are, Lord knows, any number of arbitrary judges. But in 1980, in a major metropolitan area, the court is less likely to give instant primacy to Motherhood (especially deserting Motherhood) and extremely unlikely to make any custody decision without some evaluation of the kid. In real life, the Kramer boy would probably have had his own court-appointed attorney, or psychiatrist.

It also struck me, during my morning-after hangover, that in the real world of divorce Mr. and Mrs. Kramer would have been more likely to share than to fight these days. They were perfect candidates for joint custody.

The fact is that while millions of Americans sat in dark movie theaters across this land, sniffling over Kramer's farewell pep talk to his boy, we are seeing a strong trend toward shared divorced parenting.

"Joint custody is not exactly sweeping the country, but the concept and actual practice is spreading," says Dr. Doris Jonas Freed, chair of the committees on child custody and on research of the family law section of the American Bar Association.

On Jan. 1, for example, a brand-new law went into effect in California which makes joint custody the first choice of the state courts. The California law was passed to assure that kids have the maximum contact with both parents and to encourage parents to share the rights and responsibilities of child rearing.

Sole custody remains an option, as it should, but if a court in California does *not* grant joint custody, it has to have a reason.

This isn't just a piece of California-ism. Five other states provide for joint custody, and courts across the country are accepting it or even ruling on it. In New York recently, in *Adler* vs. *Adler*, each parent asked for sole custody of an eleven-year-old, but the court ruled on joint custody.

This doesn't mean splitting weeks or years down the middle, shuffling children back and forth from one school or town to another. It doesn't necessarily mean a fifty-fifty deal. It establishes a legal principle of the sharing of decision making and of physical time, according to any sensible plan the parents can devise.

It seems that if two parents can fashion an agreement together (and it does require cooperation) they are more likely to avoid the pitfalls of divorce—from child snatching to defaulting payments to disappearing acts.

Even the father's rights advocates have turned their interest from sole male custody to shared. As Dr. Freed said, "It's more important for children to have access to both parents, the love and affection of both. You know the old cliche; 'You won't divorce your children'? This will make it a reality." Neither parent need "lose" his or her child.

I grant you that a scene of the Kramers sitting down and bargaining would have meant fewer handkerchiefs. But what's bad for the movies may well prove better for many of the million kids who go through divorce each year. After all, a tearjerker isn't much fun in real life.

JANUARY 1980

The Baby Louise Clinic

It's been a year and a half since Baby Louise, the first child ever conceived in a dish, was born. Since then, at least two more babies have come into the world with the aid of this technique. One of them was born in Calcutta, where the streets teem with Sister Teresa's unwanted refuse.

Today these three sets of parents are, I am sure, more worried about their children's development than their origins. To them, at least, the procedure has seemed an unmitigated good.

Now, in Virginia, a private clinic has been okayed by the state. In about two months, if the opposition is unsuccessful, the clinic will begin fertilizing eggs, implanting embryos, creating new life in America.

And so the controversy is open again begween the claims of the would-be parents and the qualms of society.

To some, this procedure is nothing more than a "bridge"

to take the sperm and egg across a gap of broken fallopian tubes. To others, it is a social tunnel into the unknown.

To some, it is just a small medical step, another helping tool which we will soon accept the way we now accept the once-diabolical diaphragm. To others, it is a step down the long road to a Brave New World in which Aldous Huxley foresaw a human hatchery and fertilizing center in the middle of London.

A fear of many protesting the opening of this clinic is that doctors there will fertilize myriad eggs and discard the "extras" and the abnormal, as if they were no more meaningful than a dish of caviar. But this fear seems largely unwarranted.

The clinic procedure is likely to mirror that of nature. The clinic will in all probability harvest one egg at a time and fertilize one at a time, the way people do. In our lives, of every 1,000 fertilizations that occur, only 400 will develop to term. Of the 600 lost, 450 have a chromosomal abnormality. Of those born, only 5 to 7 per thousand are abnormal. The statistics of the scientists in terms of discards and abnormality may be no more harsh than those of nature.

But whether this is acceptable or not depends on whether we consider each two-cell embryo a human being and how seriously we regard the desires of the would-be parents.

Our attitudes also depend on which we see as more humane: helping the infertile couple, or keeping the human body as the sole vessel of creation.

Leroy Walters, the director of the Center for Bioethics at the Kennedy Institute of Ethics at Georgetown University and a member of the HEW advisory committee that has put together an 860-page report on "in vitro" fertilization, sees it as "an entirely pro-life activity":

"I take the desire of couples who wish to have children very seriously. Should they be legally prohibited from seeking help? My answer to that would be a very decisive 'no' unless it can be proved that it would mean serious damage to the society in general or to the offspring."

He sees neither of these, saying, "In the spectrum of

risks that we as a human race face, the risks from some couples using in vitro fertilization are very low-level."

But two other members of the ethics committee, Leon Kass and Paul Ramsey, see it as "a giant step toward the full laboratory control of human reproduction."

As one committee member who did not want to be quoted by name put it, "What really concerns me is 'intervention,' our posture that we are in the world to master and control and manipulate. It seems to me that this is the posture of a community headed for a fall. I take this to be a very grave matter, far more grave than the providing of children to couples who want them."

Those who are for and those who are against in vitro fertilization agree with Dr. Walters' statement that, "I see it as another step in the control by human beings of reproduction." But they disagree about whether this is good or bad. Should we, they ask, respond like a consumer society to the demands of the buyer? If we don't stop here, where do we stop?

The questions are cosmic. But the issue in front of us at this moment is quite specific: one clinic.

As a person with qualms, it seems to me that fertilization and transplant is no more or less dehumanizing than artificial insemination, no greater or lesser a moral issue than the I.U.D., no more unsettling to some than it is hopeful to others.

I think we should neither fund such a clinic at this time, nor prohibit it. We should, rather, monitor it, debate it, control it. We have put researchers on notice that we no longer accept every breakthrough and every advance as an unqualified good.

Now we have to watch the development of this technology—willing to see it grow in the right direction and ready to say no.

Checks on
Parental Power

First, consider the stories.

An eleven-year-old retarded boy was brought to a mental hospital with a teddy bear under his arm. His parents were, they said, going on a two-week vacation. They never came back.

A twelve-year-old "tomboy" and truant was committed to a mental hospital by her mother after school authorities threatened the woman with prosecution.

A seven-year-old boy's mother died one year, and he was committed the next year by his father—two days before the man's remarriage. The diagnosis: a reaction of childhood.

Consider, too, the story of one child committed because he had "school phobia," another because she was "promiscuous," a third and fourth because they were "difficult" or even "incorrigible."

Then, when you've heard the stories, listen to Justice Warren Burger insist that the "natural bonds of affection lead parents to act in the best interests of their children."

Last Wednesday the Supreme Court assured all parents— the confused and the pathologically indifferent as well as the caring and concerned—an equal right to put their kids in mental hospitals. Last Wednesday they denied all children—the odd and the unwanted as well as the ill—an equal right to a hearing before being institutionalized.

And they did it on a wish and a myth: that parents—and those bureaucratic "parents," state agencies—know best. It took seven years and four separate Supreme Court hearings to achieve this disappointing decision.

Lawyers from Pennsylvania and Georgia, and children's advocates, argued that minors deserve the same treatment adults have: a simple hearing before incarceration. They argued that children facing a mental institution deserved the same treatment as children facing a penal institution: a hearing.

But the Justices, especially Burger and Potter Stewart, were convinced that these children didn't need any advocate other than their parents, or any check on parental power other than the institution's own medical team. In roughly thirty-eight states, they left the fate of children up to parents and hospitals.

"That some parents may at times be acting against the interest of their child creates a basis for caution, but it is hardly a reason to discard wholesale those pages of human experience that teach that parents generally do act in the child's best interest," wrote Burger.

The conflict was between the right of the parent to make decisions about bringing up their children, and the rights of children to their liberty, and to due process. Burger and Stewart, both ardent advocates of extreme parental supremacy, interpreted the Constitution to read, Families First.

I agree that most parents do want to act in the "child's best interest." But the law is not necessary to protect children from wise and sensitive parents. Nor is it made to "interfere" with families functioning smoothly on their own.

As David Ferleger, the Pennsylvania lawyer who argued this case, put it: "We all want to protect the integrity of a family where it exists. But when the family wants to incarcerate a member, it has already created a break. There is no longer a united family to protect."

At that point, the question is whether it's more important

to protect a possible, and devastating, infringement of the child's liberty, or to protect the right of a parent or state guardian to dispose of that child's fate.

A family in stress may not have the information and emotional stability to make a good judgment. A state agency may not care. Nor can we trust the hospital for an impartial judgment. If surgeons have a bias toward surgery, institutional psychiatrists often have a bias toward institutional psychiatry. Psychiatry is hardly an infallible science, as Burger knows, and there are many children in hospitals now who are simply not mentally ill.

The justices compared signing a child into a mental hospital with signing him into a general hospital to have his tonsils out. But a tonsillectomy takes hours, not years. And it does less harm.

Parents obviously have and must have a wide range of decisions over their children's lives. But they don't have absolute power and never have. They cannot refuse immunization for their kids or keep them uneducated. They cannot (at least yet) forcibly sterilize them, order them to become a transplant donor, commit incest or abuse them.

Nor should they have the right, without another impartial source, to deprive children of something equally as fundamental as their liberty, by putting them away in an institution. In this case (which bodes badly for other children's rights cases coming before the court), the majority of the justices have sided with a parental power that is virtually unchecked.

Chalk one up for the folks who dropped off the boy with the teddy bear.

JUNE 1979

Sparing the Rod Won't Spoil the Society

I have known dozens of people who use the Bible as if it were a Rorschach test rather than a religious text. They read more *into* the ink than they read *out* of it.

They form their opinions first and then search for the piece of scripture that will back them. They study the Book, in short, the way lawyers study the statutes—not to find out right and wrong, but to shore up their defense.

So it was hardly surprising to see the controversial Brother Roloff of Texas waving his Bible over his "students" in a "Sixty Minutes" CBS-TV rerun last Sunday saying, "Last September they were nothing but a generation of hoodlums. . . . Here's the secret to our success: 'He that spareth his rod, hateth his son, but he that loveth him, chastens him.' We give them spankings because we love them."

Robert Roloff was defending the policy of his Homes for Wayward Children in Texas. There, this fascinating character "disciplines" teenagers sent to this imprisoned environment by their despairing parents. His method is a graduated system of corporal punishment.

But what hooked me on this story wasn't the brotherly homes or the mail overwhelmingly in favor or Roloff's "methods." It was his headlong plunge into the issue of "licks," spanking, love and punishment, parents and children—an issue as loaded and divisive as any in our society.

Corporal punishment is to wounding as capital punishment is to murder. It is the official bureaucratic word for inflicting pain on those in our custody, especially children. It is a specter surrounded by confusion and guilt and tinged by the horror of child abuse, on the one hand, and the fear of "permissiveness" on the other.

The arguments about spanking seem to go on and on, wherever there are parents. One parent says out loud how much children need discipline, and another agrees vehemently. But the first is thinking of a stern lecture, and the second is thinking of a cat-o'-nine-tails. A third parent then speaks against hitting, and across the room, a fourth automatically labels her as a patsy. We live with a sense that parent-child relationships are power plays, that if we are not victor we are victim. We seem to believe that our only parenting tool is force.

In Sweden, it is now illegal for parents to strike their children. But in forty-eight of our states, we give unrelated teachers the right to hit our children without our permission. As American parents we are horrified by child abuse, but believe in corporal punishment the way we believe in vitamins—good for growth. The line between abuse and discipline is most often drawn by the hand of the punishing adult.

Of course, the Swedish law is absurdly unenforceable. It would be impossible and outrageously invasive for the state to try every parent for a spank, a slap, a verbal abuse. But the magistrate who wrote it was right: "Children just do not respond when they are hit or threatened. Their reaction is the opposite; they think in terms of revenge."

Spanking, for example, is nearly always inflicted by the powerful on the less powerful. Small children are the ones who get it the most. Parents and teachers stop hitting, not when the children are "cured" but when they are big enough to threaten the adults with retaliation, "revenge."

In the meantime, corporal punishment has not taught children discipline. It has taught them about the lack of self-discipline on the part of adults. Taught them that hurting is okay.

Surely every parent has felt a sense of frustration build into fury. It is understandable when our rage occasionally turns into force. But force is a last and desperate resort—an admission of our failure. When we rationalize violence as "justice," we appoint ourselves judge, jury and executioner of the attitude that two wrongs make a right.

The real disaster is a systematic equation of love and violence. Brother Roloff said that he spanked the children because he loved them. How many other parents have said that. The parent who was both loved and hit as a child himself may protectively assume some connection and believe that physical abuse is a part of love.

In fact, as children instinctively know, beating is the darkest side of our most intense feelings toward those we love.

To express violence coolly—as if it were right to trick children into distorting reality until they, too, make some sick connection between affection and pain—that is a form of inherited abuse that does leave the deepest sort of "lasting marks."

JUNE 1979

The Age of Consent

This isn't a subject I'm dying to leap into. Just whispering "teenage sex" is like yelling fire in a crowded theater. Perfectly sane people panic. Reason rushes out the exit doors and we are left stranded in the murkiest emotional alleyways.

But the events of the past weeks in New Jersey are too intriguing to ignore. So stay seated for a minute, and hang onto your fire extinguishers, while we replay the show.

Act One began several years ago when the New Jersey legislature began to consider a number of reforms for its penal code. Among the more archaic laws on the books was the one governing something called statutory rape.

The concept of "statutory" rape was based on the notion that there is an age below which no one can be said to have "consented" to sexual relations. Sex without consent is, by definition, rape. A child of eight, for example, obviously doesn't have the wherewithal to willingly engage in sex. An adult of eighteen, on the other hand, has the "will" to be willing.

The problem, however, has always been in defining the

time when millions of minors—all different—can be said to have that mysterious power called "consent."

So, the laws vary wildly from one state border to another. In California, the age is eighteen and in Alabama the age (of a female) is twelve. In New Jersey, the law was typically atypical. Sex with anyone under sixteen was a crime, a crime punishable by up to ten years in jail and/or a fine of $100,000

This led to an assortment of delightful situations worthy of dimestore magazines headlined *Jailbait!* More than one luckless soul of sixteen got entangled with what was essentially a Dirty Old Man Law, as the seducer of a fifteen-year-old partner.

Well, in Act Two, the State of New Jersey reduced the age of consent to thirteen years of age. The revised code was to go into effect in September. But when this small item leaked out, as one observer put it so eloquently, "The (blank) hit the fan."

Hold onto your fire extinguishers.

The notion was bandied about on assorted T-shirts and petitions that "consent" was the moral equivalent of approval. The distinction between the age at which a person could consent to sex, and the age at which that person should consent, was trampled by the crowd.

People seemed to believe that it was the Assembly which had reached the age of consent, and that it was all too willing to be a partner to the sexual activities of its young people.

Well, this is, after all, the home of "Scared Straight." So, with amazing speed, the New Jersey Assembly voted 71−2 to restore the age of consent to sixteen.

Now, may I pause for a brief intermission. Or should I say disclaimer. I do not, I assure you, approve of thirteen-year-olds having sexual intercourse. I was stunned at the figures which showed that one fifth of the eight million thirteen and fourteen year olds were sexually experienced and that eleven million teen-agers between fifteen and nineteen were sexually active.

But I am not willing to criminalize some teenagers under

the illusion that the law will have a chilling effect on this hot issue. Teenage Sex, as it is written large on our national marquee, is worthy of parental supervision, but not court action.

The supreme irony is that, for all the uproar, the New Jersey bill will have no effect on two kids of the same age, even thirteen, who have sex with each other. It will only affect the partner over sixteen having sex with the partner under sixteen. It is written so crudely that a kid sixteen years and one day old could be prosecuted for being with a kid fifteen years and 364 days old.

There are real issues in this crowded alleyway: the issue of serious child abuse, the issue of teenagers who are coerced into sex by their elders, the issue of children too young to have anything like "informed" consent.

The compromise bill suggested in the New Jersey Senate made far more sense than the one adopted. It was based not only on age but on age differential. It would have restored the age of consent to sixteen, *but* with an exception. Kids between thirteen and sixteen would not be liable for prosecution if the difference in age between the partners was three years or less.

That would have appeased our legitimate fears of coercion, and our fear that a young person could be prosecuted just for being a welcome partner.

It's too bad that in the stampede that followed these two little words—Teenage Sex—reason was trampled into the ground.

MAY 1979

Rape: A Crime of Violence, Not Sex

*O*nce upon a time there was a charming judge named Matthew Hale who made a certain reputation for himself in seventeenth-century England for the ardor with which he ordered the hanging of witches.

This fellow Hale was also one of the earliest recorded advocates of "spousal exclusion," the notion that husbands couldn't, by definition, "rape" their wives because, as he put it, "The wife hath given up herself in this kind unto the husband which she cannot retract."

Well, lest you burn Hale's effigy at the stake, remember that, in those days, husbands also were encouraged to "discipline" their wives. As Blackstone recorded in the eighteenth century, "The law thought it reasonable to entrust him with this power of restraining her by domestic chastisement..."

Historically, wives were regarded as property. Once a man bought his own acre, he was allowed, if you will forgive the analogy, to plow it, fence it in, and generally do with it what he would.

The primary function of the law was to protect the property owner from any interference or trespassing.

Well, after centuries of rule by this English common law, during which sex was coyly referred to as "exercising marital rights," there has finally been pressure for what might be called new zoning laws.

The law is now more concerned with protecting the individual from violence, even domestic violence—such as child abuse and wife battering. Moreover, in four states marriage is no longer a defense against the accusation of rape.

The rape laws were reformed in order to protect women from random sexual attacks by their estranged husbands and they have been used effectively this way.

But last week in Oregon, for the first time, a woman named Greta Rideout accused her husband, John, of rape while they were living together as husband and wife.

The jury of eight women and four men in Salem, Oregon, was faced with some extraordinary questions. They were asked to determine the essence of the Rideouts' private relationship—the marital context in which this act took place. They were asked to decide the difference between what the defense described as a neurotic relationship and what the prosecution described as criminal behavior.

They were not asked to determine, constitutionally, whether a husband should be immune from rape charges, but whether this man should be found guilty, convicted and jailed as a rapist.

Full of what I think were reasonable doubts, they found John Rideout not guilty of first degree rape.

I don't believe that this ruling is a renewed license for every husband who wants to "exercise his marital rights" by using his wife as a gym mat. Nor do I believe, as Greta Rideout said, that this verdict is a "terrible, terrible setback for women."

I suspect that we will go on striking spousal exclusion clauses from rape laws because they are a holdover from the mind set of the days when judges hung witches and men married property. And we will go on using these laws carefully, sparingly.

The case is a good reminder that it is far more appropriate, accurate and practical to deal with the issues of sexual assault—in or out of marriage—as a crime or violence rather than as a crime of sex.

The cry of "rape," especially in marriage, is often too loaded an accusation to be useful. It's not enough to say, as the sign in the women's crisis center in Salem, Oregon, did, that, "When a woman says no, it's rape." That's a fine piece of consciousness raising, but not a good piece of law enforcement.

Every psychological profile shows that the rapist is out to harm women—not to "have a good time." The husband who forces sex upon his wife is more interested in punishment and power than in pleasure.

It was violence, which, according to both Rideouts, preceded their sexual encounter. Forced sex should be dealt with like any other assault, according to the degree of physical and emotional pain inflicted on the victim.

The issue, after all, is to protect people from harm. Forced sex is to normal intercourse as battering is to caressing.

Changing the accusation from "rape" to assault might not make these decisions easier for a jury. But I think they would clarify the issues—removing from our mind layers of sexual fantasies and historical "rights."

Forcing sex is not making love. It's making war.

JANUARY 1979

Future Shockleys

A dozen years ago, when William Shockley first began talking about improving the stock of the human race, nobody knew that he was going to try to do it all by himself.

Back then, you may recall, the man who won a Nobel Prize for making transistors started talking about making babies. He believed that the world would be better off with more smart people than dumb people, and that intelligence was inherited.

Therefore, he suggested that the best way to improve the world was to set up sperm banks for very smart men and impregnate very smart women. As an amateur geneticist, he sounded like an expert in making transistors.

Well, now it turns out that a seventy-four-year-old California businessman, Robert K. Graham, has actually founded an exclusive sperm bank. In what sounds like a Woody Allen script, he solicits donations from Nobel Prize scientists only—Peace Prize and literature prize winners need not apply. And guess who was among the first three donors? William-Father-of-the-Year-Shockley.

When I first heard this piece of news out of the Los Angeles *Times,* I was stunned by the sheer conceit of the donors. The belief in the superiority of your sperm—even seventy-year-old sperm—can only come from long nights spend rereading the Stockholm speeches. If ego is carried along by the DNA, the three women impregnated so far in this program will give birth to a trio of miserably conceited little monsters.

The Repository for Germinal Choice (I did not make that name up) is a phallic symbol... without the symbolism. But there is more here than meets the ovum.

In the past two weeks, we have had this bulletin about a sperm bank for propagation of elite in California and another tale about a program for sterilization of 4,000 "misfits" from 1922 to 1972 in Lynchburg, Virginia. These are both entries in the historic annals of genetic control.

For over a century, this country has debated whether heredity or environment is most important in determining the physical, mental and "moral" health of a human being.

In mid-nineteenth century Massachusetts, the poor Irish who lived in slums with virtually no health care had a higher infant mortality rate than others. An extensive study conducted by Massachusetts Brahmins blamed it on their "weaker genetic stock." After World War I, when the country went through a fit of xenophobia, they used I.Q. tests at Ellis Island to "prove" that most of the Jewish, Hungarian, Italian and Russian immigrants were "feeble-minded."

In the same vein, an old study of Harvard College graduates lamented the fact that the educated Harvardians underreproduced themselves. Early birth-control advocates put it bluntly: "More children from the fit; fewer children from the unfit."

In short, the situation at Lynchburg was only a more efficient example of a fairly popular concept. People categorized rather blithely as retards and "misfits"—including young women who were committed for being sexually active—were to be prevented from polluting the genetic pool. No one ever proved that they had genetic diseases.

Well, in the 1930s, due to a well-known eugenicist named Adolf, a lot of these theories fell into disrepute. But they started percolating up through the surface of social reform again about ten years ago when Arthur Jensen, and, yes,

"Papa" Shockley started putting forth theories that I.Q. was largely inherited.

Shockley not only endorsed the concept of "increasing the people at the top of the population" but also of "reducing the tragedy of the genetically disadvantaged at the bottom." Not coincidentally, he believes that blacks are genetically less intelligent than whites. Here we go back to Ellis Island.

There are reasons why the notions of "genetic inferiority and superiority" become popular from time to time. When we lose confidence or interest in reforming the environment, we are more likely to blame genes.

If an underclass exists in a democratic society, we want to blame their "stock" rather than our system. When the economic times are hard, I think we are also more likely to think in terms of controlling people rather than helping them. When social programs seem messy and complicated and exhausting, we turn to the efficient engineering of science.

It all sounds so logical. Cast genius sperm upon the world, like Johnny Appleseed, and you will get a crop of geniuses. But genetically it just ain't so. Furthermore, the definition of a successful human life isn't as simple as that of a successful race horse. Genius is more than genes.

And if you're in the market for some Shockley sperm, think about this: You might end up with the genes of a lousy geneticist instead of a decent transistor.

MARCH 1980

The Pope's
Nostalgic Vision

Religion is once again off the front page and morality off the evening news. The people who followed the pope's trip as if he were a candidate and the people who tracked him as if he were a celebrity will soon be after other stars. Those who care are left to sort out the dashed and renewed hopes.

But for a week we witnessed the impressive behavior of a religious incumbent in an age of political transients. For a few days we heard the sound of authority in an age of relativity.

People who long for such certainty greeted the embodiment of it, wrapped in splendor and human warmth, with admiration—even envy. John Paul II spoke of eternal truths when most of us are playing catch-up to change. He represented unity when we were so aware of disparities.

Americans responded to the pope more than to his programs, and displayed a kind of nostalgia for a world that seems more stable.

But in the end, nostalgia doesn't change the way people live.

The part of John Paul's message at greatest odds with the daily life of the Catholic laity was his unwavering opposition to birth control. On this issue, his words were as clear and conservative as they are likely to be ignored. As one woman put it: "The pope is in Rome and I am on the pill."

But the words of the pope on birth control were, in a way, central to his nostalgic vision. He spoke of a world in which pleasure has a biological purpose and sex is part of nature. There is an intellectual purity and wholeness about this ideal which appeals strongly to people like us who have such mixed feelings right now about the ways in which we have "controlled nature."

I suspect that the real revolutionaries of the past hundred years have not been politicians, but technocrats and medical scientists. In this century, medicine has learned to do something it rarely did before: save lives.

Doctors are the ones who have "interfered with the natural order" in the deepest way: by preventing so many deaths. Today, in the western world at least, far fewer women die in childbirth, as did the pope's own mother. Fewer children die of infectious diseases.

Because of medicine, the world eventually will be faced with over-population or with birth control. It is not a question of wanting to provide each child with a color television set. It is a question of protecting the existing life and exhaustible resources.

We have already breached the natural order. The question is how we respond.

In the same vein, the sanctity of human life, of which the pope spoke eloquently, is clear as long as we don't define life. Again, science has upset order: It has enabled us to save the most handicapped, and wounded, and to extend "life" in the form of breathing. We are forced every day to make very human decisions about what life is. Is pulling the plug "euthanasia" or ensuring a "natural death"?

We have, to a certain degree, displaced nature in our attempt to soften its rule. Today, biomedical sciences are the greatest challenge since astronomy. In the seventeenth century, it was heresy, a burnable offense, to say that the earth was not the center of the universe, but just a planet that circled around the sun.

In Brecht's famous play about Galileo, an old cardinal gasps: "Mr. Galileo transfers mankind from the center of the universe to somewhere on the outskirts. Mr. Galileo is therefore an enemy of mankind and must be dealt with as such."

Even his pope, Urban VIII, a man educated in science, allowed Galileo to be arrested by the Inquisition. As the head of the Church he had to defend harmony.

If astronomy violated the order of heaven and earth, today biomedical sciences, like technology, change the human place in the balance of nature.

At the very end of Brecht's play, the pope cries, "I do not want to hear the battle cries: 'Church, Church, Church! Reason, Reason, Reason!'" Eventually those battle cries died down: The earth moved around the sun and the Church accommodated.

Unless we are willing to go back to a world in which people give birth to eight children to ensure the survival of two, in which death was often swift and arbitrary, or willing to accept a world in which nature eventually rules again through famine, we have to accept birth control. Surely on this issue, too, the Church will accommodate.

OCTOBER 1979

Doctors' Dilemma

When I was a kid we used to march into the school auditorium every few months to see a film in some never-ending series on the Wonders of Science.

In those postwar years, there was the notion that the scientist was the Handmaiden of Progress. If there was a gap between what we wanted to do—like go to the moon—and what we were able to do, we were sure that, given enough time and money, science would Make It All Possible.

But now, ironically, the old gap has widened in a different direction. From the people who brought us Baby Louise to the machinery that supported Karen Ann Quinlan, we are now able to do all sorts of things we're not sure we want to do.

Doctors especially, as the trustees of the issues of life and death in this society, are caught today in a variety of bioethical dilemmas in the courts, the legislatures, and the hospital rooms.

This is painfully obvious in the most controversial issue of all, abortion. Last week, the New York Court of Appeals ruled that a doctor must advise a patient if she is facing the special risk of bearing an abnormal child, or he may be held liable for paying the lifetime costs of special care.

The ruling means that, for example, any doctor who is suit-

230

conscious (and if you find me one who isn't I'll save the city of Lot) must now advise any woman over thirty-five or forty of the higher risk of Down's syndrome. The doctor must surely also recommend a test called amniocentesis which is given in the second trimester to detect this defect.

Presumably then the patient can learn if the fetus is unhealthy and decide whether or not to have a mid-term abortion.

But while this was going on in a courtroom in New York state, another group of doctors in a California hospital announced that they had apparently saved the tiny life of Muntaha Ibrahim. Muntaha had been born a month ago weighing only one pound eight ounces—the size of an average six-month fetus.

These two stories show a near-collision of our scientific know-how—between the ability to detect Down's syndrome and abort a mid-term fetus and the ability to save a twenty-four-ounce baby. Rather than resolving old problems, our new skills bring up a host of new problems. And once again physicians carry the burden of solving them.

Since the 1973 Supreme Court abortion ruling, the two most famous abortion trials have been physicians—Kenneth Edelin in Boston and William Waddill in California—on trial for homicide.

In Akron, Ohio, last year, the city council adopted a severe anti-abortion ordinance. Among other things, they ordered doctors to lecture women seeking abortions all about the stages of fetal development. They required that two doctors be present for late-term abortions and take extraordinary efforts to save the "viable unborn child."

Now if you lump all of these doctor-laws together the possibility exists that the same doctor could be responsible for (1) telling a woman that she might have an abnormal birth; (2) informing the woman of the entire fetal development; (3) overseeing an amniocentesis; (4) performing an abortion; (5) saving the abnormal fetus; or (6) for a homicide case.

This scenario is deliberately farfetched. Only a small minority of abortions are performed after the first trimester or because of birth defects. It is impossible to save a twelve-week fetus which weighs half an ounce. At least it is impossible right now.

But I think we can get a hint of the conflicts. Only the Right-To-Life believers enjoy the luxury of moral absolutism. The rest of us, whether we support the Supreme Court decision or back the narrower options of the recent federal compromises, are relativists. We try to find our way through the ethical thicket, issue by issue, case by case, tracing the path of lesser evils until we make a judgment call.

Scientists can't really show us this way between our abilities and our values. We have to do that ourselves.

But it seems to me unreasonable, and unfair, that doctors should find themselves now on the hot seat in this gap, taking the rap for our own uncertainties.

JANUARY 1979

Just Woman's Work?

The young woman stood up before the college audience and talked earnestly about her new job and her new confusion.

A June graduate, she was now a teacher. She was lucky and she knew it. Yet each day she carried a sheaf of self-doubt to school along with the ditto papers and work sheets.

The women her age, you see, have been encouraged to

become astronauts and senators, corporate vice-presidents and assorted firsts. Though she had elected to go through the more traditional door, somehow she couldn't shake the feeling that she was "just" a teacher.

As a parent seated with her on the podium, I felt a wave of concern. There is no outsider more important to our children's lives than their teachers, no job that we weigh more heavily in cost-accounting their futures. We want our children to be taught by the best, the brightest, the most lively and sensitive. To us, there is no such thing as "just" a teacher.

Yet, in her era of change, when the status and stroking of society has gone to the innovators, how many others have felt left behind: "just" a teacher, nurse, secretary, homemaker. And what effect does that have on the choices that young people are making?

I know it isn't popular to talk about this, even in an era when everyone is worrying about teacher "competency," but we are witnessing a young brain-drain from the old "women's jobs."

The young people planning to be teachers don't rank as high scholastically as they did. Dr. Timothy Weaver of Boston University studied this decline and it's a substantial one. In 1970, the high school students planning to be education majors tested in the top one-third of all students on their English boards. Six years later they were found in the bottom one-third.

On the graduate record exams taken by college seniors in the same time period, the scores of ducation majors dropped eighteen points in verbal aptitude.

There are other reasons for this decline. The teaching job market isn't what it used to be. Neither are the salaries. In 1972, teaching salaries were about 25 percent above the national average. Now, says Weaver, they are just about on a par.

But 70 percent of the teachers in this country are women. Their test scores were typically higher than those of men, their salaries relatively higher than those of other women. Now the opportunities for young women are greater and the decline in the test scores of women planning to teach is sharper.

Teaching isn't the only job or the best job for the ambitious and academically talented young woman today. As Weaver put it: "Women do have more opportunities. They are encouraged to feel they have more opportunities in higher-paying professions and that is reflected in the data."

It isn't just teaching that's been affected. In nursing, where there are many jobs, the scores have also declined. And in clerical work, employers continually moan to each other that, "We just can't find the same kind of young secretaries anymore."

But this isn't just a case of Liberation Chic. It isn't just the lure of the new, and the prestige of the different. The fact is that a rise in status for women is associated, for better and for worse, with entry into the male world. That's where the prestige has always been.

We have simply done a better job at letting some women into "men's" jobs than at raising the status of "women's" jobs.

The care-takers—those who are helpers, nurturers, teachers, mothers—are still systematically devalued. We don't put our money where our mouths are.

Now the job market competes for the brightest women as well as the brightest men. If the projections are right and we have a teacher shortage, not a surplus by the mid-1980s, we'll have to do some fancy status shuffling.

Competency tests are nothing more than the last resort of despairing parents. There's no real secret to attracting and keeping the highest caliber applicants for any job. They need the rewards of independence, growth, initiative, respect, personal satisfaction and money. With these, no one is a "Just."

The Art of Living

The story ran across page one like a chill up my spine. It was a nail scratched across the blackboard of the morning newspaper. There, under a photograph of a robust woman brimming with life, was the report of her preplanned suicide.

On June 10, Jo Roman, a Manhattan artist and long-term advocate of what she called self-termination, "took command of making life's final brushstrokes." Her elaborate preparations ended with a final round of farewells and champagne toasts. After a shower, she dressed in a pink nightgown, took an overdose of Seconal, and went to sleep next to her husband. None of those who knew stopped her.

It wasn't her suicide that put this story in the front of our consciousness. People commit suicide every day. They act out of desperation. Some are ending excruciating pain—physical or psychic, and others are crying for help when no one is listening.

But Jo Roman, an artist, did it coolly—did it to complete her own self-portrait. She signed her life, framed it, and went with celebration.

There was, we are told, a reason: cancer. Fourteen months ago, the sixty-one-year-old woman was diagnosed as having breast cancer. The best prognosis gave her three to five years of life.

But was cancer a reason or rationalization for death?

A bizarre suicide note left by Italian author Cesare Pavese read in part, "No one ever lacks a good reason for committing suicide." Jo Roman was not in anything like the final stages of her illness. Indeed, as a friend said, "I was opposed if she had a chance to live any substantial time—well, Jo would have made a week substantial."

But it seems that Jo Roman, as it was said of the Japanese writer and suicide, Yokio Mishima, was impaled on her own imagination. She believed that life could be transformed into art and that her act was artistic.

Suicide has always held a dark fascination for people. It isn't only Camus who believed that the only important question is why not suicide. Death stands for most of us as the ultimate alternative which forces us to evaluate life.

Suicide is, Wilfrid Sheed once wrote, "the sincerest form of criticism life gets."

The notion of rational, planned suicide, the idea of self-termination as simple self-determination, is a gripping one. It is discussed more and more frequently, especially in the context of cancer—a disease whose treatment is as dreaded as its symptoms. We are encouraged now to think of suicide as not necessarily an act of insanity, not necessarily immoral, but perhaps even rational.

Artists in particular, those people who attempt to personally create order out of chaos, have often believed they could at least thwart randomness, accident, and chaos by controlling their own life canvas, their own final lines.

On the surface, this woman said that she was simply shortcutting her disease, aware and unwilling to go through what she read about. But perhaps, more importantly, she was trading a few years of mortality for a shot at controlling her fate. Surely she planned her early afterlife. She left behind a legacy of manuscripts, videotapes and this most personal statement. Her best-known work of art is her death.

Jo Roman was not, her friends say, "flaky." And I believe that. She was clearly a powerful personality, able to use her own will to override any objections of her family and friends.

Yet in her case, cancer appears to have been merely the trigger, while suicide was the obsession.

For years she had planned her own death at seventy-five. Perhaps this notion pushed the demons away. Perhaps she appeased what A. Alvarez called "the Savage God" by planning her own self-sacrifice.

She was among those who ardently advocate rational suicide. Yet I think this is little more than a powerful conceit: that by choosing death we can control it; that by embracing death, rather than letting it come for us, we have won a victory, when we have really lost time. We try to put the imprimatur of reason over the darkness of despair.

Years ago, Alvarez debunked, at least for me, the glamorous notion of stoic suicide. He showed in his fascinating book that reason deteriorates into obsession before the act. If a person is serious, then, as Wilfrid Sheed put it, "he must surrender his fine cool and enter the closed crazy world of suicide, where no phones ring, where children sleeping in the next room make no case for life."

No amount of videotape and manuscript can convince me that this suicide was rational except in one sense: a woman lost her reason, her reason to live.

JUNE 1979

PART 7

Public Lives

Mother Teresa and Her Endless Fight

In the photograph, she is holding an emaciated child. There have been, surely, enough of them, a ready supply of emaciated children in Mother Teresa's life. She has lived in a sea of sick, a Black Hole of Calcutta's poor.

Even now, if she were to distribute every dollar of her $192,000 Nobel Peace Prize, one by one, she would run out of money long before she ran out of poor in that one teeming city.

The portrait of this woman is absolutely awesome. She is no statesman who makes a treaty in an air-conditioned chamber and then goes home to a ticker-tape parade. Here is a woman who gets up every morning of her life to tend endless streams of victims of life's longest war of attrition. Without an expectation of victory.

Most of us in her place could not have stood a week or a two-year tour of duty before being overwhelmed by pain and a sense of futility. There are times we all look at good work and good workers as if they were shoveling sand into the wind. But here is a woman who always sees people.

So, the awarding of the Nobel Prize for Peace to Mother Teresa is a pinch at our consciences—that unpopular and obsolete part of our ethical anatomy. People today don't talk about their consciences and how to appease them; they talk about guilt-trips and how to avoid them.

But Mother Teresa reminds us how often we think of the poor of the world as sand. Most of us live according to self-interest. The truly selfless are as rare as Nobel Prize winners.

But it is a question of how wide our definition of self-interest is and how much it rules our lives.

It is hard, at a time when many Americans feel desperate about their heating bills or their ability to buy a home of their own, to think about the emaciated child. It's hard when we haven't eliminated poverty in America to think about Calcutta. I don't fault this. It just is.

We can't measure one person's pain against another's. But it isn't hard to measure one person's standard of living against another. The anxiety of the couple worried about a 12 percent mortgage and the anxiety of a couple worried about food is utterly different.

When the Nobel committee awarded its peace prize to Mother Teresa (and I do not forget that they also awarded one to Henry Kissinger), they did so because "poverty and hunger and distress also constitute a threat to peace."

The gap between the rich and the poor of the world makes this country look like an egalitarian utopia. The gap between the rich and the poor of the world is a true source of insecurity and hostility. We are the rich and it is harder and harder to get away from it.

It's odd to quote Fidel Castro and Pope John Paul II in one breath. But in their back-to-back visits to this country, they both gave the same message: "Some countries possess abundant resources while others have nothing."

However dubious Castro's credentials or motivations, his words ring true and we know it. "I have come to warn that, if we do not eliminate our present injustices and inequalities peacefully and wisely, the future will be apocalyptic. Bombs may kill the hungry, the sick and the ignorant, but they cannot kill hunger, disease and ignorance. Nor can they kill the righteous rebellion of the people; and in the holocaust, the rich who are the ones who have the most to lose in this world will also die."

Mother Teresa said that, "The great thing about the poor

is that they are not discontented. They don't hate us despite their immense suffering. It is a mystery we cannot understand."

Perhaps she is right. Perhaps they are too tired or too concerned with survival for hatred. But I doubt it. When "have nots" see the "haves," they want to know why.

The Nobel Prize award and the words of two visitors from two different worlds suggest that each year we need a broader definition of self-interest: one that sees the world as our neighborhood, one that sees our conscience as a guide, not as a guilt-trip.

"I have been told I spoil the poor by my work," says Mother Teresa. "Well at least one congregation is spoiling the poor, because everyone else is spoiling the rich."

Few of us are or can be as selfless or dedicated as this woman. But perhaps, for a few minutes, she helped us wipe the sand from our eyes, so we could see the people.

OCTOBER 1979

Knowing Eleanor Roosevelt

Now it is Eleanor Roosevelt's turn to have her private life exhumed. Someone has said that the woman we buried was not who we thought she was, and so they have disinterred her letters, dissected their vital organs and sent them to the cruelest coroner of all, the public.

Those who think her prose was purple are arguing with those who think her life was tinged with lavender. Across the tabletops and country, people are talking about her "sexual preference" as if it were hair color: Did she or didn't she? Only her friend knew for sure.

Well, they say that every generation writes its own history. Ours, it appears, is sexual. We thrust our own obsessions back into time and come up with JFK's promiscuity, Thomas Jefferson's black mistress and, now, Eleanor's friend Lorena Hickok.

It seems, moreover, that we have greater taste for suspicions than for facts, for the unknown than for the known. We continually want to unmask our heroes as if there were more to be learned from their nakedness than from their choice of clothing.

It is odd in this case, especially, because what we do know about Eleanor Roosevelt is so much more vital than what we don't know. A tall woman with a voice that begged caricaturing, she grew up in an era when form dictated feelings—when, as she said, "you dressed, not according to the weather but the date."

We know that by all accounts, including her own, she had a miserable childhood. Regarded coolly by her mother, who called her "Granny," she was told that, "In a family that had great beauty, you are the ugly duckling of that family."

We know, too, that she worshipped—and struggled to please—her father long after that attractive, self-destructive and unreliable man was gone.

At forty-three years of age she could still write, "I knew a child once who adored her father. She was an ugly little thing, keenly conscious of her deficiencies, and her father, the only person who really cared for her, was away much of the time...(but) he wrote her letters and stories telling her... she must be truthful, loyal, brave, well-educated.... She made herself as the years went on into a fairly good copy of the picture he had painted."

From the time she was ten and an orphan, she spent a

neglected childhood with her grandmother in a dark, gloomy house where, as a cousin recalled, "We ate our suppers silently."

At a very young age, then, Eleanor knew too much about life's blows. As a young wife, she learned more. After ten years of marriage and six children, her husband fell in love with Lucy Mercer, and: "The bottom dropped out of my particular life, and I faced myself, my surroundings, my world, honestly for the first time. I really grew up that year."

Even when her husband died, Eleanor knew, ". . . he might have been happier with a wife who was completely uncritical. That, I was never able to be. . . . Nevertheless, I think I sometimes acted as a spur even though spurring was not always wanted or welcome. I was one of those who served his purposes."

She became a great lady, then, not because she was a first lady, but because she was able through enormous will to turn her pain into strength, to turn disappointment into purpose. It was as if her backbone had been permanently strengthened by the brace she wore in childhood.

The facts, just the facts, of her life might have defeated any of us. Add to that list a dead child and a husband stricken with polio. But she used them, the way she used her rigorous discipline of calisthenics and ice-cold showers, to make herself stronger.

With this gutsiness, she cared about the poor even when the press accused her of interfering, and supported civil rights in the days when an antilynch law was highly controversial with southern Democrats. She promoted women in government when others disparaged them and, as a widow, worked for human rights in the world and the United Nations when others grew resigned.

And, yes, she was also effusive and loving in letters to women friends. She was as intimate as her husband was remote. As James Roosevelt once wrote: "Of what was inside him, of what really drove him, Father talked with no one."

All this, the important facts, the fundamental truths, are

known, not suspected. As Arthur Schlesinger once added them up: "Her life was both ordeal and fulfillment. It combined vulnerability and stoicism, pathos and pride, frustration and accomplishment, sadness and happiness."

That is still the best epitaph.

OCTOBER 1979

A Three-Piece Jerry Rubin

Once upon a time, in the mythical 1960s, Jerry Rubin looked into the media mirror and learned that he was the Yippiest of them all. In those wonderful yesteryears, when someone asked what he did for a living, he answered, "I'm famous. That's my job."

Well, this vocation has kept the lad busy.

Jerry Rubin has proved himself to be the Duddy Kravitz of the Sixties Kids. He has hustled himself with more consistent skill than a Harvard MBA.

First he made a living off The Movement, no mean feat in itself. He wrote books and made speeches about how kids should drop out and turn on and "Do It!" He penned everybody's pet paranoid phrase, "Kill your parents."

Then he turned thirty and the 1960s turned into the 1970s. After a panicky moment or two of being passé, he moved right along into the Self-Searching Seventies. He was rolfed, est-ed, and massaged until he got in contact with his inner feelings. He also got in contact with a publisher who paid him to write about it all in *"Growing (Up)"*.

But then the Self Biz hit the skids (life is not a bed of roses for The Human Trend) and the seventies dropped like a stone into the eighties. If the challenge of 1976 was to get in touch with your feelings, the feeling of 1980 is that you'd like to get in touch with some money.

Enter stage left (but moving right), Jerry Rubin of Wall Street, New York.

Rubin once again used the *New York Times* the way his more crass classmates use the alumni notes. He announced on its op-ed page: "I accepted a position on Wall Street this week."

In what was inadvertently a hilarious piece of journalism, he went on to say: "I know that I can be more effective today wearing a suit and tie and working on Wall Street than I can be dancing outside the walls of power. . . . Politics and rebellion distinguished the '60s. The search for self characterized the spirit of the '70s. Money and financial interest will capture the passion of the '80s."

And J.R. will be there.

Here is Rubin at his best, announcing every turn of his life as a sign of the times, mixing the outrageous and the naive, doing social work in self-indulgence.

He is now a marketing analyst. But not your everyday marketing analyst. He is a consciousness-raised marketing analyst and self-certified good person ready to reach out and affect the system on his own terms.

To put it another way, he is now available to accept customers with a social conscience who are looking to invest their money in firms with a social conscience (not to mention a good profit picture) at John Muir and Co.

"Welcome, Wall Street, here I come! Let's make millions of dollars together supporting the little companies engaged in social environmental positivity. Let's rescue American capitalism from overemphasis on the huge organization. Let's make capitalism work for everyone."

Well, it is nice to know the man has retained his chutzpah

inasmuch as he has lost his sense of humor. His job announcement is almost charming in its outlandish, childish sincerity.

Reading this, it is hard to believe that he was ever very "bad." It is easy, however, to believe that he was never very bright.

It took Rubin until he was thirty-seven to come up with blazing banalities like: Hate is a very strong bond.

It took him until he was forty-one to discover "Money is Power."

Now he has also "discovered" that "the challenge for American capitalism in the eighties is to bring the entrepreneurial spirit back to America."

This, at last, and at least, is a task that suits his talents. Through all the years of tripping the trends fantastic, Rubin has maintained a stunning consistency. He is now and always was the 100 percent pure American archetype: The Happy Capitalist.

After all, he is the man who read Dale Carnegie for hints about how to perform on the radical-left platform and had $20,000 in the stock market when he was manning the barricades.

The lad has finally come home. Rubin's the name: Money and Fame's the game. *Yippee!*

AUGUST 1980

Pablo Picasso: Living in His Own Shadow

We were one hour into the Picasso exhibit when we stopped in front of a cubist painting called "The Accordionist."

Behind us were five huge rooms full of gorgeous Impressionist children and massive seated women, of perfectly reproduced realism, of shattered forms of revolutionary cubism.

At the bottom of this one picture, we checked the date: 1911. He had done all this before his thirtieth birthday.

The age impressed me more than it did the twelve-year-old next to me. We live on opposite sides of that dividing line. Yet, we were both struck by the volume and versatility of Picasso's life work in this exhibit.

Surrounded, even overwhelmed, as we moved among the 900 Picassos that have taken over the Museum of Modern Art for the summer in a massive retrospective, it was obvious why this man still dominates art the way Shakespeare dominates literature or Mozart dominates music.

It is said that when Picasso was a teenager, his artist-father gave the boy his own palette, brushes and colors, and never painted again. It is known that when he died at the age of ninety-one, Picasso was arranging for a show of his latest work. In between he was astonishingly productive.

Here was a man who produced some 13,000 to 14,000 canvases, 100,000 prints or engravings, and 34,000 book illustrations. He worked in virtually every medium from stage sets to ceramics, ranging back and forth from one to the other with as much energy as genius.

Yet as we wandered through the last thirty years of his life, you could see it all slip. The exhibit kindly excluded the commercial peace doves and greeting-card poster art of the last years.

But still, it is easy to see the versatility turning frenetic, the search turning downhill. There is even a sense that perhaps he began to imitate himself—not just to create, but to create "Picassos."

There is nothing bad on these walls. The worst of this artist is very, very good. But winding down through his age and out again onto 54th Street, it was hard not to wonder what it was like to be Picasso at seventy, or eighty, or ninety, competing with Picasso at forty.

What is it like to keep working in the present while your past has already been written into history books? What is it like to compete with your own best?

It is something that I've thought of before. I've thought of it whenever Tennessee Williams turns up in the news, alive but rarely well, writing poorly in comparison to his own brilliant retrospectives. I've thought of it when Frank Sinatra goes on stage, all blue eyes and strained vocal cords. They are pale versions of themselves.

Living in your own shadow is a problem of aging athletes and beautiful women and artists and actors and, to an extent, all of us.

The American ideal is that people should quit with the gold medals around their necks and the stars on their doors.

We want them to stay on top or move on. We want to laurelize them like Jesse Owens or ignore them like Mark Spitz. We hope that, like Beverly Sills, they will "move on" at the right moment, off of one stage and onto the next . . . before their voices crack in public.

There are very few ways for our stars to retreat gracefully back into the chorus line. We live in such an achievement-oriented world that anyone who is not doing his or her best, breaking records, going onward and upward, is somehow or other failing.

We feel saddened that Joe Di Maggio sells coffee-makers and uncomfortable that Willie Mays "stayed too long." Few of us know quite how to deal with the man or woman who "used to be" somebody.

Picasso was hardly a failure in his later life. He refused to be canonized. He refused to rest on his laurels. He chose productivity. He got up in the morning, nearly paralyzed by pessimism about his own ability, and went to work.

There is something, not sad but remarkable, in this refusal to "act his age," or to retire gracefully. Surrounded by his own collection of his favorite cubist work, he must have known his limits. But out of compulsion or conviction, he kept working.

"Creation," Picasso said, "is the only thing that interests me." So for ninety-one years, he did something remarkable. He stayed interested.

JULY 1980

Anita Bryant:
Between Her Husband
and Her Conscience

Spare me the Saturday night snide jokes about this. I am no fan of Anita Bryant's politics, but I don't want to poke through the ashes of her marital eruption for the laughs.

Yes, another self-appointed smug savior of the American family has become a shaken survivor. The story seems familiar, but not really very funny.

A few years ago Bryant was questioned about her wifely role in a *Playboy* interview: "If Bob (Green, her husband) asked you to do something right now that was against the grain of your thoughts," she was asked, "would you simply submit to him?"

She answered then, "I might rebel against it—and I have many times—but biblically, I would submit, yes."

But last week, she said no. She would instead divorce her husband after twenty years and four children, because he "violated my most precious asset—my very conscience." Her husband and others, she said, "conspired to control me and use my name and reputation to build their personal careers instead of my ministry."

This woman who once described submission as a choice

she had freely made, faced another choice: between her conscience and her marriage, between her beliefs and her husband. It happens, in real life, all the time.

Still, The Anita Bryant saga is not just another tale of disillusionment and divorce. She is part of a long tradition of women who enter the public sphere only to "defend" the private one: conservative women who become part of change.

The nineteenth century defined women as the Keepers of Moral Values. As duly appointed moral superiors to men in the home, they often became mother superiors to the country. These Domestic Women of the World founded not only the Social Purity movement against prostitution but the mass movement against saloons, called Temperance.

By the thousands, they worked without guilt and crusaded without criticism because they were, after all, protecting the family.

In the twentieth century, too, traditional women have founded very popular and public "moral" crusades. Anita Bryant's controversial second career began to "save the children" from her bizarre nightmare vision of homosexual recruiters. Phyllis Schafly, for her part, has made a full-time profession out of defending homemaking. Again and again, "mothers" have founded and filled the antiabortion, antihighway, antinuclear energy, antichemical, and antiwar movements.

For many, it has been a logical extension of first concerns. But for others it also has become an attempt to have it both ways, to justify working outside the home by defending the home. After all, in traditional times and marriages, the woman crusading "for her family" is more acceptable than the woman crusading "for her own rights."

A century ago, for example, the press condoned the illegal acts of the Temperance women because "these women were not agitating for suffrage." And only last week, a husband of a Love Canal leader supported his wife's activism, saying, "The hell with all the equal rights stuff— they're fighting for their families."

But as women go into the world, join causes, become

leaders, they change. In his new book, *At Odds*, historian Carl Degler says that the nineteenth-century movement women "saw things and learned things that moved them in new, often quite unexpected and even unsettling directions. . . ."

The women who wanted to save the nineteenth-century family from prostitution inevitably started lobbying for women's employment, if only to save them from "sin." The women who wanted to kill the Demon Rum realized that to do so they would need the vote.

Their twentieth-century descendants have irresistibly drifted in the same directions. Even conservative women battle now against second-class status in the political parties. The neighborhood women who fight highways or school policies begin to run for statewide office. At the Love Canal, the "mothers" fight to be taken seriously, to be aggressive and knowledgeable and powerful—in order to be heard.

Rarely do any of them "go home" again. Rarely are their homes untouched.

Anita Bryant, too, a public defender of the family and the traditional female role, was pushed or grew out of submission. Hardly a feminist then or now, she has still followed a familiar course: She has chosen her individual conscience over her role.

The lady tried to be a leader in the world and an obedient follower in the marriage. But these are the two ways you can't have it anymore.

MAY 1980

The Sounds of
Richard Rodgers

He came into our house with the first Victrola...and
stayed. By the time I was ten I knew every song on our
boxed and scratched "78" records: songs from *Oklahoma!*
and *Carousel* and *South Pacific*. They were, very simply,
the earliest tunes in a house that was more alive with the
sound of politics than the sound of music.

As I grew older, I knew he was no Beethoven or Verdi,
or John Lennon for that matter. By then his songs had been
orchestrally overkilled into the sort of Muzak that kept you
company in elevators or "on hold" at the insurance company
line.

But the fact is that from the time I was a child, to the
time I sat with my own child watching the Trapp family
escape again over the mountains, there has always been a
Richard Rodgers song in the background.

His work has been, very simply, our musical common
exchange—as familiar and contagious as the composer ever
hoped.

By the time he died last Sunday, he was that rare man,
someone who accomplished what he set out to do: "All I
really want to do is to provide a hard-working man in the
blouse business with a method of expressing himself. If he
likes a tune, he can whistle it and it will make his life
happier."

And, at seventy-seven, he was something ever rarer, a man who remained centered in his work over six decades.

The numbers were overwhelming: 1,500 songs, 43 stage musical scores, 9 film scores, 4 television scores. He wrote music when he had a heart attack and music when he had cancer and music when he was learning to talk through his esophagus. He wrote music when his plays were huge successes and music when they were not; music when he needed the money and music when he didn't.

At fourteen, he composed his first song and at sixty-seven he still wrote to a friend: "I have a strong need to write some more music, and I just hope nothing stands in the way."

Yet when he was praised, he said, "I admit with no modesty whatever that not many people can do it. But when they say, 'You're a genius,' I say, 'no, it's my job.'"

Music was his job. It is a curious phrase. Yet it seems to me, looking back over his career, how little attention we've paid recently to the relationship between a life and "a job." For the past several years we've been more intrigued by life-styles than by work-styles, more curious about how someone sustains a marriage or a health regimen than how someone sustains an interest in his work.

The magazines we read are more focused on how we play than how we produce. We assume now that work is what we do for a living and leisure is how we enjoy living. When we meet people who do not understand this split, we label them "workaholics."

But Richard Rodgers was never seen in *People* magazine wearing his jog-togs. His "job" was writing music and his hobby was listening to it.

Usually we think of creative work as either inspired or tortured. We remember both Handel writing "The Messiah" in three weeks and Michelangelo mounting the scaffolding of the Sistine Chapel year after year. Rodgers for his part once wrote a song in five minutes. But when asked about it, he said, "The song situation has probably been going around in my head for weeks. Sometimes it takes months. I don't believe that a writer does something wonderful spontaneously. I believe it's the result of years of living, or study, reading—his very personality and temperament."

The man knew something about the relationship between creativity and productivity. He knew something about the satisfactions of both, and managed to blend them. He could write music when handed the lyrics and write it before the lyrics. He could and would write a song to fit a scene. If Woody Allen is right in saying that "Eighty percent of life is showing up," well, Richard Rodgers showed up.

"Some Enchanted Evening" will never go into the annals of great classics. *The King and I* is not *Aida*. Rodgers was a workaday artist and he knew it. But he also knew that for some people there is a fuzzy line between work and play, between what is hard and what is fun.

"I heard a very interesting definition of work from a lawyer. Work, he said, is any activity you'd rather not do. . . . I don't find it work to write music, because I enjoy it," said Rodgers. Yet he also said, "It isn't any easier than when I began, and by the same token it isn't any harder."

He was a man who was lucky in his work and lucky in his temperament. In an era when we tend to doubt the satisfactions that can come from work and tend to regard hard workers as a touch flawed in their capacity for pleasure, this composer showed what work can be: how it can sustain rather than drain, heighten rather than diminish, a full life. He leaves us a legacy in the sound of his life as well as his music.

JANUARY 1980

Margaret Sanger: Flawed Heroine

The Margaret Sanger Centennial year has begun rather quietly, especially for as catalytic an agent of change as the woman who invented the very term, Birth Control. As H.G. Wells once wrote, "When the history of our civilization is written, it will be a biological history, and Margaret Sanger will be its heroine."

It was her intense commitment and energy which almost singlehandedly promoted contraception in this country— something which wasn't fully legalized until 1972.

Still it's hard to pin a nice unequivocal label like "Heroine" on the lady, even as a 100th birthday gift. Her history is a whole lot more complex than that.

Sanger was born one of eleven children to an Irish immigrant free-thinker who sculpted gravestone angels. She began her career as a public health nurse on Manhattan's Lower East Side, where she became comvinced that the solution to poverty was birth control.

In 1914, when Sanger was on the lam in London—she had broken the pornography laws by distributing birth-control information—she became an admirer of Havelock Ellis. Ellis was one of the more prominent eugenicists of the period who applied (or misapplied) Darwinian notions to a creepy philosophy of selective breeding. He wanted only the "best people" to reproduce.

Under his influence, Sanger panned one of her early and least attractive slogans, "Birth control—to create a race of thoroughbreds." Shades of the Third Reich. In fairness, Sanger didn't advocate birth control out of a desire to breed a super race, but made an alliance with eugenics out of a desire to push birth control. It was her one and only cause.

She came to believe contraception was a panacea. It would not only control poverty, end child labor and improve health but also give women "the key to the temple of liberty." Birth control would allow them to plan their lives without sacrificing their sexuality.

Despite her own support of what she saw as women's liberty, Sanger was hardly a favorite with the feminists of her era. Most of them looked at her rather ecstatic views on sex—a "psychic and spiritual avenue of expression"—with a jaundiced eye.

Suffragist Carrie Chapman Catt chided that "merely to make indulgence safe does not do enough." She and others were in favor of restraining male sexuality instead of freeing female sexuality.

Charlotte Perkins Gilman was uninterested in birth control because she thought that in an ideal feminist society—like the one she described in *Herland*—the energy of adults would and should be directed toward child raising, not sex.

Still others, including many of the progressives, were sure that Sanger had the whole thing backwards. She thought that large families were responsible for the evils of the system and that a wife could control the entire organization of society with a diaphragm. But the progressives thought the birth-control issue came in second at best to the issue of social reform.

By the 1920s and 1930s, birth control was overwhelmingly adopted by the middle class, not the poor. It was not accepted as a solution to economic injustice, but as part of the "sexual revolution" of the post World War I period.

At that time the ideal of middle-class womanhood switched to the vision of a wife primarily as a companion and sexual partner, not mother. This was an overwhelming social change. For the first time, the credo, as author Sheila Rothman describes it, was marriage "based on passion, sexuality and, of course, birth control."

Margaret Sanger is not the first flawed "heroine" to facilitate a vast social change. Contraception, for all of its failures and problems, has enabled millions and millions of women as well as men to plan their lives as well as the size of their families.

But the most profound effect of the availability of birth control has been on the ability to separate sex from reproduction. This simple and revolutionary fact has been accepted by most of us with relief or joy or unease. The way we feel about the separation often underlies the attitudes we have toward the second sexual revolution—from extra-marital sex to *The Joy of Sex* to the availability of abortion.

In that sense, this most fantastic and controversial woman was prophetic when she said that birth control demands "the frankest and most unflinching reexamination of sex in relation to human nature and the bases of human society." One hundred years later, this reexamination still goes on.

SEPTEMBER 1979

John Lennon: It's The Promise That's Gone

I had seen his face only last Sunday: he and the other three looking out from the 1960s buttons and posters. The four were all encased in glass, like cameos of Queen Victoria. They were captured in a Beatles Booth at an antique show.

It startled me then to see the Beatles sold as something old. But it is always surprising when our youth becomes a collector's item.

On Tuesday, I saw his face again, on the front page. John Lennon, the most complex of the Beatles, had been shot dead by a looney, a cuckoo, a nutcake—the New York police used all the familiar words, including "allegedly." The killer apparently was some crazed cousin to all the crackpots and criminals who can buy guns as easily as Christmas trees. Amen to that.

But the Lennon I'll miss isn't the brilliant Beatle of the sixties with his hair "rebelliously" grown below his ears. That John Lennon exists on my records. The man I'll miss is the one I just met again, the man of the eighties, moving in new ways, making new sounds. Five bullets wiped out this father, husband, musician... human work in progress.

I am more a member of the Beatles' generation than the fans' generation. So I was moved by the emergence of John Lennon at forty.

It was good to see him selling Promise at Forty. Not

depressions, not complacency, not mania, but Promise. "It's quite possible," he said, "to do anything."

The new record he made with his wife, Yoko Ono, "Double Fantasy," was the work of a survivor. "You have to give thanks to God or whatever is up there (for) the fact that we all survived—survived Vietnam or Watergate, the tremendous upheaval of the whole world," he said in an ironic prelude to his death.

But it wasn't just the decades he'd survived. He'd overcome something else: other people's expectations.

John Lennon got lost for a time, wandering in the body of The Famous John Lennon. He became so public a person that his life became a role he was playing. Other people were the directors.

There were the fans who expected him to be a Beatle Forever, until he ended up singing "I Wanna Hold Your Hand" in Las Vegas nightclubs. There were the business managers who wanted him to be their product. "I was a machine," he said, "that was supposed to produce so much creative something and give it out periodically for approval to justify my existence on earth."

There were even people who expected him to self-destruct like Dylan Thomas or the rock stars with needle tracks up their arms. "I'd just naively accepted the idea," he said, "that an artist had to self-destruct in order to create."

He survived all these expectations by getting better, saner, older. In 1975, he jumped into his private life as if it were a lifeboat. His fans called it seclusion. He called it becoming a "househusband." But he got in touch with the routines that root all of us, with daily-ness. He took care of his child, instead of being taken care of like a child. He let himself go into his new rhythms.

Five years later, this fall, he and his wife came out with music and words. He talked about men and women "Starting Over," about balancing family and work, about growing up.

"Is it possible to have a life centered around a family and a child and still be an artist?" he asked one reporter.

"When I look at the relative importance of what life is about, I can't quite convince myself that making a record or having a career is more important or even as important as my child, or any child," he told another.

The man changed, and typically refused to apologize or simplify it. "The attitude is that when you change when you get older there's something wrong with that. Whatever changes I'm going through because I'm forty I'm thankful for, because they give me some insight into the madness I've been living all myself."

In a way he was talking to and for his own generation. "I'm saying, 'Here I am now, how are you? How's your relationship going? Did you get through it all? Wasn't the Seventies a drag, you know? Well, here we are, let's make the Eighties great because it's up to us to make what we can of it.'"

John Lennon of the sixties survived so much—even pessimism—only to get murdered. He made a life late and died early.

Did his murderer aim for the Sixties' Superstar, the Beatle, the face under glass? What craziness and waste. You can't kill what a man has already done. You can only kill what might have come next.

The antique John Lennon had already been preserved. Dammit, it's the promise that's gone.

DECEMBER 1980

PART 8

Thoughts At Large

Class
Struggle

Now they've gone, carrying school lunches and school jitters. Soon they'll have settled into class, and memorized the hours and the corridors, the teachers' names and foibles.

But the children carry something else with them past the crossing guards and playgrounds today: a loaded bookbag of expectations. Their own, their parents', their society's.

If there's a single message passed down from each generation of American parents to their children, it is a two-word line: Better Yourself. And if there's a temple of self-betterment in each town, it is the local school. We have worshipped there for some time.

Most of our ancestors left countries where poverty, caste and class were inherited. They came to a country founded on the notion that they were born equal. So they lived, and we still live, not with the reality of an equal society but with the ideal of equal opportunity—especially for the children.

Americans have, in a sense, always laid their dreams on their children. As long ago as the late 1830s, people like Edward Everett, the governor of Massachusetts, said: "The wheel of fortune is in constant operation, and the poor in one generation furnish the rich of the next." It was the hope for the chances of the "next" which kept the country relatively stable.

Our children's chances have been invested in the schools since Horace Mann, denouncing visions of redistributing wealth, instead advocated free and universal education. He was one of the first to give children and schools the job of equalizing America. In 1848, he wrote: "Education, then, beyond all other devices of human origin, is the great equalizer of the conditions of men—the balance-wheel of the social machinery."

That notion has been behind reformist public policy— from the schools to the Head Start program to parent education.

It has also formed the outline of the most popular tales of the poor boys who made good through study.

But to a certain extent, the text has now been revised. The relationship between schooling and success, education and equality, classes and class has been scrutinized anew.

It is still true, according to Harvard's Christopher Jencks in *Who Gets Ahead?*, that the best indicator of economic success—among men at least—is how much education a man has had. A college degree of any kind still makes a great difference. But at the same time, Jencks finds that we can tell soon after a child is born whether his chances for success are good or bad "for reasons that have nothing to do with anything he did."

It appears that, to a large extent, the status of the family determines the education of the child, which in turn determines his status.

"Most people, when they speak of school as an equalizer, mean that advantages obtained through schooling will cancel out socially inherited disadvantages as children become adults," writes another "revisionist," Richard deLone, for the Carnegie Council on Children. But he notes that (1) education hasn't closed the gap between the rich and the poor and (2) only one man in five will succeed in surpassing his father.

While education may be the best, or only, route out of poverty for the individual, on the whole status is inherited today in America not through the genes but through the class structure.

". . . Schooling by itself cannot produce interclass or interracial equality," writes deLone. Even among the immigrant fables, the reality was that most families achieved some economic stability first and then insisted on their children's education.

The point isn't to denigrate school, but to gain perspective on the idea that each child starts with an equal chance and that education itself can solve inequality by lifting the next—always the next—generation out of poverty.

If we truly want to reduce poverty or inequality, we may have to start with parents—not kids and economics, not education.

"I don't think there has ever been any question that a society can narrow its social extremes if it wants to," says Jencks. "The question is one of political will."

Instead, we have thrown the issue of equal opportunity onto the backs of our children, and that's a heavy burden to carry off in a school bag.

SEPTEMBER 1979

The Not-So-Good Old Days

On the top of my desk there is a green button. No, not the kind of button you push. The kind of button you normally put through a hole. The hole is still on my sweater. The button, having been used three times, has been cast out of work by the unraveled thread.

It is an American sweater.

On the wall of my kitchen there is a new clock. Another new clock. The first clock would, from time to time, start going backwards. The next one had a second hand which struggled upward from the number six to the number seven and then collapsed in an exhausted heap back at six. After twenty-four hours of this, I replaced it with the third.

All three are American clocks.

You are now, I am sure, expecting another diatribe on "The Decline of Quality in America," and let me assure you that I can launch one with the best. Give me a minute and I'll gather together my personal exhibits in the case against quality.

Step right up! Touch the abominable toaster tray! See the disintegrating book! Taste the inedible tomato!

I can then also Point with Pride to the products of a simpler and sturdier time. The indomitable oak table of 1900, the unfailing railroad clock of 1860, the unbreakable sewing machine of the 1930s, the unfrayable silk blouse of the 1940s.

This is, after all, how we all play the most popular game of the year, "The Rise and Fall of American Quality."

But after weeks listening to the rising ardor of the fans, forgive me if I use halftime to question the rules.

I am not a great believer in The Good Old Days. I think we all tend to idealize the past. A hundred years ago, people were no doubt ruing the decline of quality. I guess I lost my rose-colored retrospectacles in history class.

I also think we tend to compare the worst of now with the best of then. The products of the past which have survived into the present are almost by definition high-quality. The rotten buildings have fallen down, the shabby furniture has been used for firewood, the crummy blouses have long ago disintegrated, the appliances are being used for landfill, the bad movies have been long forgotten.

But it's also worth remembering that some high-quality products often depended on low-quality lives. It's one thing to miss the delicate handmade lace of another time. It's quite another to miss the long hours at low wages in a desperate cottage industry.

It is equally easy to admire the intricate molding on the walls and stairways of another decade. But it's hard to admire the enormous gap between what the rich could afford and the working poor were paid. The high cost of labor is, after all, good for the laborer.

We talk about lost quality as if we were the potential buyers rather than the producers. The Chinese always remind foreign visitors that while The Great Wall was a wonderful achievement, the lives of the people who built it were rotten.

Most of us did not live in the mansions of the nineteenth century, unless we were in the scullery. Most of us didn't eat luxurious meals off elegant silver. At best, we made the meals and polished the silver.

In fact, we could make a pretty decent, if unpopular, case that the quality of life has improved in the past century along with the quality of things like food and housing. It seems that the distribution of goods has raised the standards for many and lowered them for some.

Consciously or not, even those who protest most loudly often choose "low quality" over "high quality" items, heading for McDonald's instead of the kitchen, for permanent press instead of the iron. We often knowingly choose "low quality" over high cost.

I'm not trying to defend things that go *bonk* in the night. I'm as infuriated by sloppy work and saddened by the loss of pride in crafts as the next person. I think we have to blame and cure "bigness," its careless management and alienated anonymous workers . . . all the rest.

But while we are playing the elite, decrying the decline of quality, the erosion of the high standards by mass production and mass standards, it's not bad to remember that we (blush) are the masses.

JANUARY 1981

Playing With the Pros

Sometimes I think there are dozens of coaches out there, all trying to recruit us, all trying to get us to root for their side of a social issue, by offering us a big chance to join the "pros."

On the abortion issue they're either Pro-life or Pro-choice.

On the regulation issue, they're either Pro-free enterprise or Pro-consumer. On the pornography issue, either Pro-morality or Pro-first amendment.

The latest grasp for our allegiance comes over sex on television. One group is encouraging us to join an advertisers' boycott and another group is enlisting us to fight censorship. It's hard to know the right team without a program.

Last month, something called the Coalition for Better Television opened up their recruitment drive in Washington. They declared a campaign to clean up the tube. They called their side Pro-morality.

For three months, they announced, several hundred of their monitors would be rating prime time shows on a score card of smuttiness. They would list what Donald Wildmon, a CBTV leader and head of the National Federation for Decency called "skin scenes, implied sexual intercourse, and sexually suggestive comments."

When the scoring was over, in June, he said they would list the sponsors of the worst shows and call on people not to buy their products. They call this game plan a boycott.

Then, last week, at the annual meeting of 4,000 television executives in New York, the other team fielded their defense. Panelists there talked about the dangerous tactics and motives of the CBTV and labeled themselves Pro-First Amendment. They said that the monitors were actually drawing up a hit list. They accused CBTV of "censorship."

So here we are again. One team claims they are holding up values and morality against the smut stream, and the others swear that they are protecting the Constitution against the censors. For whom are we supposed to root?

Well, I bow to no one in my scorn for the TV shows that come complete with a snigger track. I am appalled at the number of programs in which sex is the plot, the subplot, and the counterplot.

So, I think Wildmon was right when he told the CBTV meeting that broadcasters have ignored protests against the creeping sexualization of the airwaves and have "rather displayed an arrogance and indifference rarely matched in the history of corporate America." The networks have had a stunning lack of regard for their own long-term self-interest. They've left all of us frustrated and vulnerable to the first group that promises us a chance to "do something." It's no wonder that 200 groups are already following the CBTV cheerleaders.

Having said that, however, I still can't sign up. I have too many qualms about the CBTV plans and planners. Morality may or may not be in the eyes of the beholder, but I'm not all that comfortable leaving the "beholding" to someone else.

The Top Three in the Pro-morality crowd are Wildmon, Jerry Falwell of Moral Majority and Phyllis Schlafly of Stop ERA. I would probably agree with them about the content of "Flamingo Road," "Three's Company," or "Dallas"— J.R. has the moral perspective of a worm—but I suspect we would part company pretty quickly after that.

I'm not willing to give them my proxy as moral arbiters. As Peggy Charren, the head of Action for Children's Television and a long-time TV critic said at the broadcaster's meeting, "What will be the next target? A production of *A Streetcar Named Desire?* A documentary on teenage pregnancy? The news?"

The anti-sex campaign looks to me like a farm team to channel people into the right wing big leagues. I keep remembering all the people who joined the Moral Majority because they were "pro-family" only to discover they were now also being counted as pro-MX missiles.

One of the other things that bothers me about this campaign is the strategy. The CBTV idea is to put pressure on the advertisers to put pressure on the broadcasters. Well, I'm not convinced that the advertiser should be handed the star role. Some of the ads themselves are mini X-rated features. If you don't believe that I'll rerun my jean reels for you.

The ad men are a big part of the problem. They kill for the privilege of sponsoring programs with the biggest ratings and never mind if the rating has been "jiggled" up a point or two. The CBTV plan would give the advertisers *more* power in programming and the results would be even worse for quality.

Does this mean we're impotent? I don't think so. There's room for an angry nonaligned third team. I believe in boycotts when they're focussed on the right targets. We should boycott the advertiser if we don't like the ads and boycott the program if we don't like the program. We should just plain turn them off.

Like it or not, the most effective way to change television and leave the Constitution intact is to play the broadcasters on their turf and the old-time ratings game is the only one they watch.

MARCH 1981

A Meltdown of Trust

When all the reports are filed about the Terror at Three Mile Island, I hope they will have studied the human reaction as well as the nuclear reactor.

The accident there is more than a test case for nuclear safety, and more than a watershed for nuclear energy. It marks, I think, a way station on the road of public mistrust.

For days, in the countryside around Middletown, Pennsylvania, and in the country at large, people were over-whelmingly certain that the authorities were lying.

Near the plant, George Meck said it gently: "I don't think they are telling us the whole truth." In another home, Hilda Lytle put it more bluntly: "I think they are lying to us."

This mistrust is not an "unanticipated transient." It is not an "event." It is not even an "abnormal evolution," as they said of the accident. It is, rather, part of a growing reality: We have become a people who expect to be lied to.

In 1960, as Sissela Bok reminds us in her book *Lying,* the country was astonished to discover that President Eisenhower had deliberately lied about the U-2 incident. But by 1975, nearly 70 percent of the people in a national poll agreed that "over the last ten years, this country's leaders have consistently lied to people."

If the attitude toward government is cynical, the attitude toward business is more so. As a movie, *The China Syndrome* didn't just hang on the breathtaking credibility of a nuclear "incident." It depended on the public's automatic acceptance of the assumption that corporate men would behave in real life like the men in the movie. That they would put their profits above our safety, and unabashedly lie.

We would not always have made that Leap of Unfaith so quickly. We have experienced a meltdown of trust.

Yet I think it's important in the weeks ahead to weed out the lies from the mistakes and the uncertainties that occurred this past week. It's important to define what a lie is and to determine how many we were fed.

A lie, says Bok in her work, carries with it the "intent to deceive." There were apparently lies, both of omission and of commission, offered by plant officials last week, particularly in regard to the emission of radioactivity. There were also lies under the label "euphemism." As Ralph Nader said, "This is an industry that calls explosions 'energetic disassemblies.'" It is also an industry that uses intentionally cool and misleading words like "incidents" and "events."

But there were many more murky areas—more examples

of truth and falsehood in this scary story. Nuclear advocates could paper the world with the written history of their safety assurances. Does this accident make liars of them? Were the people of Metropolitan Edison Company guilty of lying, or of wishful thinking, or of genuine, if incorrect, belief?

During the critical weekend, scientists and industry officials offered different explanations of the accident and different versions of the solutions. Was one of them a lie, or was the situation simply confusing, infused with genuine doubt?

Were the officials who denied the need for evacuation lying about the dangers in order to calm them, or were they in disagreement?

There is a difference between a lie and a mistake (however lethal), between a lie and ignorance, between a lie and confusion. There is even a difference between not telling the whole truth and telling an untruth.

Past lies have already had a disintegrative impact on our whole society. As Bok said, in thinking about this: "Much of our distrust is for good reason and yet much of it is incidental. The honest professional suffers and we can all become paralyzed in our effort to work jointly."

I find it sad and yet understandable that we no longer give anyone the benefit of the doubt. We give the benefit to the doubt. One of the tasks of this cleanup operation must be to discern the confusion from the deceit and the errors from the lies.

What has gone wrong in the public trust is nearly as crucial as what went wrong in the plant. After all, lying creates a destructive human chain reaction of its very own.

APRIL 1979

Designer Genes

In case you haven't noticed it yet, genes are back in style.
Designer Genes.

You can hardly open a publication these days without being confronted by the latest recycled fashion. Once again we are being told that the Designer of Us All created men and women out of entirely different patterns.

Now, frankly, I never bought much off of the unisex rack. When I looked at the label, they were almost always male goods which women were supposed to accept. They rarely fit me right. But this new offering is about as comfy as a corset and a wing collar.

Designer Genes can be found at the moment on any magazine rack. In the December *Science* magazine there is an article about the scientists at Johns Hopkins who suspect that males are born better at math. In *Newsweek*, they ask the question: Do Males Have a Math Gene?

In the October *Quest* magazine there is an article about the University of Chicago research on the differences between male and female brains.

And in the recent *Commentary*, there is an article by Michael Levin which lumps together selective "scientific facts" to "prove" that the biological differences between men and women make equal rights an impossible and irrational goal. Levin makes mental leaps that rival Nureyev in energy. Unfortunately, he thinks with his feet.

The Designer Gene debate is cut out of old cloth. It's an argument about human nature, between biology and environment, nature and nurture, that has gone on for centuries. To what degree are people born "that way," relatively fixed beasts of biology? To what degree are they formed, as relatively flexible creations of their environment?

It's no accident that those who believe in changing society place more importance on our environment. Those who are against change, place more importance on our biology.

Nobody really knows, you see, how much we are a product of our genes or our culture. It is most likely that we are a mix, neither wholly free of nature nor dominated by it. But the argument is fascinating because it is really a product of politics more than science.

Science, that most "objective" of disciplines, is often as trendy as Seventh Avenue. Not only do we pick and choose from the wardrobe of scientific ideas, but scientists themselves often back one or another notion as it fits their own prejudices and politics.

The history of the Scientific Facts about Men and Women is particularly outlandish. In the nineteenth century, for example, very serious sorts of men went around measuring skulls. Paul Broca, a French anthropologist, came up with the theory that women's social position in the home was due to the fact that they had smaller brains.

In the 1920s and 1930s, the common wisdom was that the differences between nationalities and races and sexes were rooted in biology. There were the Anglo-Saxon males and the inferior "Others." This notion went out of style with Hitler.

A similar notion that hormones made women incapable of doing male work went out with the national need for Rosie the Riveters.

It's not surprising that now the right wing has reemerged wearing Designer Genes. As Harvard biologist and writer

Stephen Jay Gould puts it, "In certain fields where the social importance is high and the data is poor, the history of scientific ideas has mirrored social history and very little else."

The research being done on the differences between men and women is fascinating. I assume some differences—beyond the physical ones—exist.

Ironically, even the ones that stand on shaky research grounds favor women. In this same *Commentary* piece, Michael Levin, who is hardly what you'd call a feminist, inadvertently made the best argument for putting women in charge. "War may be loathsome but only males have ever been capable of waging it," he writes. This is as good a reason for keeping men in the kitchen as I have read.

The problem is how research is used and by whom. "What we see is that the pendulum is shifting," says Gould, from change to antichange. "At the base of it is politics, not science."

Politics can use science to serve the status quo. Politics can use the work of a woman brain researcher to prove that women can't be scientists. Politics can find some biological reason why a nurse should be paid less than a bus driver.

Designer Genes are becoming the uniform of the conservative camp followers. All the old arguments against women are being hauled down from the attic.

DECEMBER 1980

The New Right of Social Interests

The more I think about the way Ronald Reagan moved into office, the more the contrasts stand out in my mind. On Inauguration Day, the Ellipse behind the White House had been covered with the mink coats and pin-striped suits of the old Reaganites.

Two days later, the same grass, muddied and trampled, had been repopulated by the waterproof boots, snow jackets and ski hats of the new Reaganites.

On Tuesday, I heard the Reagans' elegant Presbyterian minister Donn Moomaw, dubbed "Hollywood's answer to God," deliver the invocation. On Thursday, I saw Joseph Sullivan, the round, ethnic-cadenced bishop of Baton Rouge, Louisiana, offer his opening prayer.

This stomping ground of the Inaugural had been quickly transformed into the marching ground of the antiabortion crowd.

From mink to down, from establishment to grass roots, the Old Right of business interests had gone back home and the New Right of social interests had taken its place.

The differences in style were striking and so were the differences in substance. In the Inaugural address, the President had talked to the majority of us about our major concern: the economy. But, two days later, in the post-Inaugural march, the minority voters were calling in their chits. As one poster declared, "Reagan, you counted on us to win, now we're counting on you to win."

The antiabortion people were quick to claim the spoils of victory. One after another, they introduced senators, congressmen and a Cabinet member with the proud, possessive phrase, "Here's another of 'our' new men."

As Richard Schweiker put it in his first day as secretary, "You have a friend at the Department of Human Services and in the Reagan administration." A little later they proved that, as the antiabortion absolutists became the first special-interest group to hold an audience with the President.

It was the eighth anniversary of the Supreme Court decision declaring that abortion was a private matter between woman and doctor. But here the dissent of the antiabortion marchers could be read on the placard—"Wanted for Murder: Five Million Mothers and Their Doctors"—and the agenda could be read on the banners waving for "The Paramount Human Life Amendment."

By mid-afternoon, the amendment to ban all abortions, no exceptions, had been introduced in Congress: "The paramount right to life is vested in each human being from the moment of fertilization without regard to age, health, or condition of dependency."

With those simple, predictable, expected words, the antiabortion people presented the first true challenge to the alliance of Old Right and New Right. On the third day of the administration, they pointed up the conflict between the old conservatives who have long protested for less government, and the new conservatives who want a government of "moral intervention."

That is what the antiabortion amendment really portends.

The paramount Human Life Amendment, like the legislation also submitted to Congress, says clearly that from the moment sperm meets ovum, this cellular creature is a human being as equally important as the pregnant woman.

Whether conception has taken place in body or test tube, through love or rape, whether it is healthy or deformed, whether it will add to the life or take the life of the woman, this fertilized egg must not be aborted.

Moreover, it says that this "right to life" is "paramount" to the right of privacy of a woman or a family.

To enforce this "right to life," aborted women and their doctors would surely be charged with murder. I.U.D.'s would, in all likelihood, also be banned. But the amendment would also ultimately require a massive hunt, a government edict to investigate "miscarriages," to oversee the habits of pregnant women and monitor research from genetic screening to amniocentesis. This is not fantasy. It is probability.

So the contrasts on the Ellipse were more than surface ones. They offered the paradoxes for the future.

We may find out soon whether the people who promised to keep government out of our family lives end up by giving government a new and omnipotent role in the most private and personal of family decisions. We may find out soon whether those who promised to get government off our backs will allow—indeed insist—that government be given control of our bedrooms and our bodies.

JANUARY 1981

The Second Battle is the Tough One

For a moment, the woman across the table looked drained of energy. If she were the sighing sort, she would have breathed out the closing line of our short conversation.

Instead she spoke in a careful voice. "All I know is that I'm in the same movement for the second time in my life and I'm not even forty."

The sentiment was a stark and simple one. The woman who had claimed some victories for the causes of her twenties and early thirties was now watching the territory erode. She felt no momentum for her "side," had lost any illusions about a swift "win." The second phase of this struggle would be, she suspected, to hold the old ground trench by trench.

Her words over lunch resonated in my mind. Though she spoke them in Denver, the same feelings were repeated all along the way from Colorado to California last week. I met people realizing that they would have to fight again for the turf they thought they'd already won. And wondering if they could.

The woman in Denver was talking about women's rights, but she might just as easily have been talking about the environment, peace, civil rights, human rights.

In Phoenix, a woman active in the anti-Vietnam War movement talked with disbelief about our increasing involvement in El Salvador. "Didn't we learn anything?"

In Los Angeles, an environmentalist who drives home through smog as dense as the fog of Cape Cod, talked about the undermining of the clean air deadlines. "It's going backwards."

In San Francisco, a civil rights activist shook his head at the critical words in Reagan's budget speech. "The taxing power of the government must be used to provide revenues for legitimate government purposes. It must not be used . . . to bring about social change."

What is a legitimate government purpose if it isn't social change for justice? he asked ardently and then reflected on his own heat. "I've said it all before. I've heard it all before. It makes me so damn tired."

Tired. It was the word I heard most often—even more than "angry"—when I talked with people called liberals, who had done time in a movement to help the poor or end the war or clean the air. People who thought they had built something solid now feel the ground crumbling, as if it had been staked on sand and not hard rock.

As Senator Paul Tsongas says again and again, "The last election changed things. Not only did we lose Democrats and liberals, but those who are left are so weary."

Weariness is not just an occupational hazard of politicians. It also infects the legions of those who care and cared . . . and now often call their own beliefs in swift victory "naive."

It hits the generation that came into adulthood in the sixties hardest. They saw their piece of time as a straight line instead of a cycle. They saw progress as an arrow instead of a pendulum. I suppose it is only the young who believe that points stay proved and fights stay won. We are all unencumbered by history until we become part of it.

Now we know that some of the movements were nourished on heady air but had weak roots. We know that some have never survived hard times in our country. We know that some simply have strong enemies. And we know that it all hangs now in abeyance.

So today, one woman wonders whether her daughters

will look back on Their Mother The Feminist the way another generation looked back on Their Mothers The Suffragettes—as terribly quaint.

One man who was there at the anti-Vietnam March on Washington wonders whether his children will think of it like some national rock concert.

Another who truly believed that we should, would, create a social policy based on justice, wonders whether this idea will be recorded as an historical oddity.

They know that the answers depend in large part on whether they learn the lessons of the old activists who learned in lean times how to regroup, change, keep a structure and dig in for a long haul.

But it also depends on how you find the energy when you are in the same momement for the second time and you're not even forty.

FEBRUARY 1981

The Era of
Medical Puzzles

"*I* don't do mastectomies anymore," said the surgeon. He stated this matter-of-factly, with neither apology nor pride.

A few years ago, he had read the research that challenged radical mastectomies, and stopped doing "radicals." Now he had studied the research that challenged simple mastectomies, and stopped doing "simples." What he does most often now, he explained, especially in early cases, is remove the cancer—a lumpectomy—and prescribe radiation.

"I don't," he adds, "believe in mastectomies anymore."

As he repeats this, my vision is suddenly filled with women: Over 100,000 a year diagnosed to have breast cancer; more than a half-million walking around who have had surgery. I think of Reach-for-Recovery pamphlets and carefully worded ads for postsurgical bathing suits. I think of *First You Cry*. I think of self-examinations and fear. And of friends.

Then I think of the women who had been to the surgeon four months ago, before he changed his mind. "What do you tell the women you've operated on?" I ask. A flicker of anxiety crosses his face and then passes. "If they hear that I've changed and they ask, I tell them that I did what I believed was best at the time."

I sigh, and in response he asks rhetorically, "What should I do? Go on performing new mastectomies because I don't want to hurt the feelings of the women who have had them?"

No, of course not, I answer. Medicine marches on. The surgeon warns me that if I write about this, I should be prepared. He is in a minority or a vanguard of surgeons who have broken with the "accepted procedure."

Furthermore, he adds, he might not have changed if it hadn't struck his family, if he hadn't been exposed and pushed and challenged.

I know this surgeon to be a good one who cares as well as he cuts, and I know that he is not alone in changing his mind and his procedure. Even Dr. Allen Lichter of the National Cancer Institute has said, "If we didn't believe strongly that a lesser operation plus radiation will prove as effective as a total mastectomy, we wouldn't be doing this."

So, the controversy that intrigues me goes beyond mastectomies. It is about trust. It is about being a patient in an era of medical puzzles, about informed consent in a time of different opinions. It is about change and research, about confidence and confusion, about being a medical consumer faced with an array of opinions that can be as dizzying as brand names in a supermarket.

Until fairly recently, medicine was a stable business. The doctors might not have been right, nor have cured many people, but their treatments were relatively constant and uniform over time and geography. The doctor's role was a combination of ministering and common sense with a smidgin of science. The patient's role was that of trustee.

Today, doctoring depends more and more on technology and research. It is a business in which it is sometimes difficult to separate the advances from the changes.

Fads come and go. Life and death can be a matter of timing. Gastric freezing, once a "new" treatment for ulcers, could now be grounds for malpractice. If Ted Kennedy, Jr., had contracted his form of cancer any earlier he might well have died of it; if he had contracted it a few years later, they might have excised the bone area instead of amputating the leg. There is today honest and deep controversy over the use of the coronary artery bypass operation. So, too, one surgeon believes that mastectomy is "safer," another does not.

The more doctors depend on statistics and science, the more patients long for reassurance and fear being guinea pigs. The National Cancer Institute study on the difference between treating breast cancer with mastectomy, or with lumpectomy and radiation, has found very few volunteers willing to have their choice made by a computer.

The change can invite total mistrust—"doctors know nothing"—or questions. Willingly or not, we have to become consumers who treatment-shop, who research disease and "cures" more carefully and more fearfully than we research the purchase of a dishwasher. And the doctor who elicits trust now isn't the one prescribing certainty, but the one who acts as a guide through a thicket of difficult scientific information—forcing and helping us to be partners.

JANUARY 1980

Of Psssst And Psychobabble

I overheard them only because I am compulsively on time in a world of Johnny-come-lates and because restaurants are as private these days as the streets of Hong Kong.

The two men were drinking white wine and speculating about marriages. That in itself wasn't unusual because speculation is everyone's favorite indoor sport. It is a chic form of gossip when mixed with psychobabble.

But because it was Washington and lunchtime, the two sitting at the table next to me weren't talking about just any marriage. They were analyzing the private lives of public people.

To be utterly and painfully specific they were delivering certainties about the relationships between Juanita Kreps and her husband and Teddy Kennedy and his wife.

I will spare you the details. But let me just say that before the white wine was consumed and the menu read, blame was assessed, personalities analyzed, and the most intimate knowledge of these people's lives assumed. Were my neighbors friends of the Krepses, of the Kennedys? Not at all. Their theories were based solely on what they read in print. Plus, of course, gossip and psychobabble.

Well, after five minutes of glibness dropped over the eaves or the edges of the table, I sat fuming, fighting a compulsion to lean over and bellow: "How the hell do you know what goes on between two people?"

I am not going to launch into a holier-than-thou diatribe against speculation. To a certain extent we all do it, and not always unkindly. Friends leave our dinner parties and we chat about them idly while we do the dishes. People at work split and we decide why.

Those of us who are slick at it, can sort the evidence and draw a brief in no time, building sound cases out of people's lives, loves, motivations.

But the fact is that we often confuse glibness with The Truth, especially when we deal with distant public figures. Today Washington is our Hollywood, the Senate our Warner Bros., the White House our Beverly Hills. People who never read a line of a movie magazine deal with the lives of leaders as if they were Elizabeth Taylor and Richard Burton. We talk about What Everyone Knows, instead of what no one can know.

It seems to me enormously difficult really to comprehend what goes on between two people, whether they are the Joneses or Jerry Brown and Linda Ronstadt. (It's even hard if you are one of the two people.) But it is virtually impossible to draw simple conclusions, single meanings from people's private lives.

Private lives don't conclude. For every set of facts there are a dozen possible meanings and for every event there are multiple sets of motivations.

What does it mean when one spouse becomes successful and the other attempts suicide? Does one person's problem force the other to be strong? Does one person's strength threaten the other into weakness? Are these facts even remotely related—as my glib luncheon neighbors assumed?

In the same vein, how do people assess blame for an estranged marriage. Is it one spouse's apparent meandering, the other's confessed drinking, the chicken, the egg, or the unknown? Knowing "so much," we know far, far too little to make judgments.

What does it mean for example when a man is called a

"womanizer"? That he likes women or hates them? That he is bringing pain to his wife or that both agreed to separateness?

Is one staying married out of loyalty, the other out of weakness; one out of hope for reconciliation or the other out of religious beliefs? What mix of emotions do we so blithely unscramble and assess? What do we pretend to know?

I am uncomfortable even raising these issues, because inevitably talking about gossip becomes a form of gossip all its own. It is rather like all of the politicians so studiously telling us how they will not talk about Chappaquiddick.

But I think it is important because it seems to me already that this is the year, and surely this will be the campaign of speculation about what we so delicately, insinuatingly refer to as "private life."

Privacy will be invaded and maintained. Gossip and psychobabble will rule. Meaning will be sewn out of scraps of facts labeled authentic by their designers. People in restaurants and living rooms will draw conclusions about private scenes from a marriage or two, and it troubles me.

It seems to me that we have always been skeptical about facts. It's time to be absolutely squeamish about conclusions.

OCTOBER 1979

Squirreling Logic

For several days last week, I found myself in a pitched battle over a priceless piece of property—a birdhouse built in Vermont for feeding chickadees, sparrows and the other small urban birds which don't own condominiums in Florida.

My enemy was a squirrel. Not an ordinary squirrel, but one which, with all the agility of the desperate, had learned how to balance on this swinging piece of real estate while he methodically chewed his way into the seeds.

Each time I saw him there, outside of my kitchen window, I bolted out of my chair, and with the righteousness of a religious zealot, drove the infidel from the holy temple of the chickadee.

But on one of these defensive attacks, broom and voice raised to a feverish pitch, I suddenly caught myself in the act. There I was, a tall woman in a navy bathrobe, terrorizing a short squirrel in gray fur. It was theater of the absurd.

Having driven away the interloper once more, I sat down and laughed. How had I decided the bird was a pet and the squirrel a pest? How had I become the protector of one and the persecutor of the other? My daughter that night wore her Stop-the-Slaughter T-shirt with a picture of a baby seal on it, at dinner, while she ate lamb chops. I remember how at one time I had argued in favor of saving the whales, while massacring a lobster. More contradictions.

Well, none of us would easily pass a logician's purity test. All of our lives and minds contain conflicts, or at least inconsistencies.

But this was just a small irony, a tiny nest of confused reasoning about birds and squirrels, seals and lambs. A minor thing. Still, it occurred to me that this is a time of much greater sensitivity about all sorts of contradictions, not only in our natures but in our public policies. A major thing.

A decade ago we worried about the contradictions between our society's ideals—such things as justice, equality, poverty—and its realities. Now we seem most conscious of the inconsistencies raised by government policies. We talk now about reverse discrimination, disincentives, government interference.

Once we focused on the problems that had grown out of our inaction. Now we focus on the problems, the "unintended consequences," of action. The relatively optimistic belief in the possibility of change and the benefits of intervention has turned into a cautious, even pessimistic, attitude against change, against interference.

I suppose part of my feeling came not from the seals but from Sears. In between chasing squirrels and harboring chickadees last week, I managed to read about the Sears Roebuck suit against the entire range of affirmative action programs.

The suit is, in many ways, a perfect New Conservative brief. It contains an effective, jabbing, antigovernment analysis. It doesn't attack the goals of equal opportunity but rather the counterproductive means. It dissects good intentions, pointing to programs that favor a veteran here, a minority there and thwart each other everywhere.

It does what the New Conservatives do best: It points out the contradictions of public policies. It ignores what they ignore best: the original inequities of society, the historic unwillingness of the business world to change.

But their goal is to remove the pressure rather than improve the programs. They are more eager to get rid of government interference than they are to rationalize its inconsistencies.

Reading all this in my kitchen chair with one eye out for the marauding squirrel made me wonder whether we are really regrouping along new political lines, or whether the important differences now are in attitude, especially in how we feel about contradictions themselves.

I think that many of us, like the lawyers for Sears, can develop terribly intricate and wise analyses for anything, and then use them to rationalize our inaction—to call for retreat. We excavate conflicts in ourselves, our plans, each other, so ardently at times that we use up our energy for change, for decisions. And then we settle for less. We can think of ourselves as very clever when we are really very passive.

We can even let the squirrels eat the seeds, and the seals be turned into coats, and injustice grow, while we pride ourselves on consistency.

I am also a sucker for consistency. I want to resolve issues the way others want to fill in crossword puzzles. But I have a sense that it's better to accept the inevitability of some contradictions, some needed adjustments along with the possibility of change and improvement.

The alternative, after all, is a grim intellectual one: to spend our days pristinely analyzing, never acting, locked in the status quo.

FEBRUARY 1979

The Sad Retreat to Private Places

*T*he church around the corner from my house has been turned into condominiums.

They held an open house last week, on Sunday of course, and we attended.

The congregants were well-behaved, respectful of property rites, awed by interest rates. The ritual was presided over by an agent of real estate.

The transformation of the church was rather a miracle. Built of nineteenth-century self-confidence and boulders, the huge structure had been saved from bulldozers by being christened a historic landmark.

But there was something so odd, awed, awesome about it. A giant white elephant of a church turned into a bonanza of real estate. An expensive assembly house subdivided into profitable units.

The gargantuan staircase that once led my neighbors up to worship, led us up to private doorways. The stained-glass windows, which once filtered out the world, have been replaced by clear panes to let the world in. The only remaining pews provide a decorative accent for a study alcove.

As for the prices, only the rich inherit this kingdom.

Walking through it on this Sunday, I wondered what the former ministers would say about this event. Had as many people come regularly on past Sundays? Had they listened as attentively to the sermons as to the tax break information?

It seemed to me that there was someting too symbolic in this secular conversion. Another meeting place had been lost. Another private living space had been created.

It looked like part of a pattern away from the communal world to the private. A pattern in which people value what we share less than what we own.

There are, already, so many converts to that.

In this state and others, where people voted for a proposition for lower taxes, the early returns are in. It is our joint education, safety, recreation, that are being cut.

Isn't this what is happening? People seem more willing to spend money on burglar alarms than on police. They seem less interested in public parks than private gardens, less interested in community recreation than in private vacations.

Last week, the Reagan Administration sounded more concerned with the price of a car than the cost to the air. The same people would, if they could, offer tax credits to private school families even while they cut funds for public school families.

It is all part of some Revival; the cult of privatization can be read in every public building that's closed down, in every mass transit system cut back.

Soon, I suppose we will begin to make police stations and firehouses into condos.

The nineteenth century was no model of virtue, but there was a philosophy of public life, of community, that stood up against the rugged individualism.

In Edward Bellamy's *Looking Backward,* he described a utopia which had an enormous impact on nineteenth-century city planners. One character explains the ideal society like this: "We might, indeed, have much larger income individually, but we prefer to expend it upon public works and pleasures in which we all share. . . . At home we have comfort but the splendor of our life is on our social side, that which we share with our fellows."

It was this spirit that built the public libraries that are now being closed. It was this spirit that built the public parks that are now neglected.

In my own town, I walk through the Emerald Necklace that Frederick Law Olmstead designed around Boston after he finished creating New York's Central Park. Weeds are untouched, and public pleasure is uprooted.

As our sense of community diminishes we retreat to our private spaces. As we retreat, our sense of community diminishes.

Public space becomes a burden on the private dweller, a white elephant on the market.

So we no longer meet on public ground but subdivide it. We sell the church and buy a living unit. We call this conversion.

APRIL 1981

PART 9

Growing Pains

Fly the
Nest Tests

They stepped carefully over the trunk and out of the cabin door. The girl glanced around the area, kiddingly but carefully, to make sure no one was looking. When the coast was clear, they shared a goodbye hug.

This time the mother had left no more than three unnecessary pieces of advice scattered around her daughter's cubbyhole. This time the girl had only one or two moments of uncertainly. It had gone rather easily.

At eleven, the girl was, her mother noted with some satisfaction, rather independent ... sturdy ... "healthy." She thought about that as she drove down from New Hampshire.

Over the years both had become more practiced at saying goodbyes. They had passed through graduated lessons in leavetaking—school, overnites, weekends, vacations, camp. It was all, surely, part of the normal process of independence programming, separation training.

Yet, when she walked into the house, saw the roller skates in the front hall, and heard the silence, she had sudden second thoughts. Why, after all, is it that we automatically equate emotional health with independence?

Picking up the bag of stationery, carefully selected and carelessly forgotten on the stairs, she thought about how we grade maturity on a scale of self-sufficiency and give out passing grades to children who learn to do for themselves.

Even our small people are supposed to learn to say goodbye without flunking composure.

Good parents, she had read somewhere, raise children who are competent and confident. enough to leave them. What a deal.

The mother chuckled at this irony. She walked into her daughter's room, picked up a stuffed owl off the floor and put it on the shelf with the rest of the motley menagerie.

Looking at it coolly, she thought: Why, the true goal of parenting is to phase ourselves out, make ourselves as unnecessary as a stuffed owl. The Ph.D's of this post-graduate course build in their own obsolescence.

If we do the job wrong, the kids may get hung up on our apron strings. But if we do the job right, why, they can feel absolutely comfortable moving to California.

Is it any wonder that people are ambivalent about signing up for the course?

Child-raising "authorities" preach independence as if it were a Universal Truth, the one correct answer on the multiple choice child-raising questionnaire. But, she thought, it was as specifically American as the mobile home and the nuclear family.

Other cultures didn't give such rigorous separation training. They didn't raise their children to see them off quite as routinely.

America, however, was founded by leavers. This woman's own ancestors had left the old world for the new. More to the point, they had left relationships for opportunities. And they were not the only ones.

The whole country was settled by one generation of leavers after the next—people who moved to a new frontier or a new neighborhood or a new job, who continually left relationships for opportunities. It was considered unreasonable, almost unpatriotic, for parents to "cling." And it still is.

A healthy adult is not supposed to suffer a syndrome,

even an empty-nest one, when the children leave. A good parent is actually supposed to hope that the children will not even be homesick. We are also graded by how well we handle self-sufficiency. And aloneness.

The mother thought about the latest Census Bureau report. One out of every five households now consists of just one person. The number of lone-livers is up 42 percent since just 1970. Is that where it ends, this curriculum? Are we better educated for living alone than for living together?

We regard it as natural, the "thrust for independence" in kids. And yet, if it is so natural why do we need so much training? And where was it writ that independence is the ultimate goal of parenting?

Well, the woman was probably just creating problems. Making a cosmic case out of a summer camp. It was just time off, and a welcome change for both of them.

She picked up a stray sock stuck under the doorjamb and quietly closed the door to her daughter's room. It was, after all, still a while until that particular test.

JULY 1979

The Long Transition to Adulthood

"*When I was a child, I spake as a child, I understood as a child, I thought as a child. But when I became a man, I put away childish things.*"—Corinthians I

What about the years in between childhood and adulthood? How do we speak then? How do we think? How do we become men and women?

For most of history there was no in-between, no adolescence as we know it. There was no such lengthy period of semi-autonomy, economic "uselessness," when the only occupation of a son or daughter was learning.

In the eighteenth century, Americans weren't legally adults until they turned twenty-one, but they did important work on farms by seven or eight. When they were physically grown, at only thirteen or sixteen, they had virtually the same jobs as any other adult.

In those days, education was irregular at best, but each child had his or her own vocational guidance teacher: the family. So the transition to adulthood was handled—though not always easily or without tension—through a long apprenticeship, on the farm or in a craft, by people who could point out a direct social path to adulthood.

It was industrialization that changed all that. In the nineteenth century, mills and factories replaced farms, and cities replaced the countryside. Children didn't automatically follow their parents' occupations and so family relations became less important for job training than something called school.

In that century, the need for child labor on farms diminished and the horrors of industrial child labor became widespread. So we passed laws against child labor and in favor of mandatory education. Decade by decade we have raised both ages.

School has replaced work not just out of our benevolence. There are also deep economic reasons. In 1933, at the height of the Depression, the National Child Labor Committee put it as baldly as this: "It is now generally accepted that the exploitation of children, indefensible on humanitarian grounds, has become a genuine economic menace. Children should be in school and adults should have whatever worthwhile jobs there are."

School became the place of reading and writing and certification. It provided the necessary paper for employment. School not only kept young people out of the marketplace but promised "better" jobs if they stayed and studied.

The result of all this is clear: Today, school is what young people do for a living.

In 1870, less than 5 percent of the high school age group were in high school. In 1976, 86.1 percent of those fourteen to seventeen were in school. In 1977, nearly one-third of the eighteen to twenty-one-year-olds were in college.

There has been a 129 percent increase in college enrollment in this country since 1960. In many places today, community colleges are entered as routinely as high schools.

While a high school diploma or a college degree no longer guarantees a job, there are more and more jobs you can't even apply for without them. So the payoff is less certain, but the pressure is even greater to go to school longer and longer, to extend the state of semi-autonomy further and further.

The irony is that society worries more when the young try to grasp at adult "privileges" than when they remain in the passive fraternity-house state of mind. We worry about teenage drinking and driving and pregnancy—all perhaps misguided attempts at "grown-up behavior." Yet we offer few alternatives, few meaningful opportunities for adulthood training. We have virtually allowed sex, drinking and driving to become rites of passage.

School just isn't enough. It demands only one skill, tests only one kind of performance. From a pre-med dorm to an Animal House, it is a youth ghetto where adults are only authority figures, where students don't get the chance to test their own identities, their own authority, their own responsibility to others.

Without enough alternatives, we have left schools the job of producing adults. But schools are where the young are kept, not where they grow up.

Adolescence isn't a training ground for adulthood now. It is a holding pattern for aging youth.

MARCH 1979

Seventh Grade Isn't Seventh Heaven

The girl has started seventh grade. This was to be expected. Nevertheless, her mother is of the confirmed opinion—based on experience—that seventh grade shouldn't happen to a dog.

If she were in charge, seventh grade would be eliminated like the thirteenth floor in hotels. Kids would go immediately from sixth to eighth grade, passing Go, without stopping to collect a set of teachers' scalps, or social wounds.

The girl is not, praise the Lord and the local school board, going to something called junior high school. Just the name gives her mother hives. "Junior" high schools are the training bras of the educational world.

Once upon a time someone—probably the same person who invented "adolescence"—decided to isolate all the children between twelve and fourteen in one institution, as if they had a social disease. Instead of finding a curse, they created an epidemic of precociousness, a generation of Jodie Fosters and Tatum O'Neals.

The mother remembers her own seventh grade, complete with terminal awkwardness, a math teacher who had deadly aim with erasers, and an English teacher who committed the ultimate mistake: She allowed herself to be vulnerable. Seventh graders go for vulnerability like a ground-to-air missile.

The funny part is that the mother loves this age, always has, loves the energy and wit and the devastating eye and appetites of the seventh graders who graze through her house.

But what is seen as energy in the world is often seen as unruliness in school. What is wit in twos or threes is often insolence in groups of twenty. What is clarity to a parent or friend could be rebelliousness to a teacher.

Again the mother thought of the tension between family and school, between the two systems in which children live out their days. It was as loaded a relationship as any joint custody.

More often than not, families and schools, like divorced parents, hold different sets of expectations and goals, different views of one child, and of childhood.

When kids are young, families are the world they live in. Our power as parents is largely unshared. We are their environment, their standard, their reality, their value-tenders and the people who interpret the outside to them.

If families work right, they are the place in which love is unconditional. If they work right, there is an assumption

of love, even under discipline or anger. Good families don't
flunk their children.

But on the first day of school—nursery school, first
grade, seventh grade, college—we give our children over
to a system that doesn't love them. Give them over to be
judged, to see if they can "measure up" to another standard.
They enter a world in which they are only rewarded for how
they perform.

I don't mean to present the schools as cold, and teachers
as uncaring. But parents see kids as special individuals; the
school inevitably sees them as part of a group. School is
the essential but scary halfway house between the home and
the world.

I suppose we also give up our own teaching monopoly
when we send them to school. There is nothing new in that.
Since the beginning schools have been the melting pots of
a complex society. They taught immigrant children English
and order; taught country people urban skills; taught everyone the "American" ways. We can only guess at how those
lessons were at odds with family tutoring.

Even today the hottest issues at school are not about new
math or phonetics, but about conflicting values. A parent
may encourage questioning, while the school has a bias
toward passivity. A parent may believe literally in the Bible,
while the children are told that Jonah and the Whale is a
story. A parent may abhor violence and the school enforces
corporal punishment. A parent may praise order, while a
school allows chaos. If sex education is the flash point, it
is no surprise.

I don't know a single parent who has not been aghast at
some attitude or information lugged home with the school
books. I don't know a teacher who hasn't felt that same
flash of horror at some family opinion. We compete (as
much as we cooperate) for influence, for space in the children's heads.

Eventually, I suppose it's the kids who make a kind of
truce, even an uneasy one, by becoming their own people.

Gradually they would pick and choose, find their own way through a thicket of teachers and parents and media.

Even now, in this miserable school year, they were becoming skeptical but dogmatic, unsure but stubborn, difficult but fascinating... self-made people. With any luck they would survive even seventh grade.

SEPTEMBER 1980

Commencement Fever

All of this commencing must have gone to my head, like ceremonial wine.

Watching the parades of graduates filing across the stages in front of cameras, I suddenly had the image of an academic assembly line. I saw a million students on a conveyer belt, each in an identical cap and gown, receiving the finishing touches: a fresh set of initials, a certificate of approval, a curriculum vitae to call his or her own.

Once stamped by the college of their origin, I was sure that each of these newly minted alumni were labeled for life. Their obituaries, half a century away, would undoubtedly describe them as graduates.

The speakers, too, seemed to have caught the commencement fever. They spoke as if the ceremony were launching new battleships made out of the newest gray matter. They broke their vintage bottles across the brows of the assembled, and allowed their favorite thoughts to bubble over.

With a sense of urgency, they poured last-minute knowledge into the ears of their students, trying to catch them while they were still hot, still thinking, still incomplete.

I am not going to bah-humbug college education.

But I think it is ridiculous to regard universities as adolescence-finishing factories that produce sanded, lacquered adults all ready to perform. It is not only ridiculous, it is terrifying.

We attribute such a large place in our lives to a mere four years that commencement is more infused with the fear of leaving than the excitement of beginning, or the sense of continuity. We tell students that they are done when they feel half baked.

College is hardly the Peak Experience or the academic end, and as one unfinished product, I say that with a sigh of relief. In the 1960s, I went to one of the Seven Sister schools where they educated women like their "brothers." It was, I am told, a first-rate education and I think I missed it.

I showed, on paper, a modest profit in the business of learning. Like many eighteen-year-olds in my class, I had been well educated in one thing: living up to expectations. So I digested history and regurgitated a thesis.

Today, sixteen years later, I carry a cum after my name like a dangling participle. But I didn't *think* until I was thirty and long past my required reading.

You can take that as depressing or reassuring, but I am grateful that college didn't finish me.

Of course, I grew up between eighteen and twenty-two when college was *in loco parentis*. But I also grew up between twenty-two and twenty-six and between thirty and thirty-nine.

At eighteen I went through the absolutely unique experience of living away from home. But at twenty-two I had the equally new experience of a first job; and at twenty-seven a first child. I am now, for the one and only time in my life, thirty-eight.

We give our Imprimatur of Importance to the four college years, as if they have a special place in the continuum of our lives. As if they are set in boldface. We regard college as an exclamation point at the end of childhood, when it is merely a comma.

Last week, Nora Ephron told the seniors of Wellesley that those people who say college was the best time of their lives didn't lead very happy lives. Maybe so. Maybe, too, their memories carefully edited out the bad, under the social pressure to make this a magnificent quartet.

I realize now that most of my friends enjoyed college one term and got through it another. Some weeks we felt euphoric and other weeks lonely. It wasn't the best of times, it wasn't the worst. It was just time, that Mixmaster of feelings.

We hadn't yet learned that this was normal. We thought that depression was unusual and loneliness a fault, and that everyone else was having his best years. You see, our thinking was as unfinished as raw pine furniture.

Commencement is an end and a beginning and all that. But maybe it doesn't merit a thunderous clap. The line between childhood and adulthood doesn't look like a stream of men and women in caps and gowns. It lurches and gropes and learns on toward some higher degree.

In the end, the degree isn't a manufacturer's guarantee that the work is done. Rather, it is a chit toward continuing education.

JUNE 1979

Alone Sooner or Later

Our friend is taking a new course in life. She is Learning to Live Alone.

She has, we tell each other, all the prerequisites for enrollment—the right background, the right training.

As a young woman she had graduated from parents to husband without a day of private schooling.

For nineteen years she had majored in togetherness.

When her marriage ended six months ago, it was only natural that she would embark on a crash course in independent studies.

Because our friend is a tough grader, she has told us: "I flunked marriage." The truth is that she dropped out, that they both dropped out. But the sense of failure is an honest one.

There was something else. In those last months of marriage she was haunted by the idea that sooner or later she would have to be alone and that she was unprepared. She had missed some sort of survival training that should have been a required course when she was younger. She expressed a sense of growing urgency. She had to learn about it now... while she still could.

So today, our friend is a determined student, even a grind at times, compelled by the need to pass this course in adult education.

Well, we are both graduates and post-graduates and we understand as we watch. She has done her homework, passed the quizzes, crammed for mid-terms. Eaten and cooked three-course meals by herself. Spent an entire weekend alone. Dealt with household emergencies, and checking accounts. Faced down half a dozen panicky moments of loneliness and self-centeredness.

We go down the checklist, nodding with approval at our friend's studies. She has gone back to basics. Even the new man who had met her and cared for her understood that she was not ready for doubles. She was still learning, slowly, about number one.

The two of us, her friends, quote statistics at each other and at her. Twelve percent of the population lives alone at one time or another. More than 20 percent of the households in America consist of one person. One out of three marriages ends in divorce. The average wife outlives her husband by a decade.

We are realistic, pride ourselves on it, and the figures tell us that sooner or later the odds are on aloneness. We have encouraged her to accept it. We have offered her a bumper-sticker truth: You have to be able to live with yourself to live with anyone else.

It occurs to me that this is our security. If one generation wanted to learn typing or teaching as "something to fall back on," now we regard Learning to Live Alone as some sort of strange security.

We take it for granted. We encourage each other and our children to learn it when they are younger. We understand when our friends enroll for refresher courses.

But I wonder about it all. Not so long ago, aloneness was regarded as a temporary condition. It was suspect. At the time of the American Revolution, less than 4 percent of the households contained only one person.

Even now in other places and other cultures aloneness is an oddity, an accident, an illness more than a luxury. Through human history, people have lived in clusters where their only privacy was in their thoughts. The Samoans did not set up single shelters. The Chinese do not learn to live alone. Hardly.

It's possible that aloneness is, in part, a modern American elective. We fall into it and, yes, we sign up for it in droves: the working young, the divorced, the widowed. Those who can afford to live by themselves choose to.

The reality resounds through the course-of-life catalogue. In fact, like our friend, we are driven now by an uneasy feeling that togetherness may be only a pause between single states. The anxious sense of what is basic has shifted. The bottom line seems to have moved.

Yet I wonder sometimes whether we struggle to protect ourselves from loneliness by liking it. Whether this independent study is an advance or a retreat. I wonder whether it is some American madness or self-improvement bravado.

Yes, I guess it is necessary for our friend to learn to live alone now. But if it felt good, would she have to study so hard?

SEPTEMBER 1980

My Mother, My Guilt

"*Oh* gawd, Sunday is Mother's Day," says one of the women, looking up from the newspapers they are sharing. "I'd better remember to call."

In a moment, guilt is streaming up from both their coffee

cups. Their feelings stand poised to be gift wrapped. Suddenly, their mothers have become an item for the checklists on their bulletin boards: Sunday, Call Mother.

Mother's Day! one says to the other, a bit irritated. She has never really liked Hallmark-card, Ma-Bell ritualizations of family life. For that matter, neither of the women likes having deadlines for their feelings. They do not blow horns at midnight New Year's Eve. They feel uncomfortable with a national mother's day to prove they remember.

But the two women are mothers as well as daughters. More than anything else, they tell each other, they don't want their children to feel that they *have to* . . . call them, gift them, feel guilty about them.

"Save me from that," says one, looking at the heavens.

The other agrees and reaches for the Margaret Atwood book, the passage that holds her own worst nightmares about the Ghost of Mother's Day Future.

"Mummy . . . Mum . . . Mama . . . Already they're preparing for flight betrayal, they will leave her, she will become their background. They will discuss her as they lie in bed with their lovers, they will use her as an explanation for everything they find idiosyncratic or painful about themselves. If she makes them feel guilty enough they'll come and visit her on weekends . . . she will become My Mother, pronounced with a sigh."

They don't want to be My Mother, pronounced with a sigh. What I want, says one, is for my kids to be free to choose to be with me . . .

The other says quickly, but do you want them to be free to choose to be without you?

There is a pause. They press each other. Would you rather have a guilty call or no call? A ritual stroking or none? "If she makes them feel guilty enough, they'll come and visit her on weekends." Will they someday settle for that?

Mothers, children and guilt. One of the women says this: My mother spoke to her mother every day. I don't do that. My mother understands and is somewhat disappointed. I feel understood and disappointing. I don't want my children to feel that way.

She has, you see, absorbed the message of her age: Guilt is the prime-time crime of parenting. The two women don't want to be even subconsciously demanding of their own children. And yet.

They have a friend who was pushed away through guilt. She escaped her mother's magnetic circle through geography. She had to physically move beyond the pull of her mother's needs and demands.

In turn, this friend consciously raised her children to be separate, to be independent, guilt-free, don't-worry-bout-me. Just like it says in the book. In June, her independent daughter will guilt-freely relocate to another coast. She says now, only half in jest, that perhaps she should have raised the child with just enough guilt to make her stick around. The two women don't laugh.

Are there two kinds of guilt: one a paddle we beat each other with, the other a kind of cement? Is there such a thing as Good Guilt—caring with a dose of responsibility?

The two women don't know a single parent who wants to ever be dependent on her kids, and they don't know one who hasn't wondered whether she will be able to depend on them. We don't want the children to be tied to us by guilt . . . or to abandon us. The centrifugal forces of society are strong.

"I want my children to call on me for the pleasure of my company," says one woman from behind the defenses of her newspaper ad pages for perfume and necklaces. Of course. We don't want pro formas. We want pleasure.

The women have a horror of being too needy. They lead different lives from their mothers because of it. They are afraid to put too many expectations in the child basket. The best protection from loss, one tells the other, is a full life of their own. Maybe.

In any case, they know this. They don't want to be "My Mother, with a sigh." Nor do they want a gift of their children's guilt. But still these casual women who do not even approve of Mother's Days, hope their kids remember.

MAY 1980

Life Begins at Forty? Baloney

I am turning forty this week. It's not all that bad. It's better than turning green, or turning sour. It's better than turning into a beetle.

With any luck, I will not wake up and find myself a metamorph. No Gregoria Samsa roles for me. I'm not up to overnight changes.

Though my friends and family have watched me for signs of imminent mid-life crisis, it seems equally unlikely that I will enter my forties with a strong desire to sing at the Met or run a skin-diving operation in the Caribbean. I don't have the voice for one or the legs for the other.

But I will wake up irrefutably middle-aged.

By forty, the way I figure it, you have already created something unique: your life. You've created it with will and energy and accident.

Life begins at forty? Baloney.

At twenty, I wanted to know who I would become. By forty, willy-nilly, ready or not, I've become. I have a web of commitments, a track record, a history. I've survived some things, hardened to some and opened up to others.

By now I have a context in which I live, a context in which to grow or a context out of which to break. Choose one of the above. I choose the first.

Do I sound smug about it? Not at all. It's not that easy. I suffer from middle-age bulge. At forty, my life is inflated, like a tire, to the maximum of pressure. It comes with the territory.

Middle age is responsible. Middle age is busy. Middle age is overcommitted. Middle age asked for it.

I spent my twenties and much of my thirties filling in the blanks, building a structure. It is the business of youth— building to avoid loneliness, uselessness, to test competence. One by one I got the basics: a career, friends, family. I have shored it up, renovated from time to time, but eventually I even added some frills: a house, a garden commitments to causes and people.

All these things nourish and enrich my life. All these things require time, and attention. I spend less energy these days on construction and more on maintenance. I am conscious of the effort needed to keep it all together, in working order. I am conscious of the strength needed to hold it up.

The support system of my life requires, of course, support. So at middle age, my life expands with other people's needs.

Middle age has botn aging parents and adolescent children. Middle age has bosses to please and deadlines to meet and bills to pay. Middle age sometimes feels useful, strong, sturdy and sometimes feels overwhelmed.

I look back over the calendar of my week. Two columns, six dinner guests, a pair of new sneakers, a family conference, a dash from the plane to my daughter's concert, plus the usual. Some weeks I am amazed at how much has been accomplished. Other weeks I am enraged that my life can so easily become a list to be crossed off.

I have, in short, all the pleasure and all the pressure of a full life. At the height of our dependability, mid-life bulges with the weight of our dependents.

Middle age also worries. It may be at work when an

emergency comes up at home. It may be on deadline when a friend calls up with a problem. It may cancel dinner with mother because daughter needs time. It may have to cut short a weekend with family because a friend is in trouble. But it tries.

At forty, I am proud sometimes to be able to deal with all the aspects of my life without more than an occasional disaster. At forty, I am distressed sometimes by the idea that I am disappointing the people I love, unable to hear enough, be enough, do enough for them.

Still, like Popeye, I am what I am. Lucky. And rushed. Torn between people and warmed by them. Strung out between responsibilities and bolstered by them. I am in a pivotal and exhausting intersection of the life I willfully created.

And I know, without the shadow of a doubt, that these are my good old days.

APRIL 1981

About the Author

Ellen Goodman is a national columnist based at the *Boston Globe*. Her column, syndicated by the *Washington Post* Writers Group, now appears in over 170 newspapers. In 1980 she received the Pulitzer Prize for distinguished commentary. She is an honors graduate of Radcliffe College and former Nieman Fellow at Harvard University.